A German panzer crewman emerging from his partly immobilized tank with his hands up, surrenders to bayonet-wielding British Commonwealth in October 1942 during one of the last — and the most hard-fought and decisive actions: the Battle of El Alamein.

TIME ®
LIFE

Titles available in this series:

WORLD WAR II

WAR IN THE DESERT

BY RICHARD COLLIER
AND THE EDITORS OF TIME-LIFE BOOKS

TIME®
LIFE

WORLD WAR II

This edition published in 2004
by the Caxton Publishing Group
20 Bloomsbury Street, London WC1B 3JH
Under license from Time-Life Books BV.

Cover Design: Open Door Limited, Rutland UK

NEW PRODUCT DEVELOPMENT: Director, Elizabeth D. Ward;
Project Manager, Karen Ingebrntsen; Director of Marketing,
Mary Ann Donaghy; Marketing Manager, Paul Fontaine;
Associate Marketing Manager, Erin Gaskins

MARKETING:
Director, Pamela R. Farrell; Marketing Manager, Nancy Gallo;
Associate Marketing Manager, Kristen N. O'Shea

Editorial Staff for *War in the Desert*
Editor: William K. Goolrick
Picture Editors/Designers: Thomas S. Huestis, Raymond Ripper
Text Editors: Jim Hicks, Anne Horan, Henry Woodhead
Staff Writers: Susan Bryan, Richard W. Flanagan,
Henry P. Leifermann, Abigail Zuger
Researchers: Christine M. Bowie, Jane Coughran,
Peter Kaufman, Helga Kohl, Karen L. Mitchell, Robin Richman,
Phyllis K. Wise
Editorial Assistant: Dolores Morrissy

Correspondents: Maria Vincenza Aloisi (Paris), Christine Hinze
(London), Christina Lieberman (New York)

Executive Vice President, Operations: Ralph Cuomo
Senior Vice President and CFO: Claudia Goldberg
Senior Vice President, Law & Business Affairs:
Randolph H. Elkins
Vice President, Financial Planning & Analysis:
Christopher Hearing
Vice President, Book Production: Patricia Pascale
Vice President, Imaging: Marjann Caldwell
Director, Publishing Technology: Betsi McGrath
Director, Editorial Administration: Barbara Levitt
Director, Photography and Research: John Conrad Weiser
Director, Quality Assurance: James King
Manager Technical Services: Anne Topp
Senior Production Manager: Ken Sabol
Manager, Copyedit/Page Makeup: Debby Tait
Chief Librarian: Louise D. Forstall

Title: War in the Desert
ISBN: 1 84447 211 6

© 1997, 1999 Time Life Inc.

CONTENTS

ITALY'S REACH FOR GLORY

Smartly uniformed Italian antiaircraft crews in Libya, their machine guns mounted on a truck, exude confidence prior to the invasion of Egypt in September 1940.

THE DUCE'S PLANS FOR A ROMAN EMPIRE

From the marble balcony of his office in Rome's Palazzo Venezia, a belligerent Mussolini announces he has declared war on Britain and France.

"Italian people, rush to arms and show your tenacity, your courage, your valor," shouted dictator Benito Mussolini to the cheering crowd that filled the immense square beneath his famous balcony *(left)*. It was June 10, 1940, the day that Italy entered the War against the Allies. Hitler was rapidly completing his conquest of Western Europe, and the Duce, not to be outdone, determined to make some flashy conquests of his own and in the process triple the size of his empire on the continent of Africa. Mussolini already held Libya in the north, and Eritrea, Italian Somaliland and Ethiopia to the southeast. Now that Great Britain was fighting for its very existence, it seemed a fine time to grab off British interests in the Mediterranean area.

On June 28, Mussolini ordered the invasion of Egypt, "that great reward for which Italy is waiting." Britain had only 36,000 men in Egypt; opposing them in Libya were nearly 250,000 Italians. Still, preparations for the attack dragged on for two and a half months. Through the summer, the Italian High Command fueled the fires of enthusiasm on the home front with grandiose pronouncements of victories elsewhere in Africa. Mussolini's armies seized posts along the Egyptian-Libyan border, drove into Kenya, penetrated the Sudan and took British Somaliland. In the heart of Rome, the Italian advances were charted on a huge map *(right)*, and people throughout Italy were soon telling themselves: "We are a revived nation. We can fight."

Finally, on September 13 the Italians launched their expedition into Egypt, hoping to make a clean sweep to the Suez Canal. Across the Libyan border they streamed, 80,000 strong. There were five infantry divisions, seven tank battalions. When the smoke and dust of the first attack cleared, the British were amazed to see a large part of this formidable force arrayed before them as though on review—first the motorcyclists, then the light tanks, then the other vehicles, all drawn up in neat rows. The outnumbered British fell back, but not before—in Prime Minister Winston Churchill's words—"our artillery took its toll of the generous targets presented to them."

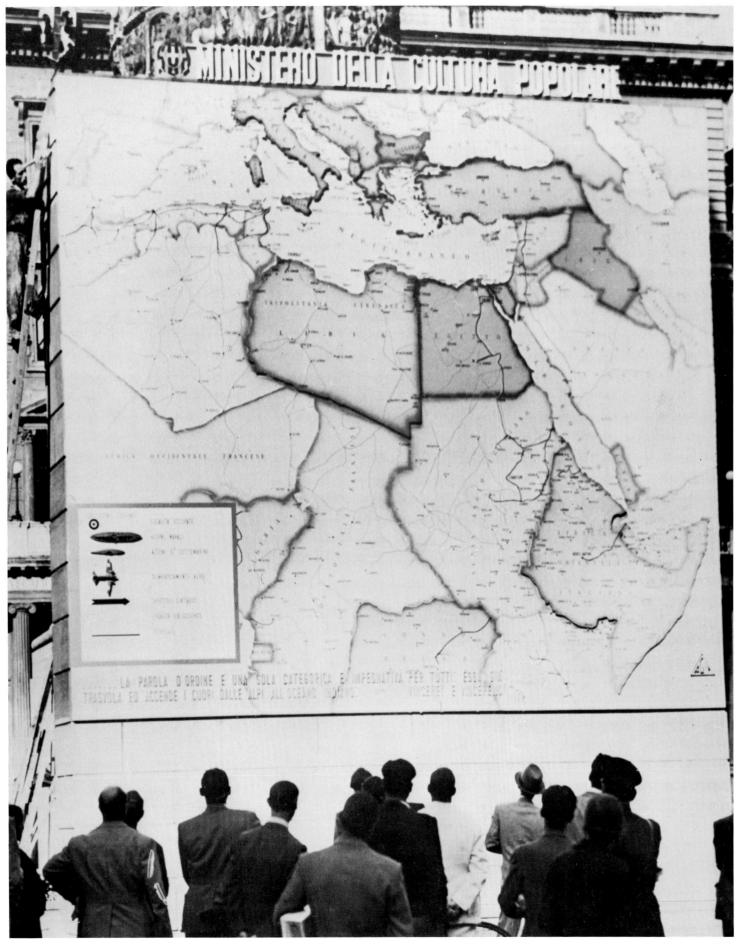

While a worker on a ladder adds the finishing touches, passersby in Rome scan a map erected to trace the successes of the Italian Army in North Africa.

Trim and cocky, goose-stepping Italian Blackshirts pass a saluting Marshal Rodolfo Graziani in Benghazi on August 14, 1940, on their way to the Libyan front.

Sun-helmeted Italian foot soldiers, carrying rifles and shouldering light machine guns, trudge across the desert during their September 1940 offensive. The greater part of the Italian Army was made up of infantrymen, who were of little use against the more mobile British.

SETTING FORTH ON THE ROAD TO DISASTER

As the Italian troops advanced into Egypt, they appeared to be a formidable fighting force. But the reality was otherwise. Their tanks were so flimsy they split apart under fire. Their solid-tired trucks were no match for desert boulders and shook to pieces. And many soldiers were poorly trained.

Nevertheless, at the start of the campaign, all went well. Four days out, the Italians occupied Sidi Barrani—a 60-mile advance uncontested by the British. Here they halted to consolidate their gains before the final push and here they had their first real taste of the desert. The land was barren and the life spartan. The officers were contented. They were well fed and slept on sheets; to them, victory seemed sure and adversity worth bearing. But the enlisted men had poor food and dismal living conditions, and their morale sagged. "This is an evil that must pass quickly," wrote one. Others began to wonder why they were there. One commented: "This is a European war fought in Africa with European weapons against a European enemy. We take too little account of this. . . . We are not fighting the Abyssinians now."

On December 9 the storm hit. The British, who had used the respite to build up their forces, launched a counterattack— and the Italians were suddenly routed.

A phalanx of Lancia trucks, loaded with Italian artillerymen, draws up on the Libyan sands, waiting for orders to advance. Officers ride in a small Fiat convertible (right); the vehicle with the oversized wheels at far left was used for pulling guns and field kitchens.

As artillery shells explode in the background, Italian infantrymen charge across the Western Desert in a December 1940 attack on British positions. Such heroics

did little to stem the tide of the British counteroffensive, which wiped out three Italian divisions at Sidi Barrani and then swept over the stronghold of Bardia.

An endless stream of Italian captives, reflecting the demoralization of defeat, marches toward a detention area after the fall of Bardia in early January, 1941. By this time, less than a month after the British counteroffensive had been launched, some 80,000 Italians in the Western Desert had surrendered or been taken prisoner.

At dawn on September 13, 1940, a fanfare of silver trumpets sounded across the barren landscape of the North African desert. From Fort Capuzzo, just inside Libya's border with Egypt, streamed a long line of tanks in single file, followed by three infantry regiments, an artillery regiment, a machine-gun battalion, and engineer and mortar companies. At the head of the column, in the flamboyant style of an earlier war, marched the black-shirted shock troops known as Arditi, armed with daggers and hand grenades. And in the wake came trucks loaded with marble monuments, which were intended to mark the triumphal progress of Italian fighting men as they swept across Egypt and wrested it from Britain's control.

Such, at least, was Benito Mussolini's fond hope. For a year, since the start of World War II, Italy's dictator had enviously watched his Axis partner, Adolf Hitler, achieve one conquest after another across Europe. Now, in the late summer of 1940, final victory in the West appeared within Hitler's grasp. Only Britain remained to be crushed, and an intensifying German air assault on its cities promised to hasten that end.

Mussolini, calculating the probabilities, foresaw an outcome not at all to his liking. Unless he put on his own show of military might while there was still time, he could hardly make a case for sharing the fruits of Axis victory. "To be able to attend the peace conference as a belligerent," he told Marshal Pietro Badoglio, Chief of the Italian General Staff, "I need a few thousand dead."

The thesis had been pretested in France, though with dispiriting results. In June, with France about to fall to the Germans, Mussolini had suddenly declared war on the Allies and sent troops into the corner of France that bordered on Italy. The foray had earned him widespread derision as a jackal trying to feed upon a corpse and had gained him only a sliver of territory—Hitler would allow him no more.

Africa, however, offered a rosier prospect. In moving to seize Egypt, the Italians would start with certain advantages. One was the current plight of the British. Though they had long dominated Egypt, first under a protectorate and more recently under a treaty that permitted British troops to be stationed there, they were now preoccupied with defending their own island. With their resources of men and

1

A GAMBLE FOR HIGH STAKES

matériel stretched thin, they could ill afford to reinforce their Middle East bastion.

A second advantage to the Italians lay in their own years of entrenchment in Africa. Libya, with nearly 1,000 miles of strategic frontage on the Mediterranean, had been in Italian hands since 1911, Eritrea and Italian Somaliland on Africa's eastern coast even longer. To his East African possessions Mussolini had recently added Ethiopia. Libya lay immediately to the west of Egypt; and Ethiopia abutted on the British colonies in East Africa. Britain's domination of the area could thus be challenged on two fronts.

Behind his bravado, Mussolini knew that his forces' quick victory over Ethiopian tribesmen in 1936 was not likely to be duplicated in combat with the well-trained British troops in Egypt. Still, given Britain's dilemma of the moment, the gamble looked possible. And it would show Hitler that the Duce was pressing the Axis cause with proper fervor.

The man chosen by Mussolini to lead Italy's North African forces was the 58-year-old Marshal Rodolfo Graziani, a much-bemedaled veteran of earlier African campaigns against rebellious natives, who was known out of earshot as "The Butcher" for his mode of dealing with his adversaries.

Graziani had expected that his task would be largely defensive—to guard Libya against British inroads from the east and against attack from French-controlled Tunisia on the west. But the fall of France had removed the threat from Tunisia. On taking up his post, Graziani was appalled to learn that he was expected to advance 300 miles into Egypt and capture the great British naval base at Alexandria. At once he flew home to Rome to plead with both Mussolini and Chief of Staff Badoglio.

His forces, Graziani argued, would be no match for the British. He had transport for no more than four battalions. Some of the weapons at his disposal were better suited to a war-surplus dump: cannons and rifles dating from the 19th Century, rusting machine guns. He was also short of up-to-date equipment—planes, tanks, antitank and antiaircraft guns, even mines. At places along the Egyptian border Italian soldiers on night patrols were forced to defuse and steal British mines to sow their own minefields.

The bleak picture Graziani painted could not have surprised Mussolini and Badoglio. The military ventures of recent years—notably the Ethiopian campaign and the in-

tervention in the Spanish Civil War—had sapped Italy's military strength.

Then, in April 1939, Italy had invaded tiny Albania, its neighbor across the Adriatic, as a rival gesture to Hitler's take-over of Czechoslovakia. Though Albania had given up without a fight, the Italians were compelled to maintain a large occupation force there, using men and arms that might otherwise have been put at Graziani's disposal.

But Mussolini hungered for some sort of victory in North Africa, and Graziani's protests proved unavailing. All he could get from the Duce was soothing syrup. "I am not fixing precise territorial objectives," Mussolini assured him. "I only ask you to attack the British forces opposing you." Egypt, the Duce predicted, would be a rich prize, its seizure "the final blow to Great Britain."

A disconsolate Graziani returned to Libya with only one tangible promise. Soon, Badoglio pledged, he would send 1,000 tanks—the weapon most effective in desert terrain. The promise was never to be kept, though for a time it gave Graziani a logical excuse to delay the invasion while awaiting the tanks' delivery. Meanwhile, hostilities with the British were confined to border skirmishes, resulting in an unequal toll that reinforced the marshal's forebodings: 3,500 Italian casualties, 150 British.

Increasingly irked as Graziani stalled, the Duce set a deadline. Ready or not, Italian forces were to move into Egypt when Hitler's presumably imminent air victory over Britain's home island brought the first German soldier stepping onto British soil. By early September, Mussolini was no longer willing to wait for this landing to materialize. He ordered Graziani to get going in two days—or be replaced.

At first Graziani's pessimism seemed unfounded. Four days after his troops left Fort Capuzzo, they were 60 miles inside Egypt and holding the coastal settlement of Sidi Barrani (map, page 27). Except for its mosque and police station, this village was little more than a collection of mud huts. But Rome Radio lost no time boosting the victory to improbable heights. "Thanks to the skill of Italian engineers," it announced, "the tramcars are again running in Sidi Barrani."

What the elated Italian listeners could not know was that the British had withdrawn from Sidi Barrani according to plan, falling back 80 miles deeper into Egypt to the sponge-fishers' village of Mersa Matruh. Once known as Paraetonium, where Anthony and Cleopatra had frolicked in the blue sea waves, Mersa Matruh was now the terminus of a narrow-gauge railroad from Alexandria. It gave the British an advantage. If the Italians continued their advance, their supply lines would be extended and exposed to attack while the British, close to their own sources of supply, could wait for an appropriate moment to launch a counteraction.

Graziani, however, was unwilling to dispatch his troops farther into Egypt. Not only their left flank, but also the flow of their supplies along the only coastal road from Libya lay open to bombardment from British warships in the Mediterranean. Graziani chose to have his men dig in at Sidi Barrani.

From his headquarters some 300 miles to the rear in the Libyan town of Cyrene, he ordered his commander on the ground, General Mario Berti, to fan out the Italian forces in a semicircle of seven defensive camps. Over the next three months these outposts took on the leisurely air of a peacetime cantonment, down to such refinements as colognes and silver hairbrushes in the officers' quarters, engraved glasses in their clubs, tinned hams and Frascati wines at their tables. Everywhere, on walls and gateways, were blazoned rallying cries from Mussolini's speeches, wryly inappropriate for an army already beginning to tire of the quest for a latter-day Roman Empire: *Chi se ferma è perduto* (He who hesitates is lost) and *Sempre avanti* (Ever forward).

The British too dug in, under the command of Lieut. General Richard Nugent O'Connor, a shy, birdlike little man with a self-effacing manner. In the long weeks of waiting, Mersa Matruh became a town of troglodytes as O'Connor's troops—fed a spartan diet of corned-beef stew and strong, sweet tea—carved trenches and dugouts in the limestone rock beneath the sand.

At British headquarters back in Cairo, the Commander-in-Chief, Middle East, General Sir Archibald Wavell, also bided his time, waiting for troop reinforcements and for a shipment of tanks designed specifically to work in close support with advancing troops. The British "I" (for infantry) tank,

THE ROYAL DUKE'S EAST AFRICAN DEBACLE

While his armies in Libya girded for the invasion of Egypt that touched off the desert war, Mussolini set in motion the other half of his scheme of African conquest: a strike at the British in East Africa. To lead that campaign he chose the Duke of Aosta, cousin of King Victor Emmanuel III and governor general of Italian East Africa.

Aosta was popular with his British neighbors in East Africa. They liked his charm, his polished manners, his "Englishness." When Mussolini ordered him to attack, in June 1940, he did so reluctantly but dutifully. In two months, parts of the Sudan and Kenya and all of British Somaliland fell to his troops. By a year later, however, the British had recouped their losses, and also controlled Italian East Africa. The Duke was captured in the Ethiopian mountains and died the following year from tuberculosis and malaria while a prisoner of war in Kenya. But his former friends treasured a token of his gentlemanly ways. Before fleeing his headquarters in Addis Ababa, he had penned a courteous note thanking the British in advance for protecting the city's women and children, "thereby demonstrating that strong bonds of humanity and race still exist between our nations."

The Duke of Aosta, in his capacity as the viceroy of Ethiopia, receives the homage of an Ethiopian dignitary in the throne room of the exiled Emperor Haile Selassie.

dubbed the Matilda, weighed some 30 tons. Its three-inch armor was impenetrable to Italian guns, while its own gun, a 2-pounder, could penetrate the best tank the Italians had.

But more than weapons would be needed in order to prevail in this parched and desolate land. Both sides would have to contend not only with each other but also with the unique challenges presented by the terrain. The Western Desert—originally a designation for western Egypt alone, but later expanded to include eastern Libya—encompassed a roughly rectangular area about 500 miles long and 150 miles wide. Behind a sandy plain that bordered on the Mediterranean lay a high desert plateau, much of its dun-colored expanse strewn with boulders and pebbles. Despite the havoc the stony stretches played with tank treads and truck springs, crossing the plateau was fairly easy; but getting to it was not. Between it and the coastal strip loomed an escarpment with cliffs as high as 500 feet and with only a few places passable by wheeled or tracked vehicles.

From a military standpoint, the worst aspect of the Western Desert was its lack of distinctive landmarks. Traversing it, except along the one coastal road, was like sailing an uncharted sea, navigable only by sun, stars and compass.

The analogy between desert and sea warfare was vividly drawn by the Australian writer Alan Moorehead, then a correspondent in Egypt for the London *Daily Express.* "Each truck or tank," he wrote, "was as individual as a destroyer, and each squadron of tanks or guns made great sweeps across the desert as a battle-squadron at sea will vanish over the horizon. . . . When you made contact with the enemy you maneuvered about him for a place to strike much as two fleets will steam into position for action. . . . There was no front line. . . . Always the essential governing principle was that desert forces must be mobile. . . . We hunted men, not land, as a warship will hunt another warship, and care nothing for the sea on which the action is fought."

Something intangible was also required: a "desert sense" that told a man never to try to tamper with this formidable environment but to use or circumvent it as best he could. The seasoned men in charge of Britain's Western Desert Force had acquired this sense, and correspondent Moore-head described some of the ways they put it to work:

"Always the desert set the pace, made the direction and planned the design. The desert offered colors in browns, yellows and grays. The army accordingly took these colors for its camouflage. There were practically no roads. The army shod its vehicles with huge balloon tires and did without roads. Nothing except an occasional bird moved quickly in the desert. The army for ordinary purposes accepted a pace of five or six miles an hour. The desert gave water reluctantly, and often then it was brackish. The army cut its men—generals and privates—down to a gallon of water a day when they were in forward positions."

In sum, Moorehead wrote: "We did not try to make the desert livable, nor did we seek to subdue it. We found the life of the desert primitive and nomadic, and primitively and nomadically the army lived and went to war."

To the Italians, settled in comfort at Sidi Barrani and hoping for no more than a static war, the British way of accommodating to the desert was thoroughly distasteful. They would learn its advantages, at heavy cost, beginning in December of 1940.

Before that time, two events with direct implications for the North African campaign occurred elsewhere in the Mediterranean. One was to be of immediate benefit to the British; the other spelled protracted trouble for them.

On November 11, night-flying torpedo bombers from the British aircraft carrier *Illustrious* swooped in on Taranto in southern Italy, home base of the Italian fleet, and crippled three battleships at their moorings. The raid substantially reduced the Italian naval threat to British supply convoys bound from Gibraltar for Egypt. It also enabled Britain's Mediterranean fleet, under Admiral Sir Andrew Cunningham, to turn more attention to harrying Italian convoys on their far shorter run from Sicily to Libya. For the next few months, the Mediterranean lived up to its Royal Navy nickname, "Cunningham's Pond."

The other event had occurred a few days earlier. On October 28, Mussolini suddenly embarked on another foreign adventure, dispatching his occupation troops in Albania to invade next-door Greece; piqued at getting no advance notice of a German move into Rumania, a new convert to the Axis cause, he had decided, as he put it, to "pay Hitler back in his own coin."

Mussolini's invasion of Greece posed a problem for the British. Though it soon met with savage resistance, it also confronted Britain with the need to make good on a pledge to the Greeks—given in April of 1939 by Winston Churchill's predecessor as Prime Minister, Neville Chamberlain—to help them with arms and men if they were attacked. Despite Britain's badly depleted resources, Churchill felt that the British were bound to honor the commitment. He wired Greek Premier Ioannis Metaxas: "We will give you all the help in our power."

At first Metaxas, fearing that British involvement would bring Hitler in to shore up the faltering Italians, rejected Churchill's proposal. But the Greeks' reluctance was only temporary, and their eventual acceptance of Churchill's chivalrous offer was destined to prolong the war in North Africa. Aid to Greece could come only from Britain's reservoir of strength, such as it was, in the Middle East.

Some of the men around Churchill were dismayed by what they deemed a rash and ill-advised gesture on his part. "Strategic folly," Secretary of State for War Anthony Eden noted in his diary. The view was unanimously shared by the trio charged with protecting Britain's Middle East dominion by land, sea and air: General Wavell, Admiral Cunningham and Air Chief Marshal Sir Arthur Longmore, area commander of the RAF. Wavell, as overall head of the Middle East forces, was especially dismayed. From now on, he had to plan his counterattack against the Italians in North Africa as a race against time and amid renewed Churchill demands for action to save Greece.

Adding to the problem was the basic incompatibility of the two men—a clash of chemistries that was in time to lead to Wavell's removal from his post. Churchill was outspoken and articulate, Wavell withdrawn and taciturn. Once, asked by Australian Premier Robert Menzies for an appraisal of the Middle East situation, Wavell replied, "That is a complicated matter," then lapsed into a brooding 10-minute silence. Churchill assessed Wavell as "a good average colonel." Wavell detested politicians who meddled in military affairs. A veteran of World War I campaigns in Palestine and in France—where he had lost his left eye—he did not regard

The North African theater stretched across more than 2,000 miles from El Alamein in Egypt to south of Casablanca in Morocco. The war seesawed in the Western

Churchill's own short tours of duty in the Sudan and in France during the First World War as grounds for claiming military expertise.

Throughout the fall of 1940, Churchill kept up a barrage of advice, comments and criticism, which Wavell succinctly summed up as "barracking"—an Australian term for the heckling engaged in by spectators at a sporting match in order to disconcert the players. Though aware that Churchill had begun to suspect him of being less than resolute, Wavell was determined not to attack in the desert until he felt his preparations were complete. He was also determined not to reveal, except to key subordinates, the plan that was taking shape in his mind.

But a visit to Cairo by Anthony Eden forced Wavell's hand. The Secretary of State for War proposed to drain off so much matériel for the Greeks that, as Wavell put it, "I had to tell him what was in my mind to prevent my being skinned to an extent that would make an offensive impossible." Eden was so impressed by what Wavell told him that he scribbled a note reading, "Egypt more important than Greece," and conveyed the secret plan back to Churchill in London. To Wavell's astonishment, it utterly charmed Churchill. On hearing its details, the Prime Minister was to recall, "I purred like six cats."

The plan hinged on a piece of information reported by scouts and confirmed by aerial photographs: the Italians had left a 15-mile gap, unpatrolled and unfortified, between two of the seven outposts they had set up as a shield for Sidi Barrani. The camps in question were Nibeiwa, south of Sidi Barrani on the coastal plain, and Rabia, perched on the escarpment to the southwest. The fortified side of all the camps faced eastward toward the British. If the British could pass undetected through the Nibeiwa-Rabia gap, they would then be able to wheel about and fall upon the Italians from the undefended rear.

As refined by Wavell and his commander in the field, General O'Connor, the plan called for the use of the two

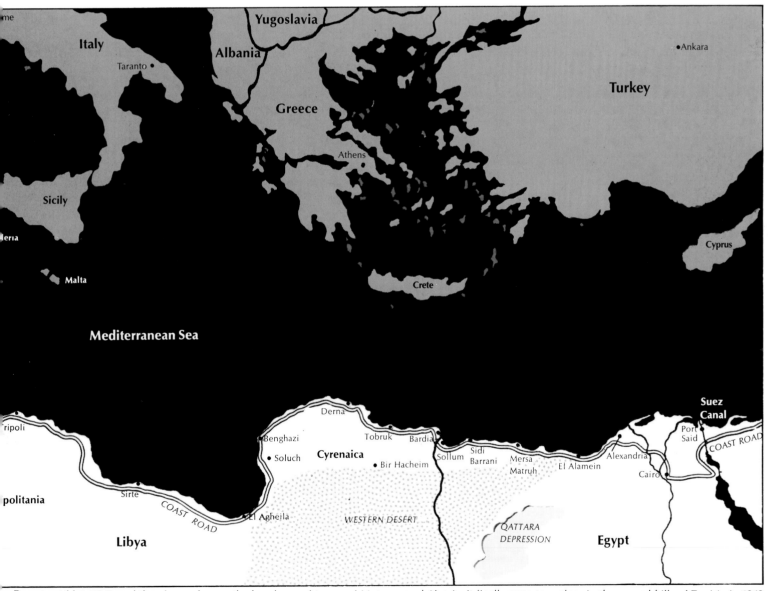

Desert until late 1942, and then focused upon the beaches and towns of Morocco and Algeria. It finally came to a close in the rugged hills of Tunisia in 1943.

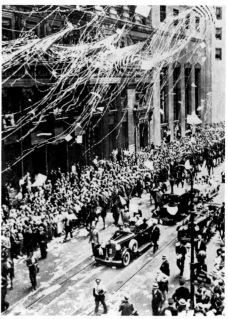

In flier's cap and goggles, Italo Balbo gets his military pilot's wings from the Duce in 1927.

Balbo is showered by New York's ticker tape.

Before beginning his 43-day air journey from Italy to Chicago and back, Balbo inspects his Savoia-Marchetti seaplane with its fore-and-aft propellers.

A MAGNIFICENT FLIER'S FALL FROM GRACE

Italian flier Italo Balbo was everything Benito Mussolini wanted to be: a handsome, flamboyant, international hero. In 1933 the bearded aviator led an armada of 24 twin-hulled seaplanes on a sensational 12,000-mile round-trip flight between Italy and the World's Fair in Chicago. Landing on Lake Michigan, Balbo was welcomed by more than 100,000 admirers, many waving the red, green and white flag of Italy. In New York, Mayor John P. O'Brien gave him a ticker-tape parade and said Balbo's name would be coupled with that of Columbus and Marconi. And in Washington, the flier lunched with President Roosevelt.

The transatlantic triumph and the world fame that it brought Balbo were not without price—the jealous Duce's secret and dangerous enmity. Mussolini gave Balbo a publicly warm welcome-home kiss on the cheek and the gold eagle insignia of Italy's first Air Marshal, but three months later the hero was packed off to be governor of the Italian colony of Libya. The post was an ignominious quasi exile for a man of Balbo's public stature and popularity, but he was stoic about it. "I obey orders," he said. "I am a soldier."

Although Balbo was an ardent Fascist—he was a founding member of the movement and was reported to have devised new methods of torturing anti-Fascists—he did not share the Duce's enthusiasm for the War. His objections undoubtedly irritated Mussolini. When the Duce warmed to an alliance with Hitler, Balbo protested: "You are licking Germany's boots." He was convinced that the Italian troops in Libya were no match for the British forces in Egypt. But he would not live to see himself proved right.

Flying over Tobruk on June 28, 1940—only 18 days after Italy declared war on Britain—he was shot down and killed by his own antiaircraft guns. Italian gunners had mistaken Balbo's plane for the enemy. (A British plane did fly over the city later—but only to drop a note of condolence from Middle East RAF Commander Sir Arthur Longmore.) Suspicion persisted that high-flying Italo Balbo was killed not by accident but on secret instructions from the resentful Duce.

Balbo and Italian King Victor Emmanuel III (left) review troops in Libya in 1938.

Seeking the dead hero's personal effects, a soldier combs the wreckage of Balbo's plane after it was mysteriously downed by Italian antiaircraft fire.

divisions in the Western Desert Force, the 4th Indian and the 7th Armored. Both divisions would move through the Nibeiwa-Rabia gap. Then the 4th Indian, supported by the 7th Royal Tank Regiment, would turn north and take Nibeiwa from the rear. After that the 4th would strike farther north to take three other camps on the coastal plain as well as Sidi Barrani itself. A frontal attack along the coast by British troops from the Mersa Matruh garrison, supported by gunboats of the Royal Navy, would take the coastal camp of Maktila and help mop up Sidi Barrani. Most of the 7th Armored Division, after moving through the gap, would head northwest for Buq Buq, a point on the coast road between Sidi Barrani and the Libyan border, to prevent the Italians from bringing up reinforcements. The rest of the 7th Armored, meanwhile, would swing westward onto the escarpment to prevent any interference from Rabia and from Sofafi, the other camp there.

Wavell did not contemplate a major offensive. He planned no more than a five-day raid, with Buq Buq, 25 miles west of Sidi Barrani, as the ultimate British halt line. His objectives were threefold: to test the Italians' fighting mettle in battle rather than in mere skirmishes, to secure a few thousand prisoners and—above all—to strike a decisive blow before the Germans moved to intervene in Libya.

Against some 80,000 Italians, General O'Connor had only 30,000 men—a polyglot force of Englishmen, Ulstermen, Cameron Highlanders, Sikhs, Pathans and Hindus.

At 7 a.m. on December 6, the two divisions moved out, tanks and gun carriers and trucks spaced 200 yards apart on a 2,000-yard front. Rocks and camel's-thorn often slowed them to a crawl. They had some 75 miles to cover before engaging in battle, but the desert-wise O'Connor, aware of the great strain imposed by the terrain, had planned accordingly. For one entire day and night, his 30,000 men would pause and lie out in the open, midway between Mersa Matruh and the Italian camps. Though they would be at the mercy of Italian spotter planes, as little as possible had been left to chance. O'Connor had even ordered windshields stripped from the trucks, lest the sun's reflections catch the eye of an enemy pilot.

Ahead of the advance, supplies lay buried deep in desert cisterns—planted there by patrols in the style of the warring Saracens more than 1,000 years earlier. Enough food, gasoline and ammunition had been stored to last the full five days until the projected return to Mersa Matruh.

Most of O'Connor's men thought they were on a routine training exercise. Briefings by the few officers in on the secret were noncommital: tank commanders were simply told that they would drive for some distance, pause for the night, then drive on the following day to an unspecified objective. The officers of the 7th Queen's Own Hussars were so certain of a speedy return to base that they dispatched a priority order to Alexandria: a special holiday feast for Christmas Day.

On the night of December 8, the troops moved on. Their way was now lit by a chain of beacons sited by patrols so as to be invisible from the Italian camps: gasoline cans, cut in half and facing toward the oncoming vehicles, shielded the steady glow of hurricane lamps. At 1 a.m., a few miles to the rear of the Italian camp at Nibeiwa, the British halted.

They were unaware of how well their luck was holding. Earlier that day, they had been spotted—by none other than Lieut. Colonel Vittorio Revetra, chief of the Italian fighter forces, while he was on a routine flight from a coastal airfield. Revetra promptly signaled Marshal Graziani at headquarters, reporting that he had seen "an impressive number of armored vehicles" moving up from Mersa Matruh. To his stupefaction, Graziani calmly ordered him to "let me have that in writing." The marshal later claimed that he had notified his subordinates in the field. But no action was taken against the British columns.

At 5 a.m. on December 9, the British awoke to darkness. In silence, the men breakfasted on canned bacon and hot tea, topped by a "fighting dram" of rum. The Muslims among them, forbidden alcohol, sucked on oranges. To the east, the fortified camp at Nibeiwa was gently astir. At 7:15 a.m., the first British tanks moved out. Incongruously, as they advanced some of the men could smell the tantalizing fragrance of hot coffee and rolls: the Italians were preparing breakfast.

It was never to be eaten. Rank upon rank of tanks came rumbling in. Riding on their flanks were Bren gun carriers, their machine guns uptilted in high-angle fire against the startled sentries on the ramparts. Then came a sound unfamiliar to Italian ears: the wild skirling of bagpipes sounding

Starting at Fort Capuzzo, Italian forces (red arrows) advanced eastward 60 miles to Sidi Barrani in Egypt, where they built seven fortified camps (red circles). The British (black arrows) withdrew to Mersa Matruh. They launched a counteroffensive three months later, moving along the coast and through an undefended gap that lay between Nibeiwa and Rabia, steadily pushing the Italians back. Most of the remaining Italian forces surrendered at Beda Fomm, nearly 300 miles inside Libya.

the charge as the Cameron Highlanders sprinted in, the rising sun shimmering from the steel of their bayonets. In the confusion, Italian cavalry horses took fright and stampeded screaming through the drifting smoke.

The Italians stood no chance. Twenty of their tanks were parked outside the camp perimeter. The Matildas shot them into smoking scrap metal and churned on. The defenders fought back with machine guns and grenades; many died bloodily beneath the Matildas' tracks. The tanks forged on, as one man would later recall, "like iron rods probing a wasp's nest."

Other men were to retain other memories: the stench from bursting creosote barrels; Italian officers, swathed in heavy blue cavalry cloaks, trying to rally their men; a litter of uneaten food and unused ammunition scattered among the tents. To Second-Lieutenant Roy Farran, the pell-mell speed of the attack was akin to "a gold rush on the Klondike." Private Jimmy Mearns of the 2nd Camerons fired as in a dream at an African manning a machine gun; standing over the fallen black soldier as the blood pulsed from a hole in his throat, Mearns felt the shock of taking his first life and retched helplessly.

On both sides there was savage determination. Nibeiwa's commander, General Pietro Maletti, sprang from his tent, firing a machine gun; then he fell, still firing, shot through the lung. Lieutenant James Muir, medic for the 1st Argyll and Sutherland Highlanders, his shoulder and pelvis smashed to pulp, lay on a stretcher under shell- and machine-gun fire, advising the stretcher bearers on how to treat the wounded.

By 9 a.m. the fighting was over. The first of the Italian outposts had fallen in only three hours. Against all expecta-tions, the attack had yielded 2,000 prisoners. As the battle moved on toward Tummar East and Tummar West, two other enemy camps 10 miles north of Nibeiwa, a sense of euphoria seized the British. It was as if, like gamblers hitting a winning streak, they could not fail now. One captain whose truck had broken down was determined not to abandon it; he had himself towed into battle backward, his soldier-servant sitting impertubably beside him. A section of the 1st Royal Fusiliers advanced on Tummar West kicking a soccer ball, until an Italian bullet burst it between their feet. Alongside them, cheering frenziedly, raced the New Zealand drivers of their troop carriers—men allotted no part in the battle plan, yet loath to miss a fight.

There were many bizarre moments. Lieut. Colonel Eustace Arderne of the 1st Durham Light Infantry, advancing with his men on the Italians' camp at Maktila, prepared to attack. But after only two bursts from Arderne's machine gunners, one of his officers shouted: "There's a white flag, sir!" "Nonsense!" Arderne snapped. But it was true. Inside the fort, a brigadier and his 500 men stood rigidly at attention. "Monsieur," the brigadier greeted Arderne in diplomatic French. "Nous avons tiré la dernière cartouche." ("Sir, we have fired our last cartridge.") Beside him, as he spoke, was a heaping pile of unspent ammunition.

The sweep to Sidi Barrani took two days, at one point through a sandstorm so blinding that the Argylls mistakenly fought a brisk skirmish with the Camerons. The town was quickly taken, and again it was much the same story as before—the British had achieved total surprise. So headlong was the Italian rout that as the first Matildas entered the gutted streets, still smoking from the shells of the prearranged British naval bombardment, a hospitalized appendicitis victim, already cut open, was found abandoned on the operating table.

By December 12, three days after the attack began, 39,000 Italians had surrendered or been captured. The British had expected 3,000 at most, and were acutely embarrassed. One tank commander radioed: "I am stopped in the middle of 200—no, 500—men with their hands up. For heaven's sake, send up the bloody infantry." A battalion commander estimated his prisoners at "five acres of officers, 200 acres of other ranks." Unending lines of Italians in dusty green uniforms choked the road to Mersa Matruh. There, the officers in charge, astonished at the size of the prisoner bag, furnished the arrivals with wood and barbed wire and set them to building their own stockade.

A disenchantment with Fascism and the Duce was quickly apparent. At Nibeiwa, captured Italian engineers, seeing British gunners set to work on a new forward gun emplacement, promptly brought picks and shovels and pitched in to help. Other prisoners showed some of their captors how to cook spaghetti and tomato sauce. One Pittsburgh-born Italian summed up the mood of many of his comrades: "If I could get my hands on that goddamned bastard Mussolini, I'd kill him right now."

In Cairo, Wavell was fast realizing that his "five-day raid" had acquired the irresistible momentum of a major campaign. Late on December 11, a message from the field reported: "We have arrived at the second B in Buq Buq"— where the British offensive had originally been supposed to stop. O'Connor's men kept going.

By December 16, a week after the fighting had begun, they had taken Sollum and Halfaya Pass and also moved into Libya to take Fort Capuzzo, Sidi Omar and other strong points that the Italians had set up on the escarpment near their stronghold at Bardia.

As fast as Wavell's planning staff could produce studies on the next phase of the combat, O'Connor, whose shyness hid a terrier-like tenacity of purpose, rendered them out of date. Conducting Admiral Cunningham on a tour of the war room at Cairo headquarters, Wavell confessed with characteristic candor: "You know, I never thought it would ever go like this."

Churchill was jubilant. Not long before he had been voicing the suspicion that Wavell might be "playing small." Now he cheered on his commander in the Middle East with the text of Matthew 7:7—"Ask, and it shall be given you; seek, and ye shall find; knock, and it shall be opened unto you." But the amity between the two men was to be short-lived. Even as O'Connor's main force, now far beyond Buq

Buq, swept on to besiege Bardia, one battalion had to be left behind on the battlefield. Its task, which was ordered by Churchill, was to salvage Italian guns and vehicles—to be sent to the Greeks when they finally accepted the offer of British aid.

The relationship between Graziani and Mussolini was also worsening. In a "man-to-man" telegram the marshal accused Mussolini of never having listened to him and of pushing him into a futile adventure. Graziani also called for massive German air support, protesting that "one cannot break steel armor with fingernails alone." Mussolini, as always when military disasters threatened, blamed his fighting men. "Five generals are prisoners and one is dead," he said to his son-in-law, Foreign Minister Count Galeazzo Ciano. "This is the percentage of Italians who have military characteristics and those who have none."

For the immediate future, the Duce was pinning his faith on a fighting soldier of the line: Lieut. General Annibale Bergonzoli, commander of Bardia, whose flaming red beard had earned him the nickname "Electric Whiskers." No cardboard general, Bergonzoli was a Spanish Civil War veteran who disdained luxury, ate and drank with his men, and slept in a noncom's simple tent.

"I am sure that 'Electric Whiskers' and his brave soldiers will stand at whatever cost," Mussolini exhorted Bergonzoli. The general's reply was suitably dramatic: "In Bardia we are, and here we stay."

He had good reason to be confident. Bardia perched 350 feet above a circular harbor, had a garrison of 45,000 men and was ringed by a 18-mile belt of defenses. Its capture required tanks, and a shortage of spare parts had temporarily robbed O'Connor of all but 23 Matildas. The brunt of the assault on Bardia would have to be borne by infantry; they would have to secure a bridgehead across a 12-foot-wide antitank ditch, and the minefields beyond it, to provide a safety lane for the lurching Matildas.

Few men were better fitted for the task than the men of the 6th Australian Division, newly sent in from Palestine to replace the 4th Indian Division. On the troop ships that had brought them to the Middle East, the Anzacs—as the Australians and New Zealanders were informally and collectively known—had made their officers' lives a hell, swimming

Burning fuel-dumps still cast a pall of sooty smoke over Tobruk, a key Italian port in Libya, two days after its fall. Australian forces overran the town on the 22nd of January, 1941—some of them making use of captured Italian tanks that they emblazoned with leaping white kangaroos so that their own comrades would not mistake them for the enemy.

ashore half-naked in Ceylon to caper in the streets, raiding Cape Town's breweries for a mammoth jag, kissing every woman in sight. Now these stalwarts thirsted for one thing only: to fight.

On January 2, Air Chief Marshal Longmore's Wellington bombers thundered in over Bardia. Along the landward arc of the defenses, a nonstop rain of bombs gouged at pill-boxes and machine-gun nests and set ablaze tanks and supply dumps. All night the RAF kept up the pounding; then, at dawn on January 3, the Australians moved in. Engineers dynamited the antitank ditch to create crossing sites, sliced at the wire surrounding the minefields, then flung grenades to detonate the mines. It was a complicated plan, requiring complicated logistics; 300 pairs of gloves for the wire cutters, flown overnight from Cairo, were doled out only as the men moved up. Behind the wire cutters came waves of Anzacs, boisterously singing "We're off to see the Wizard, the wonderful Wizard of Oz" and clad against the cold in sleeveless leather army jerkins that the terrified Italians took for some sort of armor. By noon the Anzacs had driven a wedge into the defenses 12,000 yards wide and 3,000 yards deep.

Meanwhile, Bardia lay under intensive bombardment by a Royal Navy force that consisted of three battleships, including Admiral Cunningham's flagship, the *Warspite,* and seven destroyers. When the bombardment was over, the gunboats *Ladybird* and *Aphis* and the monitor *Terror,* a heavily armored warship that was used chiefly for coastal action, glided toward the shore. At point-blank range they began to lob shells at the defenses beyond the cliff on which Bardia was situated.

By dawn on January 4, a heavy cloud of black smoke hung over the battered town. Then a whole section of the cliff gave way and slid roaring to the sea, wiping out many of the defenders' gun positions at one stroke.

As the day wore on, Bergonzoli saw that his position was hopeless. The bombing had cut off his water supply and wrecked his food depots. With a handful of troops, he slipped out of Bardia dressed as a private, passing close enough to the British lines to smell their cooking fires.

Bundled against the early-morning chill, Lieut. General Richard O'Connor (left), commanding Great Britain's desert forces, and General Sir Archibald Wavell, Commander-in-Chief, Middle East, confer near Bardia the day before the Italian stronghold fell to their offensive.

Hiding in caves by day and traveling by night, Bergonzoli escaped toward Tobruk, 70 miles west.

At sunset on January 4, the Italian flag was hauled down from Bardia's Government House, and the British had more than 40,000 new prisoners of war.

Tobruk, a major port, was the next target. O'Connor's tanks and trucks swept on like a battle fleet, their sides adorned with proud emblems—the leaping white kangaroos of the 16th Australian Infantry Brigade, the scarlet desert rats of the 7th Armored Division. Captured Italian trucks, emblazoned with such slogans as "Benito's Bus," were also in the ranks, rumbling past freshly posted road signs that read: "If you lika da spaghetti KEEP GOING. Next stop TOBRUK—27 kms."

But even as O'Connor's forces reached Tobruk's perimeter—120 miles beyond their original goal—Wavell, in Cairo, had a new reminder that the campaign was operating on borrowed time. Churchill again urged the Greeks to accept British aid. Metaxas again demurred, but Churchill remained adamant. In a message to London, Wavell questioned the Prime Minister's policy toward Greece; "nothing we can do from here," he said, "is likely to be in time to stop the German advance if really intended."

Churchill's reply was a stinging rebuke. "Nothing must hamper capture of Tobruk but thereafter all operations in Libya are subordinated to aiding Greece," he informed Wavell, adding acidly: "We expect and require prompt and active compliance with our decisions."

Throughout the autumn of 1940, Adolf Hitler's thoughts about the Mediterranean theater of war had been meticulously recorded in the diary of the Chief of the German General Staff, Colonel General Franz Halder. An entry for the 1st of November read: "Führer very much annoyed at Italian maneuvers in Greece . . . not in a mood to send anything to Libya . . . let the Italians do it themselves." And on November 3: "Führer stated that he has written off the Libyan affair."

But Britain's raid on Taranto eight days later, and a warning by Grand Admiral Erich Raeder that the British "had assumed the initiative at all points in the Mediterranean," changed Hitler's mind. Early in December he ordered that a number of German air units be transferred to bases in southern Italy to take part in attacks on British shipping in the Mediterranean.

This decision, put into effect less than a week after the Italian defeat at Bardia, was to alter the course of the desert war. The Luftwaffe's intervention conferred virtual immunity on Axis supply convoys and spelled deadly peril for those of the British.

The results were quick, dramatic and devastating. On January 10, 1941, Lieut. General Hans-Ferdinand Geisler, commander of the Luftwaffe's X Air Corps, was barely settled in his headquarters at the splendid Hotel San Domenico in Taormina, Sicily, when word came of the sighting of a British convoy with a large escort of warships. They were en route eastward from Gibraltar with troops and planes for the island of Malta, Britain's vital air and sea base in the mid-Mediterranean.

Among the warships escorting the convoy was the 23,000-ton *Illustrious,* whose torpedo bombers had struck at Taranto. One of Britain's newest carriers, she boasted an armor-plated flight deck. She was a terrible threat to Italy's supply convoys, and Geisler received a succinct message from Berlin: "*Illustrious muss sinken.*"

At 12:28 p.m. Captain Denis Boyd, on the bridge of the *Illustrious* 100 miles west of Malta, was anxiously scanning the sky. Minutes earlier, a flight of his Fulmar fighters had zipped off toward Sicily, pursuing two Italian Savoia torpedo bombers. On the flight deck, another group of Fulmars, engines turning over, were due to take off in seven minutes. Boyd briefly debated whether to get them airborne sooner, then decided against it.

In those seven short minutes the fate of Britain's Mediterranean fleet swung like an overweighted pendulum. Boring toward the convoy at 12,000 feet came 30 to 40 Junkers-88 medium bombers and Stuka dive bombers. The Stukas, plummeting in a perfectly coordinated attack, screamed down on the *Illustrious.* Six 1,000-pound bombs struck the carrier. One sliced through the flight deck and burst in the paint store, sending sheets of flame clawing skyward. Another burst on the No. 2 starboard gun, wrenching it from its mounting and killing the crew. A third struck the lift platform, blasting a plane and its pilot to smithereens. Other bombs burst in the heart of the ship, disintegrating the fire screens and punching the stricken hangar into the shape of a giant arch. A torrent of fire swept through the *Illustrious*.

Boyd now faced the crisis all carrier commanders dreaded: with his flight deck out of service, not one of his planes could either land or take off. Biting down on an empty pipe ("to stop my teeth from chattering with fright," he explained later), Boyd made for Malta at 21 knots with the *Illustrious* belching inky clouds of smoke and listing to starboard. Three times on the way, Axis planes—Savoias, Stukas, then Savoias again—swooped to attack, rekindling the carrier's fires and ripping apart her sick bay and wardroom. But by 10:15 p.m. she had docked at Malta's Parlatorio Wharf, hailed by a band and a sea of waving hands.

Her ordeal was not over. Repeated Stuka attacks greeted the carrier at the wharf, piercing her below the water line and flooding her boiler room. Two weeks later, with the repair scaffolds still swinging at her sides, she slipped out of Malta at dusk and eventually reached Alexandria—still afloat but operationally useless for 11 months.

The bombing of the *Illustrious* signaled the start of an intensified aerial assault on Malta that would last almost two years and make the island one of the most bombed targets in the War. More than 14,000 tons of bombs would fall on the Maltese before the nightmare ended.

By January 20, O'Connor was poised before Tobruk. His men had smashed eight Italian divisions; only about 125,000 poorly armed enemy troops—out of the original North African force of some 250,000—remained. But unless he could decisively break the Italian Army in Libya within a month and put the entire eastern province of Cyrenaica under British control, the Germans were likely to intervene.

Tobruk's more than 30 miles of perimeter defenses were breached in a day and a half. Advancing through a sandstorm that forced some of them to don their gas masks, the Australians wedged explosives beneath the wire entanglements and blasted them to shreds. By sunset on January 21, the first units had pushed on eight miles to Tobruk itself. One Australian who had served in Palestine commented: "The police in Tel Aviv give us a better fight than this." As they drove for the center of town, a greeting from an Australian airman the Italians had captured set the tone of the day: "Welcome pals! The town's yours."

Derna, 100 miles west of Tobruk, fell eight days later. O'Connor, tense and edgy and racked by stomach trouble, now faced the most critical test of all: Could he catch the Italians before they evacuated Cyrenaica? They were fast retreating along the southward-curving coast road from Derna through Benghazi toward Tripoli. If he moved quickly enough he might be able to cut them off before they could escape. Furious that a strong force of Italian tanks had escaped an attempted British trap at Mechili, a fort inland from Derna, O'Connor gave vent to a rare burst of temper. He stormed at Major-General Sir Michael O'Moore Creagh, commander of the 7th Armored: "You are going to cut the coast road south of Benghazi, and you are going *now*, repeat *now!*" Shortly, the word passed through the ranks: "The code word is Gallop."

At daybreak on February 4, the 7th Armored, now down to 50 cruiser and 80 light tanks, moved out of Mechili across the interior wasteland of Cyrenaica to try to cut off the retreating Italians beyond Benghazi. For some 30 hours, striving to cover 150 miles, men jounced in tanks and trucks over rocky, bone-jarring ground, harried by blinding squalls and vomiting from sheer fatigue. Racing in their wake came O'Connor and Brigadier Eric Dorman-Smith, Wavell's envoy with the Western Desert Force. Alarmed by the spectacle of abandoned broken-down British tanks that marked the way, O'Connor had sudden doubts. "My God," he burst out to Dorman-Smith, "do you think it's going to be all right?"

But at noon on February 5 came the signal that all his men had awaited, from an armored car near the village of Beda Fomm south of Benghazi. The road was cut. Thirty minutes later, trailing a plume of dust, the first trucks of the retreating Italian column loomed on the road from the north. O'Connor had sprung his trap with half an hour to spare.

For a day and a half a battle raged. Time and again the Italian tanks charged en masse, in a desperate attempt to break through; but they had only one wireless set for every 30 tanks, and coordination proved almost impossible. During lulls in the fighting a bizarre note intruded: local Arabs, their camels grazing peacefully nearby, would appear to sell eggs to both sides.

By February 6, with one British brigade down to 15 cruiser tanks, bluff began to count as much as armor. When a non-com complained that his gun barrel was bent all out of shape, his tank commander suggested that he stay put and simply *look* dangerous.

At first light on February 7, O'Connor received word that Marshal Graziani had decamped to Tripoli and that the army he had abandoned was surrendering; it could fight no longer. In their car, O'Connor and Dorman-Smith crossed a battlefield strewn for 15 miles with the debris of war. Every rise was littered with burned-out tanks. Softly shifting sand covered the dead; desert birds circled overhead. "Dick, what does it feel like to win a complete victory?" Dorman-Smith asked. O'Connor replied quietly, "I'll never believe I'm a successful general until I've commanded my forces through a retreat."

All through the day, in the battlefield mess tent and at O'Connor's new headquarters near Beda Fomm, there was a strange sense of anticlimax. Some men wondered whether the fighting was really over. Told that 400 Italians were ready to surrender, Lieut. Colonel John Combe of the 11th Hussars remarked wearily, "Tell them to come back in the morning." Sipping a victory drink, O'Connor apologized politely to one captured Italian general for the makeshift accommodations, commenting that not since 1911, when he had attended a particularly resplendent international gathering in India, had he seen so many Italian generals in one place. Among them was General Bergonzoli. Sheepishly, Bergonzoli pronounced what might have served as the campaign's epitaph: "You were here too soon."

Everywhere were reminders that the Italians had paid a terrible price for Mussolini's North African dream. Second-Lieutenant Roy Farran and his men, detailed to bury an enemy tank crew, found the task beyond them. All four of the Italian crew had been decapitated by a shell while sitting in their action stations; the stench inside the tank was unbearable. Suddenly, in a ghastly parody of combat, the tank rolled downhill, its engine turning over, a dead man's foot still jammed on the accelerator. Appalled, Farran and his men at last approached the tank, laid a trail of gasoline, and set fire to it.

On February 12, Brigadier Dorman-Smith was back in Cairo on an important mission: to persuade his commander in chief to approve O'Connor's request to drive on toward the Libyan capital of Tripoli. But even as he entered Wavell's map room he knew the answer. The desert maps had vanished from Wavell's wall, replaced by maps of Greece.

Wavell swept an arm toward them. "You see, Eric," he said wryly. "You find me busy with my spring campaign." Premier Metaxas of Greece had died suddenly, and his successor, Alexander Koryzis, had finally accepted Churchill's offer of help.

There was another bitter irony for Wavell. In two months O'Connor had advanced 500 miles and taken 130,000 prisoners, some 400 tanks, more than 1,000 guns and the major fortresses of Bardia and Tobruk. But he had defeated the Italians too quickly. Four months later, all of Hitler's resources would have been irrevocably committed to his obsessional attack on Russia, and other military ventures would have been out of the question. Now the seeds of trouble had been sown for the British in Africa.

On Sunday, February 9, Major General Enno von Rintelen, German military attaché in Rome, arrived at Mussolini's 40-room mansion, Villa Torlonia, with news that left the Duce beaming. A panzer division and a light mechanized division were to be dispatched from Germany to serve as a blocking force in Tripolitania, the Libyan province to the west of Cyrenaica.

Germany was now coming to the rescue of the Italians in North Africa.

THE DESERT FOX

Lieut. General Erwin Rommel, sporting a jaunty plaid scarf and a pair of captured British sun goggles, leads his panzer troops through the North African desert.

A LEGENDARY SOLDIER WITH A SIXTH SENSE

As an instructor of Army recruits in 1912, the youthful Lieutenant Rommel was a sober, serious man who was fascinated by military minutiae.

In January of 1942, as Allied forces in the North African desert struggled to regain ground lost to the Germans, Prime Minister Winston Churchill stood in the House of Commons and paid a singular tribute to one of Britain's most determined foes: "We have a very daring and skillful opponent against us, and, may I say across the havoc of war, a great general."

That general was Erwin Rommel, an aggressive, indefatigable and audacious soldier, whose exploits in North Africa earned him the nickname "Desert Fox" and made him a legend among his enemies. As commander of the Afrika Korps, Rommel applied blitzkrieg tactics to warfare in the desert with a mastery that awed the British. Among the troops opposing him his name came to be synonymous with success—so much so that any British soldier who performed well might be described by his comrades as "doing a Rommel."

Born the son of a schoolmaster in the German village of Heidenheim, Rommel joined the Army at the age of 18 and won high honors for his courage and skill in combat against the French and Italians in World War I. By the time he was 25, senior officers were seeking his advice on battlefield tactics. Two decades later, by then a major general, Rommel drove a panzer division through France in an operation so successful it made him a German national hero.

In the desert, Rommel's pace was as furious as a driving sandstorm. He directed his panzers from the front lines, oblivious to crackling shellfire and the threat of capture, protected by what his soldiers called *Fingerspitzengefühl*, "an intuition in the fingers," a sixth sense. "No admiral ever won a naval battle from a shore base," he said, fond as he was of comparing desert combat to warfare at sea. His split-second ingenuity under fire often violated textbook principles of military tactics and threw his enemy into confusion. He was a master of the unexpected, with a gift for improvisation. Outside of waging war, he had few interests. "He was 100 per cent soldier," recalled a general who served under him. "He was body and soul in the war."

In a portrait made by Hitler's chief photographer, Heinrich Hoffmann, Rommel displays the field marshal's baton awarded by the Führer in September 1942.

Rommel, outfitted in his new German Army uniform, displays a stony countenance in a 1910 photo with his younger brothers, Gerhard and Karl, and his older sister, Helene.

The 24-year-old Lieutenant Rommel manages an air of insouciance during a lull in combat in 1915 in France's Argonne Forest. He had only recently recovered from his first wound.

QUIET MOMENTS ON THE RISE TO FAME

"My Dearest Lu," began the letters Rommel wrote nearly every day to his wife from the far-reaching battlegrounds of his fighting career. Apart from military matters, Rommel's concerns in life were limited to his wife, Lucie Maria Mollin, whom he married in 1916, and Manfred, their son. As a soldier of the old school, Rommel had no taste for the heady revolutionary maneuverings that took place in Germany between the world wars. Although devoted to Hitler, Rommel never joined the Nazi Party. He disliked the Führer's SS troops and in time came to regard most of the Hitlerian entourage with disdain.

In 1937, Rommel published a book on infantry tactics. Hitler read and admired it, took an interest in its author, and assigned Rommel to his personal staff. As the Führer's protégé, Rommel was assured a key role in the war soon to come.

A decorated Rommel poses with his wife,
Lucie, in 1917, following his greatest triumph of
the First World War—the capture of
an Italian mountain and its 9,000 defenders.

During the Second World War, on leave from
the campaigns, Rommel visits his wife and son,
Manfred, at home in Wiener Neustadt, a
town in the mountains to the south of Vienna.

Poring over a battle map, Rommel ponders tactics with his staff officers in northern France in the late spring of 1940. During the pell-mell drive of his 7th Panzer Division through the French countryside to the Atlantic coast, he exposed himself repeatedly to frontline action and narrowly escaped capture.

Poring over a battle map, Rommel ponders tactics with his staff officers in northern France in the late spring of 1940. During the pell-mell drive of his 7th Panzer Division through the French countryside to the Atlantic coast, he exposed himself repeatedly to frontline action and narrowly escaped capture.

THE GHOST DIVISION STALKS NORTHERN FRANCE

"What do you want?" Hitler asked Rommel a few months before the German invasion of France in 1940. "Command of a panzer division," Rommel quickly replied.

The Führer's resultant gift—the 7th Panzer Division—played a devastating role in the defeat of France. Rommel crossed the Belgian border on the 10th of May, 1940, and charged steadily ahead for five weeks, his panzers firing on the move, their turrets roving like those of battleships. Called the "Ghost Division" because of its sudden and unexpected appearances, the 7th Panzer surprised barracks full of French soldiers, overran retreating French detachments and terrified unsuspecting civilians. Patting Rommel's arm, a villager asked him if he was English. "No, Madam," he replied. "I am German." "Oh, the barbarians!" she screamed, fleeing home.

The Ghost Division pushed to the English Channel, then swooped west along the coast to capture Cherbourg, covering as much as 150 miles in a day. Rommel's calculated boldness in waging tank warfare had set the stage for his brilliant performance in North Africa the next year.

On a rocky French beach, Rommel plants his combat

40

boot symbolically in the waters of the English Channel. "The sight of the sea with the cliffs on either side thrilled and stirred every man of us," he later wrote.

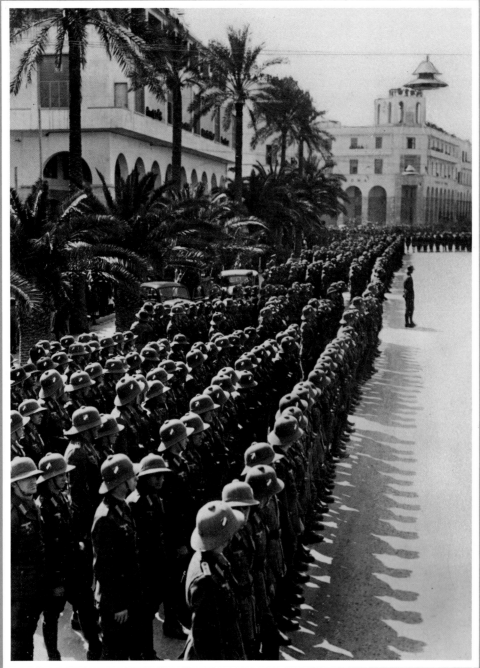

The first soldiers of the Afrika Korps to arrive from Germany stand at parade rest on a street in Tripoli.

FROM VICTORY IN FRANCE TO PALM-STUDDED SANDS

"It's one way of getting my rheumatism treatment," Rommel wrote his wife before leaving for arid Libya in February 1941. It was his coded message to her that his two-year desert campaign was beginning.

In his role as commander of the Afrika Korps, Rommel tended to be impatient and abrupt with his senior officers, but kind and understanding with the younger soldiers, who bore the brunt of combat. He shared their hardships and earned their respect. In his dashes about the front he ran the same risks his troops did. Tough-

ened by mountaineering and skiing in his youth, he subsisted on snatches of sleep and the basic rations—canned meat and black bread—of common soldiers. He appeared impervious to the harsh desert life.

Almost immediately after he had arrived in Africa, Rommel began to shove the British eastward through the sands toward the gates of Alexandria. On June 21, 1942, he led his men to their most spectacular victory when the British fortress of Tobruk fell to his panzers. Later that same year, however, hamstrung by supply shortages and the German High Command's disinterest in the desert war, Rommel's forces began their slow slide to ultimate defeat.

Rommel rides in a procession in Tripoli beside

General Italo Gariboldi, the Italian commander in North Africa. Later, the Desert Fox would say of many of the Italians: "Certainly they are no good at war."

43

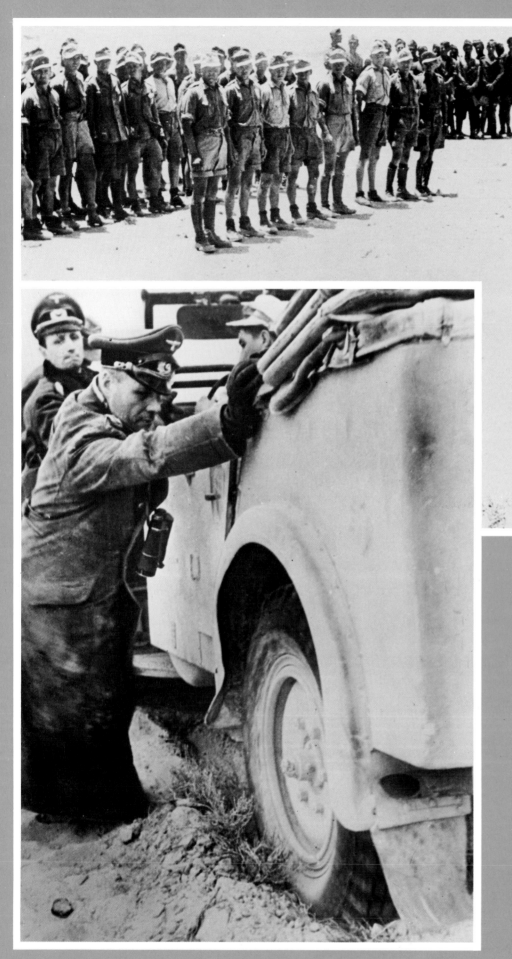

Fond of giving impromptu speeches or detailed lectures on battlefield tactics, Rommel thanks his men for their performance in combat near the desert town of Sollum in 1941.

The ever-present binoculars dangling from his neck, Rommel strains to help his officers free his staff car from the desert sand. He was not above dirtying his hands alongside his men.

Although he possessed no pilot's license, Rommel was an eager and confident amateur aviator who often took to the air for desert reconnaissance missions.

45

In field headquarters set up at the site of an old well in May 1941, Rommel uses a telephone to direct the siege of Tobruk on the Libyan coast. Tobruk's stout defenses would frustrate the Desert Fox for an entire year, until, on June 21, 1942, the town finally fell to him after only a single day of concentrated attack.

HELL'S OWN BATTLEGROUND

In a howling desert wind, an Italian soldier ventures forth from a command post near Sidi Barrani. The horn on the stick at left was meant to be a good-luck charm.

THE WESTERN DESERT: A SECOND FOE

Late in April 1941, on the edge of the Western Desert, infantrymen of Lieut. General Erwin Rommel's Afrika Korps captured a desolate ridge south of Tobruk. Shortly thereafter a British artillery barrage pinned them down. In their attempt to dig in, the Germans found they could not make even a dent in the desert's underlying limestone layer. All day they lay motionless beneath a scorching sun as they tried not to draw more British fire. Swarms of black flies viciously attacked them. Darkness only increased their misery as the temperature plunged and left them shivering throughout the night. The following day the sky blackened and a sandstorm raged over them.

For soldiers in the desert war these were not unusual experiences. The Western Desert, where much of the fighting occurred, formed a rectangle 500 miles long and 150 miles wide. Although fringed by a fertile coastline, its inner reaches were a wasteland devoid of almost all life except for a few Bedouin nomads and such drought-adapted species as poisonous scorpions and vipers, and prickly camel's-thorn. Water could be obtained only from widely scattered cisterns or by drilling deep into the ground. Every item a soldier needed or wanted had to be brought in by truck.

The desert's torments were many. Temperatures fluctuated as much as 60 degrees in a single day. Sand that was as fine as talcum powder routinely clogged rifle breeches and inflamed eyes, and when driven by the hot southerly wind, it filled nostrils, permeated cracks in vehicles and tents, buried food and equipment, and reduced visibility to a few yards. On clear days mirages played tricks with vision, and concealment in so bleak and featureless a land became a conjurer's art.

And yet the desert was uniquely suited to the waging of war. The open spaces and the lack of natural obstacles made it ideal tank country. So did the absence of permanent human settlements. As Fred Majdalany, chronicler of the British Eighth Army's exploits, put it: "There was absolutely no one and nothing to damage except the men and equipment of the opposing army."

Afrika Korps troops advancing into the desert wear tight-fitting goggles to protect their eyes from flying sand churned up by wind and vehicles.

Partially concealed behind a hastily improvised rock shelter, a German forward observer peers through a periscopic instrument used to adjust artillery fire.

A STINGING MENACE
BORNE BY THE WIND

The British called it *khamsin*, Arabic for the hot wind that blows out of the Sahara; the Germans used another Arabic word for it, *ghibli*. Most frequent in spring, the wind raised temperatures by as much as 35°F. in a couple of hours and sapped friend and foe alike. Bedouin tribal law permitted a man to kill his wife after five days of it.

As the wind roared in, it swept up sand and sent grains billowing across hundreds of square miles. Visibility dropped to zero, and soldiers gasped for air through makeshift sand masks while gusts of hurricane force overturned trucks and whisked telephone poles from the ground. Whirling particles of sand created electrical disturbances that drove compasses crazy. On the Gazala line south of Tobruk, in May 1942, such storm-generated electricity during a *khamsin* was blamed for an explosion that destroyed an ammunition dump.

Goggles and a mask were issued to early Afrika Korps troops for protection against sandstorms. Later in the war, the helmet was replaced by a cloth cap.

A swirling sandstorm advances on trucks and men southeast of El Alamein in September 1942. Such desert storms blotted out the sun, raised the temperature and sometimes stopped battlefield movements for days, pinning down troops, halting tanks and grounding planes. Their winds raged up to 90 miles an hour.

MAKING DO IN A LAND OF EXTREMES

The most precious item in the desert war was water. When the Afrika Korps attacked the Gazala line, 350 miles west of El Alamein, in the summer of 1942, it carried with it only a four-day supply: three quarts for each man per day, four quarts for each truck and eight quarts for every tank. If the water ran out before the battle was over, the soldiers would have to survive on whatever they could capture or find—or die of thirst. Fortunately for the Germans, the battle soon ended—in victory.

The lack of water in the outlying desert areas posed a major challenge to both armies. Not a drop could be wasted. Dirty water was hoarded and filtered through cloth into radiators. Obtaining fresh supplies was a matter of critical importance. The British copied a sturdy German water can—theirs leaked—and called it the jerry can after the enemy, known as "Jerry" to two generations of British soldiers. Loaded with these four-and-one-half-gallon receptacles, fleets of trucks crisscrossed the desert to bring water to thirsty outposts.

Water that was distilled from the salty Mediterranean and chemically treated left much to be desired. The British boiled it for tea, but found that when they added milk it curdled and went to the bottoms of their cups in big lumps.

Pausing on the march to Benghazi in spring 1941, German soldiers strip to the skin for a rare bath at a desert cistern. Such reservoirs caught and held rain water, but since rains were infrequent, the cisterns were often empty and the armies used them as storage tanks.

Lacking water, a German soldier scrubs his uniform with sand to rid it of salt, oil and grime. The British often used gasoline as well as sand to clean their clothes and save water. Without such makeshift methods, clothes would become stiff from dirt and salty sweat.

Swathed in head nets to protect their eyes, nostrils and mouths from swarms of flies, German troops tackle another desert hazard: dust and grit in their weapons.

Gauze dressings like those on the legs of the two men to the right were essential to keep sand away from even the smallest sores, which otherwise would not heal.

A German desert warrior fries eggs on the sun-heated hull of a tank. Cooking in this way was more a stunt than normal practice, but metal that was exposed to direct sunshine was sometimes hot enough to inflict serious burns on bare skin if tankers or others accidentally touched it.

Huddled in a slit trench and bundled up against the desert's chill night air, a British soldier sleeps with his gear close at hand. Such trenches not only provided protection from anything short of a direct hit by bomb or shell, but also offered their occupants a modicum of warmth.

2

It was a spectacle designed to awe Tripoli's Italian population and impress any British spies who might be watching. Across the city's main piazza rumbled a seemingly endless column of formidable 25-ton Panzer III and Panzer IV tanks, painted in the newly fashionable desert-camouflage shade of sand yellow. The tank commanders, wearing tropical uniforms much the same color as their vehicles, stood at attention in their turrets, as impassive as the death's-head badges adorning their lapels. Taking the salute on the reviewing stand was the man who had ordered this parade as a display of armored power, a short and muscular German lieutenant general with clear blue eyes: Erwin Rommel, commander of the newly formed Afrika Korps.

Standing near Rommel a young aide, Lieutenant Heinz-Werner Schmidt, watched the continuous line of tanks clattering through the square and out a side street with growing amazement. "I began to wonder at the extraordinary number of panzers passing by," he later recalled. After some 15 minutes, when he noticed a Panzer IV with a distinctive faulty track and realized he had seen it earlier in the procession, Schmidt chuckled. In a speech to German officers the previous evening, Rommel had stressed the importance of deceiving the enemy about the weakness of the Afrika Korps, which was still awaiting the arrival of most of its forces from Europe. Now, Schmidt realized, his chief was running the tanks around a few blocks to stretch a panzer regiment to the proportions of an armored corps.

The date was March 12, 1941. Rommel, who had arrived in North Africa only four weeks earlier, was already demonstrating his mastery of audacity and deception, qualities that were to play as great a part as real armored power in the next phase of the desert war. They were qualities the British had yet to master or learn to cope with. Even Rommel's identity had been successfully hidden from the British until the past few days. Before March 8, General Wavell's staff could only refer to the new German commander as "General X." Now, from their intelligence, they knew it was Rommel, and the knowledge caused some uneasiness in Cairo.

Rommel had the reputation of being a fighting general with an intuitive sense of his enemy's weakness, dedicated to the twin concepts of speed and surprise. His maxim was *Sturm, Swung, Wucht:* attack, impetus, weight. As commander of the 7th Panzer Division—the "Ghost Division"—

ROMMEL'S STUNNING BLOW

in May 1940, Rommel had time and again outsmarted the British retreating across France, repeatedly turning up in strength where least expected.

A 49-year-old self-made man from a family without money or influence, Rommel was proud and strong-willed and did not always conceal his contempt for some of the German Army's top brass. He considered Field Marshal Walther von Brauchitsch, the Army's commander in chief, to be an overly sensitive, withdrawn patrician. Rommel viewed the Army Chief of Staff, the acerbic and ambitious Colonel General Franz Halder, as an ineffectual deskbound soldier. Rommel himself was a field man, who enjoyed action and little else. He did not smoke and drank very little. He wrote almost every day to his wife, Lucie, but apart from his family his only pleasure in life seems to have been fighting—and winning. Joyful as a schoolboy when victorious, he became angry and petulant whenever he lost.

This galloping exponent of the open-ended offense had been sent to North Africa to fulfill an assignment that was clearly limited. The Italians were holed up in Tripoli, expecting the British to move along the coast and attack the port city at any moment. Many had their bags packed, hoping to be ordered aboard evacuation ships for a one-way voyage to Italy. Although Hitler considered North Africa a low-priority theater, he nonetheless felt that Germany should not let its Axis partner be pushed out of the region. He had agreed to send help. But Brauchitsch had made clear to Rommel when briefing him that his task was strictly defensive; for the moment Germany would not be able to send sufficient forces to drive the British from Cyrenaica, Libya's eastern province.

One of the two divisions allotted to Rommel, the 5th Light, began its transfer to North Africa in mid-February, planning to complete it by mid-April. More formidable than its name, the 5th Light Division included the 5th Panzer Regiment, which had 80 medium tanks (Panzer IIIs and IVs) and 70 light tanks. By the end of May, Rommel was told, he would receive a full-fledged panzer division, the 15th. What was left of the Italian motorized forces in North Africa—chiefly the Ariete armored division with 60 obsolete tanks—would also be under Rommel's command. But for the sake of diplomacy, the German was to serve under 62-year-old General Italo Gariboldi, who had succeeded the defeated Marshal Graziani as the Italian commander in North Africa.

When Rommel arrived in Tripoli on February 12, he fully expected the British to resume their westward thrust soon. He knew that if they attacked immediately, before his reinforcements arrived, there was little chance of stopping them. Lacking the men and equipment for a strong defense, he put his faith in a strong show of defense. "It was my belief that if the British could detect no opposition they would probably continue their advance," he wrote later, "but that if they saw they were going to have to fight another battle they would first wait to build up supplies. With the time thus gained I hoped to build up our own strength until we were eventually strong enough to withstand the enemy attack."

Within a few hours of arriving in Tripoli by plane he was back in the air for a flying reconnaissance of the desert east of the city. He decided to establish a forward defensive position in the area of Sirte, a village on the coastal road about halfway between Tripoli and the place where the British had finally halted their advance, El Agheila. General Gariboldi was reluctant to risk his few remaining troops by moving them 250 miles in the direction of the enemy, but Rommel insisted. "I had already decided, in view of the tenseness of the situation and the sluggishness of the Italian command," he said, "to take the command at the front into my own hands as soon as possible."

The next day two Italian infantry divisions and the Ariete Division were put on the road to Sirte. On February 14 the first German troops—one reconnaissance and one antitank battalion—arrived at Tripoli, and left for Sirte the next morning. Meanwhile, "to enable us to appear as strong as possible and to induce the maximum caution in the British," Rommel resorted to a ruse. He had a workshop make dummy tanks of wood and canvas mounted on Volkswagen chassis. By February 17, Rommel was sufficiently happy with his hastily assembled little army, half substance and half shadow, to write to his wife, Lucie: "Everything's splendid with me. . . . As far as I am concerned they can come now."

But the British did not come. They were going to Greece instead. The expedition to Greece, launched on March 4, stripped British defenses in eastern Libya to the bone. Cyrenaica was now "a passive battle zone" policed by the

THE DESERT FOX AS CAMERA BUFF

Among the many talents that Erwin Rommel employed in North Africa was his skill at photography, a peacetime hobby. Just hours after arriving in Libya he flew off in his Heinkel-111, camera in hand, to "get to know the country" he was to defend. Rommel thus opened the African chapter of a wartime scrapbook that ranged in subject matter from aerial panoramas to destroyed British tanks. Over the months in the desert Rommel took thousands of photographs. Besides being mementos of his campaigns, they were intended to illustrate a postwar book he planned—and was fated never to write. But in amassing his visual record, Rommel carefully avoided one subject. As he explained to his son: "I don't photograph my own retreat."

With his Leica, Rommel snaps one of his own weapons, a camouflaged 150mm gun.

On his first reconnaissance flight over the Libyan desert, Rommel shot this photograph of an Italian antitank ditch east of Tripoli.

One of the general's pictures records the escarpment that separates Tripoli's coastal plain from the Libyan plateau farther inland.

"minimum possible force." In theory, this consisted of the 9th Australian Division and the 2nd Armored Division. But both had been cannibalized for the campaign in Greece. What was left amounted to little more than an ill-trained, badly equipped infantry division and a weak, inexperienced armored brigade with tanks that kept breaking down under desert conditions. The western flank of Britain's Middle East command was thus dangerously vulnerable.

Moreover, the one man whose battle intuition might have been a match for Rommel's, Lieut. General Richard O'Connor—badly in need of a rest after his victorious campaign against the Italians—had been promoted to command of British troops in Egypt. At February's end, he was replaced as commander in Cyrenaica by Lieut. General Philip Neame, a soldier known for his bravery, but an engineer unversed in desert warfare.

As Wavell later was to admit, he had miscalculated fatally in making arrangements for Cyrenaica's defense. Not until mid-March—"when it was rather too late"—did he make a personal reconnaissance of the Benghazi area and the forward British positions. With dismay he discovered that he had "an entirely erroneous idea" of the escarpment south of Benghazi. He had thought that it was a barrier to tanks that could be scaled in only a few easily defended places. "When I actually went out and saw the escarpment, I realized that it could be ascended almost anywhere and was no protection." He found Neame's tactical dispositions "just crazy" and ordered some redeployment immediately. "But the really alarming feature," he recalled, "was the state of the cruiser tanks of the 2nd Armored Division, which were the core of the whole force." Of 52 tanks, half were in the workshop and more were breaking down every day.

Wavell instructed Neame that if his frontline troops at El Agheila were attacked they should fall back to Benghazi, fighting delaying actions along the way. If necessary, Neame was to yield Benghazi itself and save his armor by pulling it up onto the escarpment east of Benghazi. "I came back anxious and depressed from this visit," Wavell said, "but there was nothing much I could do about it. The movement to Greece was in full swing and I had nothing left in the bag."

Still, Wavell did not think Rommel would be capable of attacking before May. Neither did the German High Command. On March 19, the day after Wavell returned to Cairo from his visit to the front, Rommel flew to Berlin. He had become aware of the "momentary British weakness" and believed it should be "exploited, with the utmost energy, in order to gain the initiative once and for all for ourselves." He asked permission to attack the British immediately. Brauchitsch's answer was a flat no.

The German High Command, Brauchitsch told Rommel, still planned no decisive strike in North Africa, and he could expect no reinforcements beyond the ones already promised. (Unknown to Rommel, there were prior demands on available German forces. Hitler was about to send troops to aid Mussolini against Greece and was secretly planning an invasion of the Soviet Union.) Perhaps at the end of May, after the Afrika Korps had been strengthened by the arrival of the 15th Panzer Division, Rommel might launch a limited attack against British forward positions, perhaps advancing as far as Agedabia (map, page 67), Brauchitsch said. Later he might be allowed to retake Benghazi. But there was to be no general offensive. Rommel pointed out "that we could not just take Benghazi, but would have to occupy the whole of Cyrenaica, as the Benghazi area could not be held by itself." Brauchitsch was adamant: Rommel was to do nothing before the end of May. Rommel listened to his orders and then returned to North Africa to disobey them.

Before leaving for Berlin, Rommel had instructed that part of the 5th Light Division that had already arrived in North Africa—chiefly, the 5th Panzer Regiment—to prepare to attack El Agheila on March 24. On his return he ordered that the attack should proceed. His rationale for defying the High Command's cautious directive was that British patrols from El Agheila had been harassing supply columns bound for a German-Italian outpost at Marada, 90 miles to the south. To maintain this outpost, he had to throw the British out of El Agheila.

El Agheila was not strongly defended, and the British soldiers there shared Wavell's feeling that they were not immediately threatened by the enemy. But, at dawn on March 24, Rommel launched his attack. Deployed across a 1,000-yard front, the tanks and armored cars of Major Irmfried von Wechmar's 3rd Reconnaissance Battalion bored toward El Agheila. Behind them groaned trucks whose drivers were doing their best to obey Rommel's order: "Rear vehicles to raise dust—nothing but dust." For the first time Rommel's tactic of deception was put to a test in the desert. Many of Wechmar's "tanks" were incapable of firing a shot; they were the Volkswagen-mounted dummies, now known as "the Cardboard Division." But their outlines in the swirling dust suggested a formidable fighting force. The British garrison of El Agheila swiftly withdrew, falling back on Mersa Brega, 30 miles to the northeast.

Learning of the German advance to El Agheila and hearing of no British counterattack, Churchill cabled Wavell on March 26: "I presume you are only waiting for the tortoise to stick his head out far enough before chopping it off." In a long, rambling reply Wavell detailed the travails besetting his forces in Libya, weakened as they had been by the siphoning off of troops to Greece, and explained that he had no reinforcements to send Neame. In any case he was convinced the Germans would not be launching a major offensive soon. On March 30, Wavell wired Neame not to be too concerned about the enemy; "I do not believe he can make any big effort for at least another month." The next day Rommel struck at Mersa Brega.

He had paused at El Agheila for a week, but he feared that if he sat there until his panzer division arrived in May the British would be able to fortify a defile that made Mersa Brega a natural strong point. The 5th Panzer Regiment, which was advancing along the coastal road, provided the main German thrust. British resistance at the defile was determined, and by the end of the afternoon the attack had ground to a halt. But late in the evening Rommel sent a machine-gun battalion through some high, rolling sand hills to the north of the road. They struck the defenders' flank and dislodged them from the defile. The British hurriedly abandoned Mersa Brega as the Afrika Korps charged through the town of shell-shattered white houses chanting

their battle cry, "Heia Safari!"—Bantu for "Drive onward!"

The next morning Rommel learned from the Luftwaffe that the British were still withdrawing to the north rather than preparing defensive positions for another stand. The gates of Cyrenaica seemed wide open. To Rommel, in spite of his instructions not to undertake a major engagement until the end of May, "it was a chance I could not resist."

He ordered the 5th Light Division to move on Agedabia. On April 2, after a short battle, Agedabia and the nearby port of Zuetina were captured. Gariboldi now tried to restrain Rommel, insisting that any further move would be in direct violation of orders. The German ignored him. "I decided to stay on the heels of the retreating enemy," Rommel said, "and make a bid to seize the whole of Cyrenaica at one stroke."

Rommel divided his forces, sending one group north along the coastal road toward Benghazi, another east toward Maaten el Grara and Ben Gania, and a third up a central route to Antelat and Msus (map, page 67). He did not have a rigid plan for his ad hoc campaign but probed the enemy here and there and pushed on as the British fell back. Soon Neame's forces were in general retreat.

At Rommel's advance headquarters near Agedabia runners scurried in and out with news of the advances as Major Georg Ehlert, the operations officer, busily scrawled the movements of German columns and the enemy on his map. Rommel himself spent much of his time in the air or on the road, checking on his forces and flogging them on. One commander, whose column was temporarily halted, was startled when a message was tossed from the cockpit of Rommel's Fieseler Storch spotter plane: "Unless you get going at once I shall come down. Rommel."

Rommel's desire for speed caused him to take great risks. On April 3 the 5th Light Division reported that most of its vehicles were extremely low on gasoline and needed a four-day break to replenish. Instead Rommel ordered all the trucks to be unloaded and sent them back empty to the divisional depot, instructing the drivers to return within 24 hours with sufficient fuel, food and ammunition to see the campaign through. It was a dangerous gamble—24 hours when the division's men were stranded in the desert, powerless to move if attacked. But it meant that the 5th Light Division was out of action for only one day rather than four.

That day Gariboldi—by now almost apoplectic about Rommel's risk taking and contravention of orders—challenged the German once more. "He wanted me to discontinue all action and undertake no further moves without his express authority," Rommel recalled. "I had no intention of allowing good opportunities to slip by unused. The conversation became somewhat heated."

That night the Germans occupied Benghazi, which had been evacuated by the British. In a letter to his wife, Rommel's boyish ecstasy was mixed with some doubts about the reaction of his superiors: "Dearest Lu, We've been attacking since the 31st with dazzling success. There'll be consternation among our masters in Tripoli and Rome, perhaps in Berlin too. I took the risk against all orders and instructions because the opportunity seemed favorable. No doubt it will all be pronounced good later. . . . The British are falling over each other to get away. . . . You will understand that I can't sleep for happiness."

Rommel was not overstating the British reaction. The general's rapid and unpredictable movements were producing exactly the effects he desired in Neame's command: confusion and panic. The Axis breakthrough at Mersa Brega had touched off a week-long, 500-mile British retreat. With gallows humor, some British soldiers later dubbed their hurried withdrawal "The Tobruk Derby" or "The Benghazi Handicap." More typical perhaps was the reaction of Roy Farran, a second lieutenant, who described that week as seven of the most inglorious days in the British Army's history. Lacking instructions to stand and fight, the British fell back in disorder—packed ignominiously 30 to a truck, nerves at breaking point from lack of sleep, faces thick with yellow dust that made them look like jaundice victims.

The traditional British qualities of a cool head and a stiff upper lip suddenly seemed to be in short supply. At Antelat,

a panicky corporal screaming "Mass retreat! The Jerries are coming!" was silenced only when Lieut. Colonel Crichton Mitchell threatened to shoot him. In Msus, one captain, told that an enemy column was approaching, blew up an entire divisional fuel dump to keep it from falling into Axis hands—and then recognized, too late, that the "enemy" was a patrol of the British Long Range Desert Group.

Neame, from his headquarters in Barce, 50 miles northeast of Benghazi, vainly tried to restore order with a series of telegrams to his subordinate commanders, but he made no attempt to visit the front. On April 2, Wavell went to Barce to assess the crisis. "I soon realised that Neame had lost control," he said later. He sent for O'Connor to come out and take over the command. On April 3, O'Connor arrived and diffidently suggested that Neame should keep the command while O'Connor acted as Neame's advisor, because "changing horses in midstream would not really help matters." Tact was not O'Connor's sole motive for demurring. He wrote later: "I cannot pretend that I was happy at the thought of taking over command in the middle of a battle which was already lost."

O'Connor's presence was not enough to alter the course of events. Rommel had developed his *Swung*—impetus—and was relentlessly maintaining it. "It was becoming increasingly clear that the enemy believed us to be far stronger than we actually were," Rommel said, "a belief that it was essential to maintain, by keeping up the appearance of a large-scale offensive." He let no opportunity pass. As the British 2nd Armored Division, losing numerous tanks in small actions and breakdowns along the way, fell back on Mechili, Rommel made that tiny desert fort the new focus of his multipronged advance. Three German columns churned toward Mechili on converging courses: the main body of the 5th Light Division and the Ariete Division from Ben Gania and Tengeder, the 5th Panzer Regiment reinforced by 40 Italian tanks through Msus, and the 3rd Reconnaissance Battalion from Benghazi via Charruba.

A fourth Axis group advanced along the coastal road toward Derna, to which the 9th Australian Division had retreated in hopes of making a strong stand there along a wadi, or dry stream bed. By April 6 the enemy forces gathering to the south around Mechili and the Axis column advancing along the coast road posed too great a threat to

Strategically placed in the desert, German dummy tanks built of wood and canvas on automobile chassis—part of Rommel's so-called Cardboard Division—create the illusion of armored strength. On sending the unarmed counterfeits into battle, Rommel quipped to the commander of this fake-tank unit: "I won't hold it against you if you lose one or two."

the 9th Australian Division, and forced a hasty withdrawal from Derna. It was so hasty, in fact, that only the rumble of departing transport alerted Lieut. Colonel E. O. Martin's Northumberland Fusiliers, who were also in Derna, to the bitter truth that they were being left behind. They hurriedly packed up and joined the retreat to the east.

That evening Neame and O'Connor, having lost touch completely with the 2nd Armored Division and realizing that their personal situation was perilous, decided it was time to withdraw from their headquarters. The two generals were among the very last to leave. In Neame's staff car they headed for Tmimi, some 100 miles to the east. During the night they took a wrong turn and ended up on the road for Derna. At about 3 a.m., Neame, who had been sleeping in the back seat, awoke to find they were in the middle of a halted convoy on the outskirts of Derna. From the darkness came shouts in a foreign language, and Neame's driver volunteered: "I expect it's some of them Cypriot drivers, Sir." Seconds later the generals were staring into the leveled barrels of German submachine guns. They would spend the next three years as prisoners of war in northern Italy.

In the immense, almost trackless desert arena, confusion did not beset the British alone. Rommel's leading units soon had outdistanced his command radio at Agedabia, and he spent hours every day in his Storch aircraft trying to find them and coordinate their movements. Frequent sandstorms threw the German columns off course and temporarily grounded Rommel's plane and other aircraft that could have guided them. Colonel Herbert Olbrich's 5th Panzer Regiment advancing from Msus was lost for more than a day. Frantically searching for it, Rommel himself came close to making a premature exit from the war. Seeing what he thought was Olbrich's column, he had his pilot circle while troops below spread out a large cloth landing cross on a smooth patch of ground. Just before the aircraft touched down, Rommel saw by their helmets that the soldiers were British. The plane banked into a climb in a shower of machine-gun fire, but was hit only once, in the tail.

In spite of straying forces and a worsening shortage of gasoline, by April 7 the Germans and Italians had surrounded Mechili. Trapped in the ring were what remained of the 2nd Armored Division, the 3rd Indian Motorized Brigade and a handful of other British units that had failed to make their getaways. Rommel sent a demand for surrender to the senior British officer, Major-General Michael Gambier-Parry, commander of the 2nd Armored Division. "Of course he refused," Rommel recorded, without surprise. On the morning of April 8 the British tried to break out at the same time that the Axis forces began a general attack. In the confusion a few Britons managed to escape, but by noon Mechili had fallen and Gambier-Parry was added to the retinue of captive high-ranking officers.

An elated Rommel watched the British general's command truck being unloaded, and reached forward to annex an oversized pair of sun-and-sand goggles. "Booty—permissible I take it, even for a general," he said, grinning as he adjusted the goggles over the gold-braided rim of his peaked cap, where they would appear in numerous photographs taken of him during the next 22 months. The legend of the Desert Fox was in the making.

On that same day, in a water-front hotel in Tobruk, Wavell announced a crucial decision to a conference of senior officers: Tobruk must be held. The 9th Australian Division, which had slipped out of Rommel's net by withdrawing from Derna, was to take up defensive positions in this coastal city, joining the British and Commonwealth units already stationed in Tobruk.

None present at the conference challenged Wavell's logic. Rommel was bound to continue his advance to the east, but as long as Tobruk was in British hands he could not go far. Holding Tobruk denied him the use of the only suitable port in Cyrenaica east of Benghazi. His troops needed 1,500 tons of water and rations a day; without Tobruk all of these supplies would have to be carried across the desert from Benghazi or Tripoli. Holding Tobruk would not be easy. Rommel would surely make every effort to drive the defenders into the sea. All their food, ammunition and replacement equipment would have to come in by ship under the bombs and guns of the Luftwaffe, which controlled the air space over the city. But there was no other choice. Noting on a map the few remaining British units scattered across 450 miles of desert—at Bardia, Sidi Barrani, Mersa Matruh—Wavell told his Tobruk officers dryly: "There is nothing between you and Cairo."

No one was more sharply aware of this than Rommel. In the next few days his Afrika Korps, bypassing Tobruk, pushed east along the coast, taking Fort Capuzzo, Sollum and Halfaya Pass, but it was futile to go farther as long as the British in their stronghold still posed a threat to his flank and rear. Tobruk was to become a thorn in his flesh, an obsession that was to dog him for seven months. Rommel, who was now intent on conquering Eqypt and the Suez, found himself halted on the threshold of triumph by a single impudent British garrison.

"We must attack Tobruk with everything we have—before Tommy has time to dig in," Rommel told one of his divisional commanders. But Tommy had already dug in. The British had begun reinforcing Tobruk's old Italian defenses in mid-March, and the 220-square-mile enclave was more formidable than Rommel supposed. The 30-mile perimeter, called the Red Line, was marked by tangled whorls of barbed wire and bristled with 140 strong points, concrete-shielded dugouts holding up to 20 men apiece. Two miles behind the Red Line lay the Blue Line, a thickly sown minefield crisscrossed with more barbed wire and studded with strong points situated 500 yards apart.

Even after German tanks probing the perimeter on April 11 and 12 were beaten back by artillery, Rommel was sure that Tobruk would fall to the full-scale armored assault planned for Easter, April 14. "Dear Lu," he wrote early that day, "Today may well see the end of the Battle of Tobruk." German troops expected that the enemy would retire as soon as the panzers approached. Heartened by Rommel's belief in a quick victory, one battalion even tagged its administration truck to the rear of the assault column.

Such confidence did not seem misplaced as the battle got under way. At 5:20 a.m. the first wave of the 5th Light Division's tanks bulled unmolested through a gap blasted in the wire south of Tobruk. The Australians manning the perimeter posts made no attempt to engage the tanks—but as the German infantry passed the strong points, murderous fire hit them from the rear. Oblivious to the carnage taking place behind them, the panzers ground on. Soon they were two miles inside the perimeter—moving deeper by the minute into a deadly and elaborate trap.

Suddenly the panzer crews found themselves in a corridor of heavy fire. Field artillery, rushed from nearby sectors, was firing from both flanks at a range of only 600 yards. One hit tore the massive turret of a Panzer IV tank clean from its mountings. German Lieut. Colonel Gustav Ponath, who had driven brashly into battle in his staff car, was killed when the vehicle was blown to pieces by an antitank shell. The panzers milled about in confusion as smoke and dust obscured the vision of drivers and gunners. Finally ordered to retire, they had to fight their way back to the perimeter through the same gauntlet. The Germans lost 17 tanks in the melee—at least one of them immobilized by an Australian who rammed a crowbar into a tread sprocket. The 8th Machine Gun Battalion suffered 75 per cent casualties. The

With his finger fixed on a point near the coast, Rommel (far left) pores over a map of Cyrenaica during his first offensive. Starting from west of Mersa Brega, his advance (red arrows) drove the British, except for a garrison at Tobruk, out of Libya by mid-April. Goaded by Churchill, British General Wavell in June mounted the Battleaxe counteroffensive, whose thrusts (black arrows) were repulsed by Rommel.

battle was a "witch's cauldron," a German tank commander wrote later. "We were lucky to escape alive."

Rommel was furious that he had been beaten. He raged at Major General Johannes Streich, commander of the 5th Light Division, saying his panzers had not given their best. He charged that both Streich and Olbrich, commander of the 5th Panzer Regiment, had "lacked resolution."

Two days later, on April 16, Rommel tried again. This time he personally took command, using the Ariete Division and an Italian infantry division against Tobruk's western defenses. As soon as they were fired on, the Italian tanks took refuge in a wadi and Rommel could not induce their commanders to resume the attack. Italian infantry, taking the brunt of an Australian counterattack, quickly surrendered. One of Rommel's officers saw a lone British scout car herding a whole Italian company into captivity. He fired on the car to give the Italians a chance to run. They did run, Rommel noted ruefully, "toward the British lines." More than 800 Italians were captured during the two-day attack; the Ariete Division lost at least 90 per cent of its tanks—to breakdowns. On April 17, Rommel called off the attack.

He still believed that when proper reinforcements arrived he would be able to take Tobruk. He consistently underestimated the determination of its defenders. There were 35,000 soldiers within the Tobruk perimeter—Anzacs, Britons, Indians—led by an Australian commander fully as tenacious as Rommel himself.

Major-General Leslie James Morshead, 51, was known to his troops as "Ming the Merciless," after a villain in the *Flash Gordon* comic strip. His concept of his task was simple. "There'll be no Dunkirk here," he told his staff. "If we have to get out we shall fight our way out. There is to be no surrender and no retreat." When an Australian newspaper ran a headline that said, "Tobruk Can Take It," Morshead was enraged. "We're not here to take it," he stormed. "We're here to give it."

Every night he sent out 20-man patrols to launch surprise attacks against the enemy. Soon Rommel was made aware of their deadly efficacy. Approaching an Italian sector of his line one morning he stopped short in amazement at the sight of hundreds of discarded helmets decorated with the cock's plumes of a crack Bersaglieri rifle regiment. An entire battalion had been seized during the night. Not all of Morshead's troops bothered to take prisoners. A patrol of Rajputs, warrior-caste Hindus from Jodhpur, rebuked for overestimating its enemy dead, returned some nights later with two small sacks of evidence: 32 human ears.

Since to stir aboveground during the day was to court snipers, the men guarding Tobruk's perimeter turned their daily routines upside down. They breakfasted at 9:30 p.m., ate lunch at midnight and dinner at dawn. Concealment was the key to life. Men entering camouflaged dugouts smoothed their footprints behind them with camel's-thorn switches so enemy bombers would not be led to the dugouts by the tracks. They had to fight not only the enemy but boredom, sunburn, lice, sand fleas and dysentery.

The Luftwaffe kept up its attacks on supply vessels. The harbor was soon littered with rusting wrecks of supply ships destroyed by German Stukas. It was with good reason that the Western Desert Lighter Flotilla, which brought food and equipment from Alexandria, contended that its initials stood for "We Die Like Flies."

On the perimeter, a consciousness of hardships shared bred a certain wry camaraderie between besiegers and besieged. Both sides endured the same desert privations—water that "looked like coffee and tasted like sulphur," as one of Rommel's officers noted, and canned meat that the Germans called "Mussolini's ass." There were fleeting relaxations of tension. Sergeant Walter Tuit, a British stretcher-bearer, seeking casualties in no man's land after one engagement on the perimeter, was assisted by Germans who delivered British wounded and dead and told him other wounded Britons had been sent to a German field hospital. They then gave him a fresh lemon drink before both sides retired to their own lines. And each night, promptly at 9:57 p.m., Britons no less than Germans turned in to Radio Bel-

The "rats of Tobruk"—the derisive Axis term for the British troops under siege in the Libyan port—make the best of their beleaguered state. An Australian soldier (right) cools off in an abandoned bathtub as his comrades wait their turn. Other amenities included mimeographed newspapers, daily church services, and meals served in one of Tobruk's many caves (far right) to avoid the danger of swooping Stuka dive bombers.

grade, to hear Lale Andersen sing—in German—the sad and sensuous lament about the girl who waited underneath the lamplight by the barracks gate, "Lili Marlene." It became the unofficial anthem of all the desert warriors.

By April 30, Rommel had been reinforced by enough of the 15th Panzer Division to try again. At 6:30 p.m. the Germans began their most furious attack on Tobruk so far. Stuka dive bombers and artillery pounded a hill called Ras el Medauer on the stronghold's southwest perimeter while German tanks burst through defenses north and south of the prominence. Within three hours the Germans had taken the hill and the panzers had penetrated two miles inside the perimeter. But they had failed to eliminate a number of fortified outposts manned by Australians who fought, Rommel said, "with remarkable tenacity. Even their wounded went on defending themselves and stayed in the fight to their last breath." These strong points were still active the next morning, harassing the German advance from behind as the British retaliated with artillery and counterattacks.

The seesaw struggle of thrust and counterthrust raged for three more days. Blinding dust storms made tactical control difficult for both sides. In the frenzied chaos, few could grasp with certainty who was winning—or for how long. One German medic, approaching the wire in an ambulance, furiously berated the Anzac who drew a bead on him; convinced that Rommel had taken Tobruk, the medic had arrived to treat the German wounded. (Seized as a prisoner, he treated both sides impartially.)

It was Rommel's most costly engagement to date. He lost more than 1,000 men in the battle. On hand to witness the slaughter was Lieut. General Friedrich Paulus, a cool and precise general staff officer who had arrived on April 27 on an urgent mission from Army High Command to somehow hold Rommel in check. (Colonel General Halder said Paulus was chosen because he was "perhaps the only man with enough influence to head off this soldier gone stark mad.") Paulus was appalled by the casualties and the fact that the German troops were "fighting in conditions that are inhuman and intolerable." He advised Rommel that there was no chance of taking Tobruk. Still, when the British broke off their last unsuccessful counterattack early on May 4, the Germans had managed to occupy a portion of the perimeter some three miles wide by two miles deep.

At about the same time an angry ultimatum arrived from Brauchitsch. The commander in chief forbade Rommel to attack Tobruk again, or to advance farther into Egypt. Rommel must hold his position and conserve his forces. The commander of the Afrika Korps was bitter at being compelled to take a defensive stance instead of being allowed to conquer Egypt. But he was soon to prove as consummate a practitioner of the defense as of the offense.

At Churchill's insistence, the British were about to launch their own Cyrenaican offensive. The groundwork had been laid on April 20, when the Prime Minister had conceived a bold, typically Churchillian idea. At the time a convoy carrying 295 tanks to aid Wavell was making ready to sail for Suez via the Cape of Good Hope. Churchill proposed that the ships cut 40 days off the trip by turning at Gibraltar and running the Mediterranean gauntlet to Alexandria.

British convoys had not dared to make the passage across the length of the Mediterranean since early January, when the Luftwaffe had demonstrated its domination of the air there by badly damaging the carrier *Illustrious*. But Churchill, knowing that Rommel was being reinforced by a full panzer division, thought the risk worth taking. If Wavell could get the 295 tanks before the new German armor was fully operative in North Africa, the recent disastrous course of battle might be quickly reversed. "If this consignment gets through," the Prime Minister, with unflagging optimism, cabled Wavell, "no German should remain in Cyrenaica by the end of June."

In fact "Tiger Convoy," as it was dubbed, lost only one ship—to an enemy mine; it delivered 238 tanks at Alexandria on May 1. On the day it arrived, Churchill quoted from Second Corinthians 6:2 in a message to Wavell: "Behold, now is the day of salvation." Wavell was not so certain. The tanks arrived in sorry shape, with cracked gearboxes, unserviceable tracks and no sand filters for their engines, so essential in the desert. Action before mid-June, Wavell told London, was out of the question.

Churchill reacted with anger and disappointment, but Wavell was not displaying any lack of initiative. On May 15, even without the new tanks, he set into motion Operation *Brevity*, a limited campaign designed to secure a jumping-off position for the major offensive to follow. Under the command of Brigadier-General W. H. E. Gott, the British threw three assault columns across the Egypt-Libya border. Two ascended the escarpment that ran parallel to the coast, one to sweep west and north toward Sidi Azeiz, the other to regain Fort Capuzzo west of Sollum. The third was to storm Halfaya Pass, a gash in the escarpment leading up onto the Libyan Plateau. The pass controlled access to the plateau as well as the coastal road to Sollum and points west.

The British quickly took Capuzzo and Halfaya Pass and were advancing on Sidi Azeiz when Rommel counterattacked, pushing them back in the early hours of May 16. Gott withdrew to the pass, which, if he could hold it, by itself would have been worth the losses of Operation *Brevity*—till then, 18 tanks and 160 casualties. But on May 27 a superior German force drove the British out of the pass, at a cost to Wavell of 173 more casualties and five more tanks. *Brevity* had gained nothing.

Churchill, aware that Rommel was strengthening his defenses every day, badgered Wavell about the need for haste in getting the big attack moving. The Western Desert offensive was not the only problem on Wavell's mind, however. Almost everywhere he looked he saw only trouble. The British had been thrown out of Greece at the end of April, and now Crete—the refuge to which most of the troops from Greece had been evacuated—was threatened by the Germans. In the meantime Wavell was being committed to campaigns in Syria and Iraq by the activities of pro-Axis puppet governments in those countries. Like a juggler frantically trying to manipulate too many colored balls, Wavell was beginning to falter.

But on June 15 at 2:30 a.m., Wavell finally got the Cyrenaica offensive—code-named Operation *Battleaxe*—under way. The plan was similar to that of Operation *Brevity*, but on a larger scale. An infantry brigade group (a reinforced brigade) with one and a half squadrons of tanks was to seize Halfaya Pass. At the same time an armored brigade and an infantry brigade were to move on Fort Capuzzo as a reinforced armored brigade swept wide to the west toward Sidi Azeiz, protecting the other British forces from the Axis troops in Sidi Omar.

The anchor of Rommel's defense, an artillery battalion in Halfaya Pass, first heard the throb of British tank motors at 6 a.m. on June 15. These defenders were known to the British as "seven-day men" because they were supplied with a week's worth of ammunition, food and water at a time and knew they had to fight to the last shell and the last drop of water. Their commander was 50-year-old Captain Wilhelm Bach, in civilian life an Evangelical minister from Mannheim, who would become known to his unswervingly loyal troops as "the pastor of Halfaya."

Through field glasses, the portly Captain Bach watched the British tanks approaching, about two miles away. "Under no circumstances fire," he told his men. "Let them come on." As the advance continued, the tanks began firing and shell craters soon pitted the biscuit-brown heights of the pass. Still Bach's men and an Italian battery under Major Leopoldo Pardo held their fire.

At 9:15 a.m., British Lieut. Colonel Walter O'Carroll, near the rear of the column moving into the pass, heard with satisfaction a radio code message: "Pink Spots"—the action was under control and going well. Then the appalled last words of Major C. G. Miles, in the lead tank, poured from the radio: "Good God! They've got large caliber guns dug in and they're tearing my tanks to pieces."

From concealed emplacements all along the cliffside, 88mm antiaircraft guns, leveled for use against the tanks, were firing 22-pound shells that could tear holes as big as basketballs in a Matilda a mile distant. In a few minutes, 11 of the 12 leading tanks were blazing like blowtorches. Five times the British tried to storm the pass and five times Bach's guns repulsed them. From that day forward, Halfaya would be known to the British army as "Hell-Fire Pass."

Up on the escarpment, meanwhile, British tanks in the center of the advance managed to drive the Axis troops back from the Fort Capuzzo area and then turned east to move on Sollum. But to the west the left arm of the British advance was stalled at Hafid Ridge by German defense emplacements that included more of the deadly 88s in use as antitank weapons. And during the day Rommel brought up reinforcements from the Tobruk area, including the 5th Light Division and part of the 15th Panzer Division.

On the morning of June 16, Rommel unleashed these reserves. The 15th Panzer Division hammered at the British at Capuzzo, but was beaten back and broke off its attack before noon. At the same time Rommel's 5th Light Division circled to the south and struck the British left flank near Sidi Omar. After a fierce battle with tanks of the British 7th Armored Regiment, the 5th Light Division broke through and began rolling east toward Sidi Suleiman. "This was the turning point of the battle," Rommel said. Here was a chance to cut right across the rear of the enemy, trap him and crush him. Rommel ordered most of the 15th Panzer Division to leave the Capuzzo area, circle to the southwest, and join the 5th Light Division in its eastward drive. Early in the morning of June 17 these units reached Sidi Suleiman and Rommel ordered them on to Halfaya Pass, happily contemplating the destruction of the British forces.

But at 11 a.m. Major-General F. W. Messervy, commander of the 4th Indian Division, unable to reach headquarters for approval, took it on himself to order a withdrawal of British forces in time for most to escape the trap. Later, on a desert airstrip, Messervy confronted a grim-faced Wavell. He recalled that Wavell stared at him for long minutes without speaking. "I thought he was going to sack me," Messervy

said. Finally Wavell spoke: "I think you were right to withdraw in the circumstances, but orders should have come from Western Desert Force."

All told, Operation *Battleaxe* cost the British about 90 tanks, more than 30 aircraft (by great effort the Royal Air Force had maintained air superiority throughout the battle), almost 1,000 men and the chance to restore morale through a desert victory. Rommel thought Wavell's planning had been "excellent" but said that the British general was "put at a great disadvantage by the slow speed of his heavy infantry tanks, which prevented him from reacting quickly enough to the moves of our faster vehicles."

Some in London were not so understanding when they received Wavell's terse admission of defeat: "Am very sorry for failure of 'Battleaxe.'" Sir Alexander Cadogan, who was Permanent Under-Secretary to the Foreign Office, summed up one of the prevalent opinions: the German Army simply had better generals. "Wavell and suchlike are no good against them. It is like putting me up to play Bobby Jones over 36 holes."

Churchill's own feeling was already well known. As early as mid-May he had discussed replacing Wavell in an exchange of assignments with Lieut. General Sir Claude Auchinleck, commander in chief in India. Churchill told Field Marshal Sir John Dill, Chief of the Imperial General Staff, that he did not want Wavell hanging around London, living in a room in his club. The Prime Minister said that in India Wavell would "enjoy sitting under the pagoda tree." Early on the morning of June 22, Wavell's Chief of Staff, Lieut. General Sir Arthur Smith, arrived at his commander's house in Cairo. Wavell was in the bathroom shaving, his cheeks daubed with lather, razor poised. Quietly Smith read out a message that had just arrived from Churchill: "I have come to the conclusion that public interest will best be served by appointment of General Auchinleck to relieve you in command of armies of Middle East."

Wavell stared straight ahead. With no apparent emotion, no visible sign of regret, he said, "The Prime Minister's quite right. This job needs a new eye and a new hand." Then he went on shaving. It was a characteristic tribute from a large-hearted gentleman to his successor. But there was no assurance that the new hand would be any more capable of outdealing Rommel than the old one had been.

EMBATTLED MALTA

Malta's capital, Valletta, is silhouetted against the smoke of bomb explosions in this still from a newsreel that was filmed during the heavy blitz of spring 1942.

HEROIC ORDEAL OF A ROCK-BOUND ISLAND

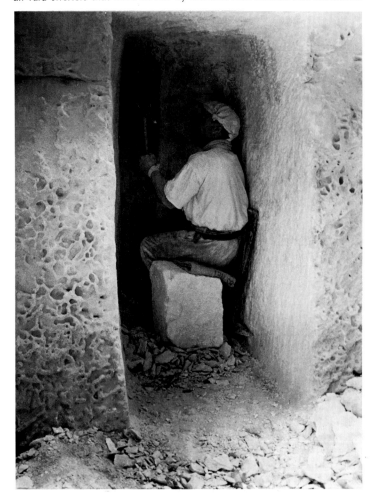

A Maltese laborer widens the mouth of one of the hundreds of tunnel-like air-raid shelters that were carved by civilians into Malta's soft limestone.

One of the most heavily bombed targets in the War was neither a great industrial complex nor a munitions arsenal. Tiny British Malta was a flyspeck in the middle of the Mediterranean, with three small, ill-equipped airfields and a superb natural harbor. But in 1941 that speck of rock became the keystone of British defense in North Africa—and a major stumbling block of the Axis desert campaign.

As long as the island's air and submarine bases were operating, the convoys that sustained Axis armies in Africa were easy prey for British attacks. By November 1941, Malta-based crews were destroying more than three fourths of all Rommel's shipping. In desperation, Reich Marshal Hermann Göring called for the island to be "Coventrated"—destroyed from the air as completely as the English city of Coventry had been in 1940.

Only 70 miles from the airfields of Sicily, Malta was a readily accessible target for the hundreds of Luftwaffe bombers dispatched to neutralize the island. During the first months of 1942, bombs plummeted down on Malta's airfields and docks, and on the capital, Valletta, an average of eight times a day. In April alone, Malta withstood 6,728 tons of bombs, 13 times the amount that had shattered Coventry. During those months virtually every British convoy carrying supplies to the island was destroyed, and food and munitions grew desperately scarce.

But Malta's plucky defenders refused to give up. RAF crews repaired the airfields daily, sending fighters up to battle the Germans whenever possible. The 280,000 native Maltese learned to endure severe rationing and mounting casualties. Then, in April 1942, during the grimmest days of the siege, King George VI conferred on the whole island the George Cross, Britain's highest civilian award for gallantry. Their morale buoyed by this tribute, the Maltese gritted their teeth and persevered. Gradually, as fortunes shifted in North Africa, the siege lifted. The Luftwaffe moved its planes from Sicily to the Russian and North African theaters, and by late fall, battered but exuberant, Malta resumed its critical role as a base for attacks on German shipping.

Queen Victoria's statue sits indomitably amid the rubble in Queen's Square in central Valletta. At right are the ruins of the lion-bedecked Governor's Palace.

Playing on the wreckage of a German dive bomber, Maltese children seem inured to a landscape of devastation. Like many of their elders, they seized every

chance to escape the dank underground air-raid shelters where, for the worst of the siege, they slept, prayed, had classes and ate most of their meager meals.

Maltese islanders examine the ruins of Valletta's Royal Opera House, one of approximately 37,000 buildings destroyed or damaged during the course of the siege.

Soldiers clear rubble from Kingsway, Valletta's main thoroughfare, on the morning after a raid.

The silver George Cross and the King's framed citation were conferred as the British Empire's formal salute to Malta's fortitude.

BUCKINGHAM PALACE

The Governor
Malta.

To honour her brave people
award the George Cross to the
Island Fortress of Malta to bear
witness to a heroism and devotion
that will long be famous in history

George R.I.

April 15th 1942.

Honoring Malta's triumph over its attackers, King George VI salutes a throng of cheering islanders on June 20, 1943, during a tour he made of the Mediterranean.

3

General Sir Claude Auchinleck seemed to be just the man for the job when he took command of Britain's Middle Eastern forces. At 57 he neither knew nor sought any other life than that of a British Army officer. He had risen steadily since graduating from the Royal Military College at Sandhurst, serving in the Indian Army in peacetime and in various campaigns of World Wars I and II.

Besides his formal credentials, "The Auk," as he was affectionately known to his troops, possessed essential qualities of leadership. To begin with he had a quick grasp of strategic and tactical problems—an urgent necessity now, in the face of an enemy personified by the seemingly invincible Rommel. With Auchinleck's jutting jaw and steady gaze went a stern self-discipline that made him impose on himself the same austerities his men endured (because his officers were barred from bringing their wives to Cairo, he left his own wife in New Delhi). He had a resolute will that inspired trust in those whom he commanded. He also possessed powers of persuasion that enabled him to have his way with superiors as well—as no less a figure than Winston Churchill learned when Auchinleck held out against the impatient Prime Minister, insisting that the next British offensive must not be prematurely launched in summer, but must wait until November when Auchinleck would have sufficient reinforcements.

Hidden behind his formidable assets, however, was one crucial failing: Auchinleck was a poor judge when choosing subordinate commanders. Once he had placed his trust in someone, he took it for granted that his orders would be carried out without the need for any follow-up supervision. And when he chose poorly, a combination of stubbornness and misplaced loyalty sometimes made him slow to rectify his own mistakes.

The first task that Auchinleck found himself called upon to accomplish when he reached Cairo was to reorganize the Western Desert Force and find a commander for it. The force was more than tripled in size—Churchill had authorized the build-up in North Africa because he was determined to make gains there while Hitler was preoccupied with the war in Russia—and was renamed the Eighth Army. Auchinleck's choice for a commander was Lieut. General Sir Alan Gordon Cunningham—and a likely choice it seemed. The 54-year-old Cunningham, who had both a quick temper

TRIUMPH ELUDES THE BRITISH

and a ready smile, had distinguished himself in early 1941 in East Africa by soundly defeating the Italians, led by the Duke of Aosta *(page 20),* in only eight weeks.

"I asked for Cunningham," Auchinleck wrote later, "as I was impressed by his rapid and vigorous command in Abyssinia and his obvious leaning towards swift mobile action. I wanted to get away from the idea, which seemed to be prevalent, of clinging to the coastal strip, and to move freely and widely against the enemy's flank and communications." Unfortunately, Cunningham had never commanded tanks and was not innovative by nature. In the face of the quicksilver moves of the unorthodox Rommel, these were to be serious liabilities. Moreover, Cunningham was enduring a personal deprivation that was to have effects far beyond its apparently petty nature. A constant smoker, he had been ordered by his doctor to give up his pipe for reasons of health. Under the pressures of the coming months, the loss of his comforting pipe was to play havoc with his nerves.

Cunningham's first major assignment as commander of the Eighth Army was to direct Operation *Crusader,* the greatest offensive the British had yet launched in the desert. *Crusader's* objectives were no less than to engage and destroy the enemy's armor, to relieve the British garrison at Tobruk from the Axis siege that had been going on since April, to reconquer all of Cyrenaica and, eventually, to move on and take Tripoli.

In mid-November on the eve of Operation *Crusader,* Cunningham was buoyantly optimistic, and so were his fellow officers and men. They had every reason to be; the War Office had spared no effort to assure the operation's success. The new army had a total of 118,000 troops, more than 700 tanks, 600 field guns, 200 antitank guns, and was equipped with a wealth of other vehicles and weapons. And it had the support of the newly strengthened Desert Air Force, which now had nearly 650 aircraft.

On the Axis side, Rommel appeared to be not nearly so well off. While he had managed to create a new division—called the 90th Light, or Africa Division—from smaller units already in North Africa, he had received no reinforcements from Europe since June. The old 5th Light Division was renamed the 21st Panzer Division, but without any change in strength. Rommel's command had been given a new designation: Panzer Group Africa. It included the Afrika Korps (now consisting of the 15th and 21st panzer divisions, and the 90th Light Division) and two Italian corps numbering six divisions. Rommel had about 119,000 troops, but he had only 400 tanks (150 of them obsolete Italian vehicles), some 50 of which were undergoing repair when the British launched *Crusader.* Moreover, the Axis air forces, with fewer than 550 planes in Cyrenaica, were now outnumbered by the British. Rommel would be hard put to get additional reinforcements from Hitler, because the campaign in Russia, which had begun with rapid success in June, was by this time showing ominous signs of trouble.

Cunningham's ambitious plan called for the armored XXX Corps, under Lieut. General C. W. M. Norrie, to advance westward from Eighth Army headquarters at Fort Maddalena, about 50 miles south of the coast, and swing around behind the German defenses running south from Bardia on the coast to Sidi Omar *(map, page 84).* Once the XXX Corps outflanked the Germans, two of its units, the 22nd and the 7th armored brigades, would move northwest to Gabr Saleh, about halfway between Maddalena and Tobruk. Gabr Saleh's only value was that it lay astride the Trigh el Abd, an inland road that was expected to be Rommel's main route of advance as he responded to the British thrust. Cunningham hoped that Rommel would send his panzers to Gabr Saleh, where the British armor would engage and destroy them. Then the British would be free to swing either northeast to Afrika Korps headquarters at Bardia or northwest toward beleaguered Tobruk.

Meanwhile, the 4th Armored Brigade—also part of the XXX Corps—would veer northwest behind German lines. It would have the dual task of supporting the right flank of the 7th Armored Brigade rolling on to Gabr Saleh and the left flank of the XIII Corps, primarily infantry, under Lieut. General A. R. Godwin-Austen, who had served with Cunningham in East Africa. The XIII Corps itself would stay south and east of the Axis front line, harassing the Italian units holding the frontier until Norrie's armored units had eliminated Rommel's tanks. Only then was the XIII Corps to join the advance on Tobruk, where it would dispose of Rommel's infantry and lift the siege of the fortress. The garrison in Tobruk would attempt a breakout to coincide with the XIII Corps' attack on the Axis siege lines around the city. All this, Cunningham hoped, would take no more than a week.

Rommel, of course, had plans of his own. He had finally won grudging assent from the German High Command for another assault on Tobruk. Since spring he had left the task of maintaining the siege to the Italians. By early November he was beginning to move his German divisions from the Egyptian frontier toward Tobruk. He planned to strike on November 21.

The British were ready before him. At dawn on November 18 the XXX Corps' brigades crossed the frontier at Fort Maddalena and fanned out across the desert. Cunningham went along, riding with Norrie's headquarters staff to command the action from the field. Meeting little opposition on the way, the 22nd and 7th brigades reached their positions in the vicinity of Gabr Saleh by evening.

Cunningham had a long and uneasy wait for Rommel's reaction. The German, at his headquarters in Bardia, was preoccupied with his proposed assault on Tobruk. He had received no forewarning at all of the British attack, because of poor German air reconnaissance and excellent British concealment of troop movements during the weeks before the offensive began. Rommel not only was caught off guard by the arrival of the British, but also was uncharacteristically slow to grasp the nature of their advance. Lieut. General Ludwig Crüwell, commander of the Afrika Korps—who was sometimes a better tactician than Rommel—advised his chief that he sniffed an offensive and urged that the two panzer divisions be moved south to counter the thrust. But Rommel was reluctant to change his plans; he thought the British were only making a cautious probe.

Cunningham, still without any real reaction from the enemy, the next day sent columns probing west to Bir el Gubi and north to Sidi Rezegh. At that point Rommel began to doubt his original assessment of what his enemy was up to. He yielded slightly to his advisers and allowed some of his panzers to move south to meet the British columns. The result was a series of heated, isolated engagements that cost the British about 50 tanks and the Axis some 30. But so far

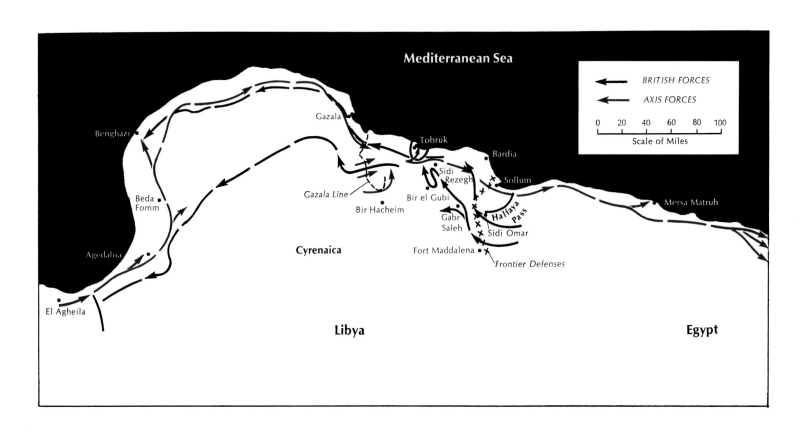

In Britain's Crusader offensive of November 1941, the Eighth Army (black arrows) relieved the siege of Tobruk and dogged Rommel across Cyrenaica to El Agheila. When the Axis forces (red arrows) rebounded in January 1942, the Eighth Army retreated to a chain of fortifications known as the Gazala line. In June, Rommel crushed these fortifications, captured Tobruk and drove the British across Egypt to El Alamein.

nothing had occurred that resembled the major confrontation of armor that Cunningham sought. The fighting did leave the British holding an airfield at Sidi Rezegh, along with 19 enemy aircraft captured on the runway. With Sidi Rezegh in the bag and no big counterblow from Rommel seemingly in the offing, Cunningham returned to his headquarters at Fort Maddalena on November 20, concluding that the operation was going well enough.

He was mistaken. Rommel, finally convinced that the British were involved in a serious offensive, had shelved his plans for seizing Tobruk and done an about-face. On November 22, some 70 tanks of the 21st Panzer Division sprang on the British 7th Armored Brigade at Sidi Rezegh. The British 22nd and 4th armored brigades rushed to the scene, but they arrived separately and too late to make much of a difference. At the end of the day the 15th Panzer Division showed up to add to British woes. It overran 4th Armored Brigade's headquarters and captured the brigade commander. The outcome of the day's fighting was that the British lost the airfield, more than 100 tanks and some 300 men.

This was only a foretaste of what they were to suffer the next day, November 23—which happened to be *Totensonntag,* "Sunday of the Dead," when Germans traditionally honored countrymen killed in World War I. Early that morning Rommel hurled his massed tanks on the British units that were scattered around Sidi Rezegh; he took them on one after another, and one after another he knocked them out. When night came the area was lighted by the flames of hundreds of blazing vehicles. Virtually every British formation took heavy punishment. Worst hit was the 5th South African Brigade, an infantry outfit that was part of the XXX Corps; it lost 3,400 of its 5,700 men. All in all Totensonntag accounted for the heaviest casualties yet endured by the British in the desert war.

Rommel was clearly the winner of the first phase of Operation *Crusader,* and he knew it. That night he wrote to his wife, Lu: "The battle seems to have passed its crisis. I'm very well, in good humor and full of confidence." Though he

General Sir Claude Auchinleck, who led the Crusader offensive, spent three years of his early childhood as well as most of his professional life in India. Unconventional and bold, he had a healthy respect for India's fighting men and lobbied to mechanize their Army at a time when some feared giving the Indians guns. His confidence in them was confirmed by the reliability of the Indians who fought under him in the desert war.

had been outnumbered and had suffered heavy losses, including perhaps a dozen senior officers and some 250 tanks, he had given the British a lesson in tactics. By consolidating his forces—massing his tanks and coordinating their attacks with infantry, antitank guns, artillery and air support—he had succeeded in achieving effective numerical advantage with a smaller force. "What difference does it make if you have two tanks to my one when you spread them out and let me smash them in detail?" he was later to ask a captured British officer. "You presented me with three armored brigades in succession."

At Eighth Army headquarters the radio had broken down and Cunningham waited anxiously for reports. When late on Totensonntag he learned the enormity of the disaster that had befallen the British, he was shattered. He thought that perhaps he should count *Crusader* lost and retreat into Egypt. There, at least, he could reorganize his forces in relative safety. Wrestling with his nerves and indecision, he sent an urgent plea for help to Auchinleck in Cairo, suggesting that the commander in chief come to see the front for himself. Auchinleck promptly flew to Fort Maddalena and

made a swift appraisal. "I thought Rommel was probably in as bad a shape as we were," he later wrote, "and I ordered the offensive to continue." Auchinleck's resolve remained firm. He told Cunningham to "attack the enemy relentlessly using all your resources even to the last tank."

In fact, not all the British plans were going awry. Two days earlier Cunningham had authorized the XIII Corps—comprising the New Zealand Division, the 4th Indian Division and a tank brigade—to begin its advance without waiting for the outcome of the armored struggle in the west. The XIII Corps moved north behind the Axis lines on the frontier as far as the coast northwest of Bardia, taking Fort Capuzzo and cutting off the garrisons at Bardia and Halfaya Pass from the bulk of the Axis forces to the west.

To relieve this pressure on his frontier forces, Rommel, heady with his successes, now embarked on a daring adventure. "Speed is vital," he told his leading officers. "We must make the most of the shock effect of the enemy's defeat." On the morning of November 24, while the British around Sidi Rezegh were still staggering, he brazenly led the entire Afrika Korps and two Italian divisions on a dash to the east,

ITALIAN UNDERWATER RAIDERS

To challenge Britain's control of the Mediterranean in late 1941, the Italian Navy resorted to employing midget submarines that were little more than manned torpedoes. On the night of December 19, three midget subs slipped into Alexandria harbor. Their mission: to destroy the only British battleships in the Mediterranean, the *Queen Elizabeth* and the *Valiant*, and set the harbor aflame by exploding a tanker.

Two of the crews attached their warheads to the hulls of the *Queen Elizabeth* and the tanker, then scuttled their subs and swam ashore. The third crew was captured in the water near the *Valiant*, after leaving its time bomb on the seabed beneath the ship. Thrown into the ship's hold a mere 15 feet above the explosive device, the Italians held their silence for two and a half hours, then warned the captain.

Minutes later three explosions rocked the harbor. The *Queen Elizabeth* and the *Valiant* listed crazily; the tanker went up in flames. The battleships were repairable, but while they were out of action, convoys with desperately needed supplies would reach the Axis forces in North Africa intact.

In this Italian wartime painting, frogmen on a midget sub cut an antisubmarine net.

straight through enemy lines. His purpose was to get beyond the frontier and threaten the British rear, a tactic that he hoped would force Cunningham to give up the offensive and withdraw. He rashly disregarded the costly losses he had sustained and the counsel of General Crüwell, who thought that prior to doing anything else the Germans should finish off the battered British forces remaining near Sidi Rezegh.

The sudden thrust was so unexpected and swift that the British rear echelons panicked and fled. It was like a replay of Rommel's first offensive in Cyrenaica. Units of both sides raced east for six hours and in their haste found themselves so hopelessly confused that many had no idea where they were or whether friend or foe was next to them. At dusk a British military policeman directing traffic suddenly realized that the vehicles he was now controlling were German. Rommel himself, along with General Crüwell, spent much of the night in the midst of British troops. No one noticed: the Germans were riding in a big, enclosed command vehicle that had been captured from the British, and its German markings were not discernible in the dark.

In making his bold move to the east Rommel had correctly perceived the Eighth Army's disarray—but he had failed to reckon with its hidden strength in the person of Auchinleck. Had Cunningham been acting on his own, the sudden Axis drive might well have induced him to call off Crusader. But Auchinleck stayed at Fort Maddalena for two days, propping up the troops as well as the flagging Cunningham. Auchinleck told his men that the enemy "is trying by lashing out in all directions to distract us from our object, which is to destroy him utterly. We will not be distracted and he will be destroyed." He said of Rommel: "He is making a desperate effort, but he will not get very far. That column of tanks simply cannot get supplies. I am sure of this."

He was right. Rommel penetrated some 15 miles inside Egypt, but on November 26 his panzers had to retire to Bardia to refuel. Ironically, during his rapid advance he had passed right by two huge, well-camouflaged supply dumps where the Eighth Army kept food, fuel and water for its Crusader forces.

In the final reckoning his dash proved to be an expensive detour. When Rommel began the raid, the balance of battle was tipping decidedly in his favor. But by the time the momentum of his dash was spent, the British had taken the offensive again. On the night that Afrika Korps tanks were refueling in Bardia, the New Zealand Division of the XIII Corps drove through the Axis forces surrounding Tobruk and linked up with troops from the beleaguered garrison who were fighting their way out. For the moment at least, Tobruk had been relieved. Farther south, the 4th and 22nd armored brigades had taken advantage of Rommel's absence to regroup and salvage some of the disabled tanks that had been abandoned at Sidi Rezegh. When Rommel's refueled panzers left Bardia on November 27, heading west to aid the hard-pressed Axis forces around Tobruk, British armor hammered them to a standstill. Only when the British withdrew to set up camp and rest for the night were the Germans able to push through the west.

After returning to Cairo on November 25, Auchinleck had made two difficult decisions. It seemed to him and to his colleagues at general headquarters that Cunningham's inclination to fall back after Totensonntag had been a sign of timidity unwarranted in view of the enemy's high losses. Lieut. General Sir Arthur Smith, Chief of the General Staff in Cairo, believed Cunningham had "lost his grip. He was not himself—he was not Cunningham." To leave him in charge would be to risk the existence of the Eighth Army and the whole British presence in North Africa. Yet to remove him might lower the morale of the already confused British troops and at the same time raise the spirits of the enemy; surely the Germans and Italians would look upon Cunningham's dismissal as an admission of defeat. Nevertheless, Auchinleck decided "it had to be done—rightly or wrongly." On November 26 he relieved Cunningham of command of the Eighth Army. Cunningham went reluctantly into a Cairo hospital, where he was found to be suffering from mental and physical fatigue.

To be Cunningham's successor, Auchinleck chose—or, in his own word, "pitchforked" into the job—Major-General Neil M. Ritchie, who had served in Cairo as deputy chief of Auchinleck's General Staff. Ritchie was familiar with Auchinleck's plans and could be counted on to know the mind of his chief.

At 44, Ritchie was the British Army's youngest general. He was handsome, wealthy and prone to take a rosy view of things, even in the worst circumstances. General Godwin-Austen, commander of the XIII Corps, said that Ritchie was "a very confident fellow—thought he was the goods." But, he added thoughtfully, universal agreement on this point was lacking. Ritchie had not led troops in combat since World War I, when he was a battalion commander.

It did not really matter. Auchinleck was virtually in command himself, with Ritchie functioning as his deputy. Auchinleck went out to Maddalena again on December 1 and stayed 10 days. With the commander in chief at Ritchie's elbow—and after that no farther away than the radio link to Cairo—the Eighth Army pulled itself together and continued Operation *Crusader*. Rommel still did not make it easy for the British. Although his tanks now were outnumbered 4 to 1, he succeeded in laying siege to Tobruk again on November 30. But without fresh supplies and replacements for his lost tanks and weapons, he could not stand up to sustained pressure from the Eighth Army. In a week the British forced him 40 miles west to Gazala, where, earlier, the Axis had prepared a fall-back defense line.

Rommel's defensive position extended some 40 miles to the southwest from Gazala on the coast. On December 15, Ritchie attacked the line from the east while sending an armored brigade sweeping around its southern end in an attempt to get behind the enemy and cut off his retreat. Rommel was determined to save what remained of his forces to fight another day. Although the Italian commanders, fearing that their nonmotorized infantry would be left

Racing headlong across the sand, French soldiers sally forth from Bir Hacheim in June 1942. In an epic 14-day struggle, the besieged Free French brigade gallantly defended the outpost that blocked Rommel's drive toward Tobruk. Determined to redeem the honor of the French Army, which had been tarnished in the fall of France, the stubborn garrison scorned surrender three times and finally fought its way out.

behind, objected strenuously, on December 16 he ordered a withdrawal, and slipped out of the trap before the British could close it. For three weeks the Axis retreated over the same ground they had crossed during their triumphant advance nine months earlier. Despite hot British pursuit, the withdrawal—including that of the Italian foot soldiers—was orderly and Rommel managed to avoid any further substantial damage to his forces as he fell back to El Agheila. In fact, on December 28 he seized an opportunity to attack a lone British armored brigade near Agedabia, inflicting a loss of 37 tanks on the enemy while losing only seven of his own.

However skilled his retreat and however determined his resistance in defeat, there was no escaping the fact that Rommel had suffered his first serious reverse. Operation *Crusader* had provided a sensational victory for the British. Early in January, Axis troops left behind on the Egyptian frontier, at Bardia and Halfaya, finally capitulated. Between November 18 and mid-January the British had taken about 33,000 Axis prisoners and destroyed 300 enemy tanks. They had lost more tanks than the Axis, but had suffered only half the number of personnel losses. Moreover, they had regained Cyrenaica—and driven Rommel back to the very point at which he had started in the desert in March 1941. "Here then we reached a moment of relief," wrote Churchill, "and indeed of rejoicing, about the Desert war."

In December 1941, events thousands of miles away suddenly exerted a powerful influence on the war in the desert. Japan's attack on British territories in the Far East forced London to divert to that area men and matériel earmarked for North Africa. Then around the end of the year, intensified Luftwaffe bombing of Malta and the arrival of German submarines in the Mediterranean—as well as successful raids by Italian midget submarines on Alexandria harbor *(page 86)*—worsened British supply problems at the same time they eased those of the Axis. On January 5, Rommel received by convoy 54 new tanks and a large supply of fuel. Now he felt strong enough to launch an attack on forward British positions, which he knew to be weak.

Setting out from his base at El Agheila on January 21, the Axis forces—now bearing a new, elevated designation, Panzer Army Africa—pushed north. Rommel quickly took Agedabia and Beda Fomm as the British fell back before him.

What began as a spoiling action to forestall any new British advance soon grew into a full-scale offensive. On January 29, Rommel entered Benghazi, which the British had abandoned, and there helped himself to large stores of booty, including 1,300 trucks. By February 6 he had pushed the British, who were now hurting badly for want of supplies, to Gazala—halfway back across Cyrenaica. In two weeks Ritchie's forces had lost 40 tanks, 40 field guns and some 1,400 officers and men.

The mounting crisis was compounded for Ritchie: his top subordinates had begun to lose faith in him. Godwin-Austen found to his discomfort that Ritchie "had a tendency to ask your advice and having received it to act in the opposite way," and—worse—that Ritchie bypassed him to issue orders to the officers of Godwin-Austen's corps. As a result, in early February, Godwin-Austen asked to be relieved of command of the XIII Corps. Auchinleck obliged, and Major-General W. H. E. Gott was pulled from the 7th Armored Division to take Godwin-Austen's job.

Other officers found the new Eighth Army commander no more reassuring than had Godwin-Austen. "Ritchie was all haywire by then," recalled Major-General F. W. Messervy, who took over Gott's post with the 7th Armored Division. "All for counterattacking in this direction one day and another in the next. Optimistic and trying not to believe that we had taken a knock. When I reported the state of 1st Armored Division to him at a time when he was planning to use it for counterattack, he flew to see me and almost took the view that I was being subversive."

Scenting trouble all the way from Cairo, Auchinleck sent Brigadier Eric Dorman-Smith, an old friend and trusted adviser, to investigate. On his return Dorman-Smith told Auchinleck that Ritchie was "not sufficiently imaginative" for his post and recommended that he be replaced. Although disturbed by the report, Auchinleck said no. "I have already sacked one army commander," he replied. "To sack another within three months would have effects on morale." He left Ritchie where he was.

Through the rest of the winter there was a lull in the fighting. Right into the spring, the Axis and British forces stayed on their own sides of the Gazala line, a 60-mile-long chain of defenses built by the British. From Gazala on the coast the line ran a jagged course southeast for about 40 miles, and then elbowed to the northeast for another 20 miles. The line was densely sown with mines, and scattered at wide, irregular intervals along it and to the east of it were a series of strongholds, each a mile or two square, called "boxes" by the soldiers who manned them. There were about six boxes in all. Some, like the one at Bir Hacheim, were known by Arabic place names surviving from early settlements; others, thrown up on unoccupied sites in the wasteland, were dubbed by the British soldiers with names such as "Knightsbridge" and "Commonwealth Keep."

Each of these boxes was girded on its perimeter with mines, barbed wire, slit trenches and pillboxes, and each had stores enough to withstand a week-long siege. Between the boxes, British tanks roamed freely. Their assignment was to intercept any tanks of Panzer Army Africa that might advance across their sector and also to race up or down the line to the aid of any box that might be attacked.

By late May, Rommel was ready to resume his offensive. While Axis infantry and some tanks launched holding attacks against the northern part of the Gazala line to preoccupy the divisions there, Rommel planned to lead the Afrika Korps and an Italian division south around Bir Hacheim, the box that formed the line's elbow. He would then swing north to chew up the British armor and attack the rest of the line from the rear. After that, he had planned a special treat for himself: the seizure of Tobruk.

The Axis struck in the north on May 26. Early on May 27 Rommel led his 10,000 vehicles around the British flank south of Bir Hacheim, leaving some Italian units to attack that box, and fanned out to the north and east. In his first encounter, about five miles northeast of Bir Hacheim, he quickly scattered the 3rd Indian Motor Brigade. By midday his forces had disposed of three more armored and motorized brigades.

But that afternoon he ran into an unwelcome surprise. The British had recently received a shipment of U.S. tanks—new 28-ton Grants, which were equipped with 75mm guns capable of firing high-explosive shells that could pierce the German armor.

By nightfall of the second day, thanks to a combination of dogged British resistance and the lethal new Grants, the two panzer divisions had lost a third of their tanks and had been stopped outside the Knightsbridge Box, some 10 miles behind the main Gazala line and midway between Bir Hacheim and the coast. The Axis forces backed into a semicircular patch of some 100 square miles with British boxes and mines all around its perimeter—an area that would come to be known as "The Cauldron" for the seething battles that took place there. While Rommel regrouped, Italian engineers opened a new supply line to him from the west, through the minefields, but British artillery fire made resupply by this route difficult. Immobilized, the Axis troops were fair game for Ritchie. Now was the time for him to mass his armor and crush Rommel. Auchinleck, perceiving this from Cairo, dispatched a message urging Ritchie to take the offensive immediately, adding, "we must be ready to move at once, whichever way the cat jumps."

Ritchie was not ready. He went into a huddle with his two corps commanders, Norrie and Gott, to consider, committee style, various plans of action. For two days the British generals deliberated, and while they did, Rommel regrouped his forces. On June 1 he smashed a bigger hole through the Gazala line, ensuring easy access to his supplies. In the process he destroyed more than 100 British tanks, took 3,000 prisoners, eliminated the 150th Infantry Brigade and knocked out the box they held. Ritchie, his irrepressible optimism still undaunted, reported to Auchinleck: "I am much distressed over the loss of 150th Brigade after so gallant a fight, but still consider the situation favourable to us and getting better daily."

Rommel now turned south to deal with Bir Hacheim, simultaneously fending off some futile British assaults from the north. Bir Hacheim, the southernmost box in the Gazala line, was crucial to the British defense—and it was more strongly defended than Rommel had expected. The Italians who had begun attacking it on May 27 had made no headway. Bir Hacheim's 3,600 troops, mostly Free French, were under the command of Brigadier General Pierre Koenig, a tall, blue-eyed Frenchman known to his soldiers as "The Old Rabbit." Rommel expected to capture Bir Hacheim in 24 hours; instead it took him more than a week. "Seldom in Africa was I given such a hard-fought struggle," he recorded in his journal.

Between June 2 and June 10 the Luftwaffe flew 1,300 sorties against Bir Hacheim, while on the ground Rommel's

German gunners wheel a deadly 88mm gun into position near Tobruk. White rings painted on its barrel, like notches on a gunslinger's six-shooter, tally the number of British tanks the formidable gun has destroyed. Originally used as an antiaircraft weapon, the 88 was turned against the armor of the Eighth Army with harrowing effect. "It could go through all our tanks like butter," one awed Englishman later attested.

surrounding forces kept up a steady bombardment day and night. Several times Rommel asked Koenig to surrender, and every time Koenig curtly refused to do so. By June 10 the fort was down to its last reserves of food, and on orders from Ritchie the defenders evacuated Bir Hacheim. Koenig led the way himself, and 2,700 of his 3,600 soldiers fought their way through Rommel's forces that night. When the Germans stormed the fort on the following morning, they found only the wounded and some equipment that had been left behind.

After subduing Bir Hacheim, Rommel moved north along the Gazala line. One by one he knocked out the remaining boxes. By his quick maneuvering he nullified the advantage of the enemy's new tanks and destroyed so much British armor that by the third week in June he had achieved a 2-to-1 edge in tanks.

With the Gazala line a shambles, Rommel turned his attention to Tobruk.

The Tobruk of June 1942 was a far weaker fortress than the bastion that had withstood Rommel's assault the previous year. This was partly because men, ships and aircraft were needed elsewhere and partly because the Eighth Army had placed unfounded faith in the Gazala line. Furthermore, Auchinleck had no plans for another last-ditch defense of the fortress. As early as February 4 he had issued orders saying that whatever developed from Rommel's advance "it is not my intention to continue to hold Tobruk once the enemy is in a position to invest it effectively." He explained that he could not afford to have a full division penned up inside the defensive perimeter. His plans went uncontradicted by London, and he went ahead with preparations to evacuate Tobruk and destroy its stores if an Axis attack made such steps necessary.

Now, in June, the garrison had a new commander, South African Major-General H. B. Klopper, who had about 35,000 men, consisting mostly of South Africans but in part of Britons and Indians. Most of the troops, like Klopper himself, were recent arrivals, and few had combat experience. Many of the mines that had earlier protected the town had been removed when the beleaguered troops had sallied out during *Crusader* the previous November. Others had been lifted and resown along the Gazala line during the winter, when Tobruk seemed to be out of danger.

In the calamitous days of early June, as the boxes of the Gazala line fell and the Germans pressed farther north every day, the troops at Tobruk made some frantic last-minute efforts to reinforce their defenses. But even as they did so, they did not know whether they should make plans to hold the fort at all costs or to evacuate it. No word came from Ritchie to guide them.

Britain's top commanders were as uncertain as the garrison. On June 15, after the last of the boxes had fallen, Auchinleck received a telegram from Churchill that read, "Presume there is no question in any case of giving up Tobruk." When, after a few more messages, this assumption of Churchill's grew to be an order, Auchinleck replied: "Ritchie is putting into Tobruk what he considers an adequate force to hold it."

Ritchie was trying to protect Tobruk by holding a new line extending some 30 miles south from the fortress. But on June 16 he authorized the British units in this line, which were suffering punishing panzer attacks, to withdraw to the Egyptian frontier to escape destruction. They fell back the next day and on June 18, Tobruk was once more under siege as Axis forces gathered around its perimeter.

"To every man of us," Rommel wrote later, "Tobruk was a symbol of British resistance, and we were now going to finish with it for good." The Afrika Korps and the XX Italian Corps—with the crucial assistance of the Luftwaffe—began to assault Tobruk on June 20. Throughout that day some 150 bombers flew 580 sorties. "They dived on the perimeter in one of the most spectacular attacks I have ever seen," wrote Major Freiherr von Mellenthin, Rommel's intelligence officer. "A great cloud of dust and smoke rose from the sector under attack and while our bombs crashed onto the defenses, the entire German and Italian artillery joined in with a tremendous and well-coordinated fire. The combined weight of the artillery and bombing was terrific."

As soon as a path was cleared through the mines that the Tobruk troops had hastily planted in the last few days, German and Italian infantry swarmed in, engaging in hand-to-hand combat with the British troops. Then the tanks rolled in behind the infantry.

Late in the afternoon, when the collapse of Tobruk appeared imminent, Klopper set about blowing up millions of dollars' worth of stores that had been meant to sustain the British desert effort. In the process he also knocked out most of his own telephone and telegraph lines—with the result that he could no longer keep in touch with his troops. At about 9 p.m., however, on one of his few remaining lines, Klopper did manage to communicate with Ritchie at Eighth Army headquarters. "Situation not in hand," Klopper wired. "All my tanks gone. Half my guns gone." Then he concluded on a plaintive note: "If you are counterattacking, let me know."

There was to be no counterattack. Ritchie's last message to Klopper, at 6 a.m. the following morning, read: "I cannot tell tactical situation and must leave you to your own judgment regarding capitulation."

At 9:40 a.m. on June 21, Klopper surrendered to Rommel. Ironically, the demolition that had cramped his own communication and movement was too little and too late to cheat the enemy. When Rommel took Tobruk, he won a rich prize—2,000 vehicles including 30 serviceable British tanks, 400 guns, enough fuel to fill up his panzers and start the drive for Egypt, 5,000 tons of provisions and large quantities of ammunition.

It had taken Rommel scarcely more than 24 hours to achieve this coup—the goal he had sought so long. "Tobruk! It was a wonderful battle," he wrote his wife that day. It was reported that, smiling broadly, he told a group of captured British officers, "Gentlemen, for you the war is over. You have fought like lions and been led by donkeys." The next day he learned that Hitler had rewarded his efforts by making him a field marshal. Later, when Rommel actually received his field marshal's baton from the Führer, he told his wife, Lucie: "I would much rather he had given me one more division."

The fall of Tobruk was a heavy blow to the Allies. Prime Minister Churchill later called it a "shattering and grievous loss." He was in Washington, conferring with President Roosevelt, when he heard the news. His only comment at the time was a laconic, "Rather disconcerting." But General Sir Hastings Lionel Ismay, Churchill's Chief of Staff, who was also present, recalled the moment as the first time he ever saw Churchill wince.

Churchill had reason to be alarmed; his own political future was at stake and—more important—so was the survival of his country. When he returned home he had to face a vote of censure in the House of Commons on his conduct of the War.

He won the vote by a wide margin, but the nation's dilemma was not so easily solved. The road to Egypt was now wide open, and Rommel was rolling along it full blast. To his troops he predicted that they would reach the Nile in 10 days. Within a week of taking Tobruk, he got as far as Mersa Matruh—140 miles beyond the Libyan border, and almost halfway to Alexandria.

As Rommel pressed deeper into Egypt, Alexandria and Cairo began to prepare for invasion. A pall of ash and smoke hung over the British Embassy and general headquarters, as officials hastily burned records. Automobiles and trucks clogged the roads leading away from the cities, and trains were packed with fleeing refugees. In Alexandria, Barclay's Bank paid out one million pounds in a single day to customers who feared a financial crash. In Cairo merchants tried to capitalize on the disorder. One, seeking the business of those who were fleeing the city, piled his windows high with luggage. Another, wooing stay-at-homes, touted bandages as a wise precaution against air raids. The only person who seemed to remain unperturbed in the crisis was the jovial, portly British Ambassador, Sir Miles Lampson. He threw a dinner party for 80 people at the Mohamed Ali Club. "When Rommel gets here," Sir Miles said, "he'll know where to find us."

Auchinleck, however, was of a different mind. On June 25 he flew to Mersa Matruh, relieved Ritchie of his command and took over the Eighth Army himself. From Mersa Matruh he retreated to El Alamein—a site that British troops had fortified in advance. El Alamein was 240 miles inside the Egyptian border and only 60 miles from Alexandria. But it stood in a neck of land that, as desert locations went, was defensible, because it was bordered on the north by the Mediterranean and on the south by hills that formed the lip of the impassable Qattara Depression, 700 feet below.

Here Auchinleck dug in. For the next six weeks, he lived among his troops, sleeping under the open sky and eating spartan rations. With his calm self-assurance Auchinleck tried to pump new spirit into the demoralized Eighth Army. Throughout July, Rommel hammered at the El Alamein line, but by a deft combination of offensive and defensive tactics Auchinleck held him at bay.

For Churchill's Cabinet in London, however—and for the British public—this was not enough. Auchinleck had to take some of the blame for the Eighth Army's losses over the past months, and for Ritchie's command in particular. Churchill and the British public were slow to forgive, and Auchinleck's reputation was clouded by the shortcomings of those he had placed in command under him. Churchill felt he had to boost public morale by bringing about another change in the desert command.

In August, therefore, two new British figures arrived on the desert stage. One was General Sir Harold Leofric Rupert Alexander, a veteran of Dunkirk, where he had been the last commander off the beach. He was wealthy, imperturbable, the possessor of a first-class military mind. It was said that during the perilous retreat from Dunkirk, Alexander, a stickler for proprieties even in the gravest of crises, sat down to a breakfast at a table set with a spotless cloth, serenely eating his toast and marmalade. Now he was given Auchinleck's post as commander in chief of the Middle East.

The other new arrival was Lieut. General Bernard Law Montgomery—eager, prickly, voluble, ruthless and unconventional. In character Montgomery was poles apart from the patrician Alexander, but that did not prevent the two from rapidly attaining an effective working relationship.

On August 12, the day before Montgomery was to take over Ritchie's post as commander in chief of the Eighth Army, he met with Alexander over afternoon tea in the mosquelike splendor of the lounge of Shepheard's Hotel in Cairo. There Alexander issued only one order to the Eighth Army's new commander. "Go down to the desert and defeat Rommel." Montgomery, at 54 about to take over his first important command, set off determined to do just that.

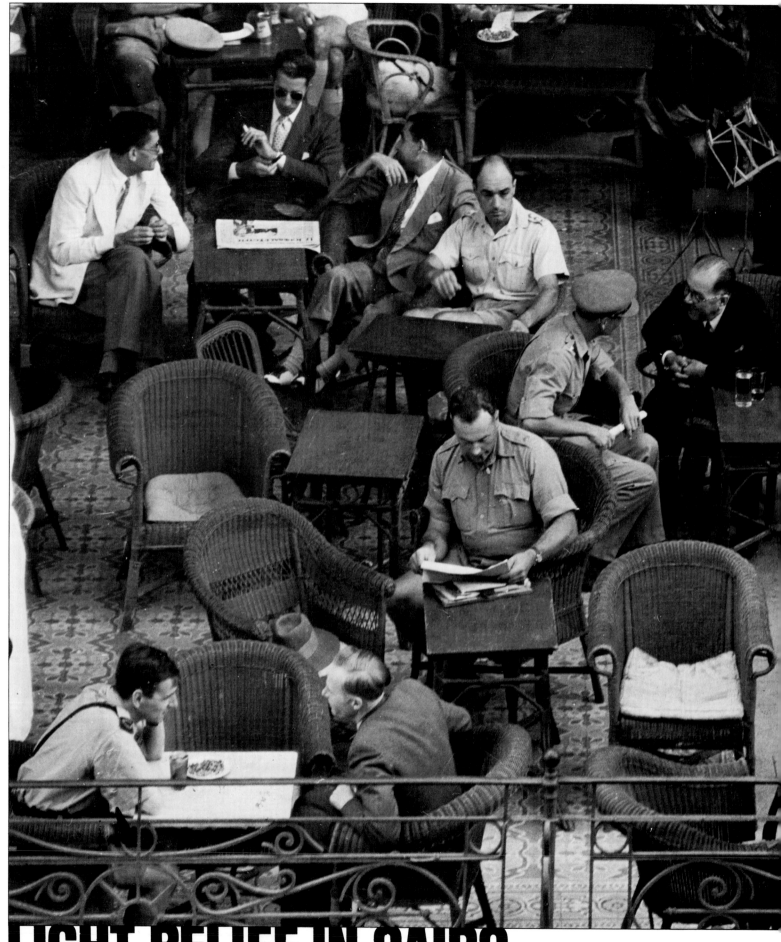

LIGHT RELIEF IN CAIRO

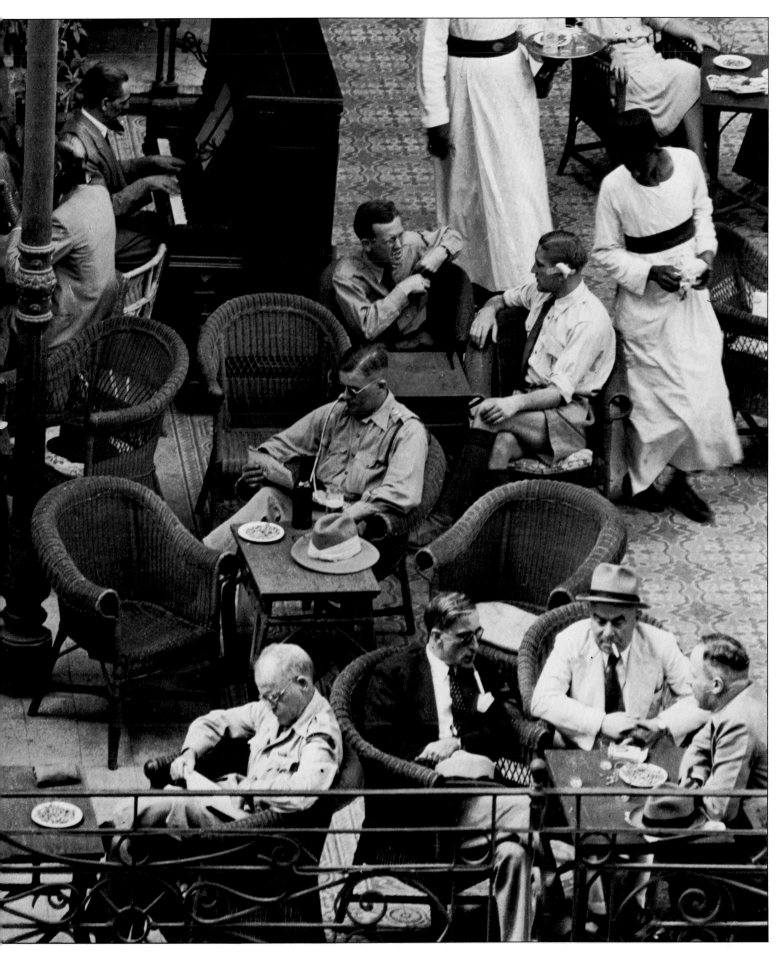

On the terrace of Shepheard's Hotel—one of Cairo's most popular watering places—British officers relax among civilians, some of whom often were Axis spies.

BEER, BATHS AND ANCIENT MONUMENTS

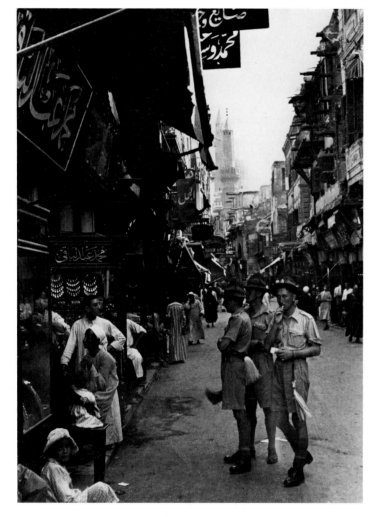

New Zealand soldiers, armed with whisks to fend off the flies that swarmed in Cairo's narrow and dirty streets, peruse the offerings of a bazaar.

To the parched and exhausted desert fighters of the Allied armies, furlough in the Egyptian capital of Cairo meant more than a respite from combat. Cairo was a rare oasis of unaccustomed luxuries ranging from the simple to the exotic, from a hot bath and a cold beer to an evening spent watching the undulations of Madame Badia's belly dancers. Soldiers momentarily forgot the war as they roamed the teeming, noisy streets of this city on the Nile, searched for bargains amid the raucous Arabic cries of vendors, or rented camels for a ride around the Pyramids nearby. Officers, off duty from staff jobs at British General Headquarters or on leave from the desert, avoided the grit and flies of Cairo proper to play polo, golf or cricket on the sporting fields of the fashionable Gezira, a verdant island in the Nile.

The grimness of war barely touched Cairo. Among the few reminders of the bitter battles being fought in the sands to the west were the ambulance convoys arriving from the desert with fresh casualties, the recuperating wounded with their bandaged limbs, and the Cairo stock exchange, where prices dipped in response to each Axis victory.

Through this atmosphere of idle complacency ran a current of innuendo and intrigue. Communications between Cairo and the desert were spotty; the truth about the progress of combat came late to the city, and in its absence, rumor prevailed. In the bars and nightclubs, gossip about the war flowed as freely as liquor. Axis spies haunted Cairo nightspots favored by British officers to garner information that might prove useful to Rommel on his drive toward the city. Although Egypt had broken off diplomatic relations with Germany, it had not declared war, and in the native population of Cairo was a vocal, if ineffectual, contingent of Axis sympathizers. Students held rallies in support of the German advance, chanting "Press on, Rommel!" And in the Egyptian Army, a cabal of officers who were bent on ending the British presence in their country waited impatiently in Cairo for Rommel's invasion of the city—an invasion that was never to come. In the meantime, Cairo remained an ingratiating host.

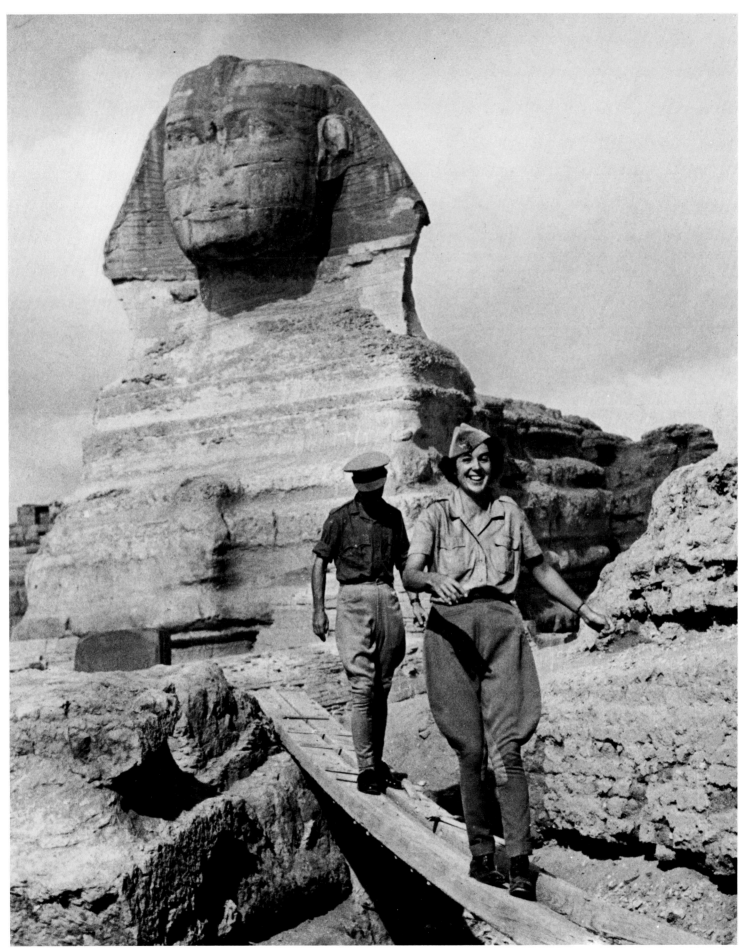

A smiling British Army woman and her companion take time off from the war to relax and wander about one of Cairo's nearby tourist attractions, the Sphinx.

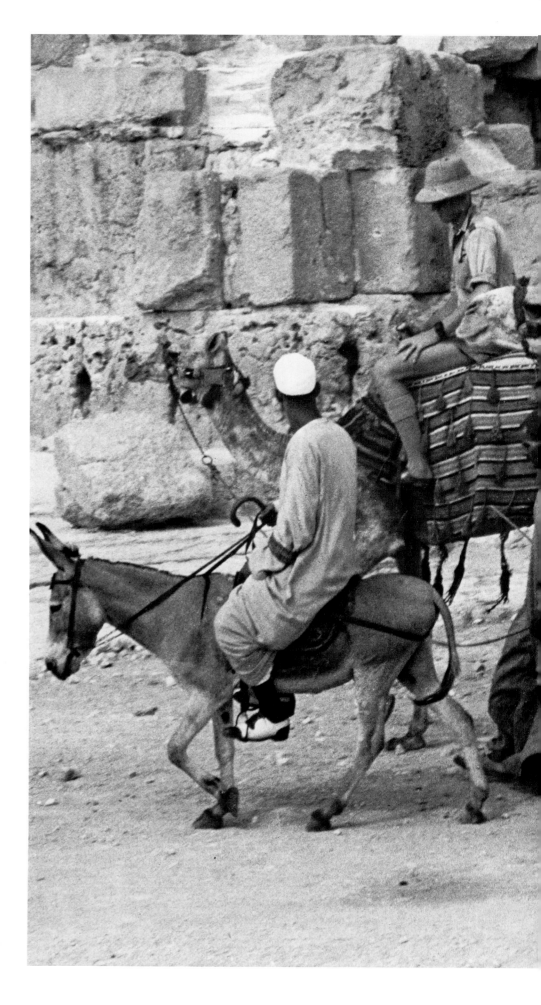

An Egyptian guide astride a donkey leads two
South African soldiers on a camel-back
expedition around the Cheops Pyramid close to
Cairo. The purses of guides and peddlers in
the city were fattened by the wartime influx of
British and Commonwealth soldiers.

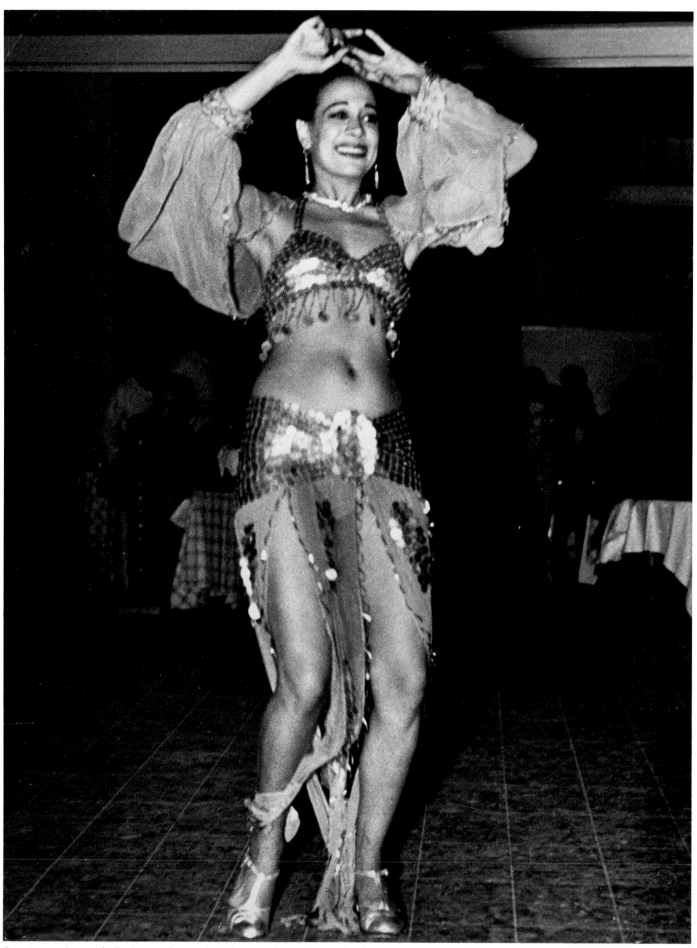

Egypt's most famous belly dancer, the supple Hekmet, performs for British admirers. Hekmet was later arrested and accused of being a German spy.

A SOCIAL WHIRL UNTROUBLED BY WAR

In the evenings, as a cooling breeze drifted in from the green River Nile, the mood of Cairo mellowed, turning gay and romantic. The officers and their ladies went dancing at the roof garden of the Continental Hotel or at Shepheard's, a Swiss-operated hostelry with grand accommodations and sumptuous meals. Soldiers of lesser rank or gentility released wartime tensions in haunts like the Melody Club, where the band was protected from brawlers by a barbed-wire fence. The highlight of an evening's revelry was often a performance by the belly dancer Hekmet (left).

As the desert war raged on—even while Rommel's panzers were less than 100 miles away—Cairo lacked no amenity for the soldiers. Its steaks were tender, its wines French and its companionship warm.

A party of officers and their companions enjoys one of the nightly dinner dances held at Shepheard's Hotel, a social headquarters for the British in Cairo.

101

For a fee of four cents a month officers bound
for combat in the desert war could leave
their personal belongings in the storeroom
at Shepheard's Hotel. Many of these trunks and
bags eventually went unclaimed after their
owners met their fate in the sands to the west.

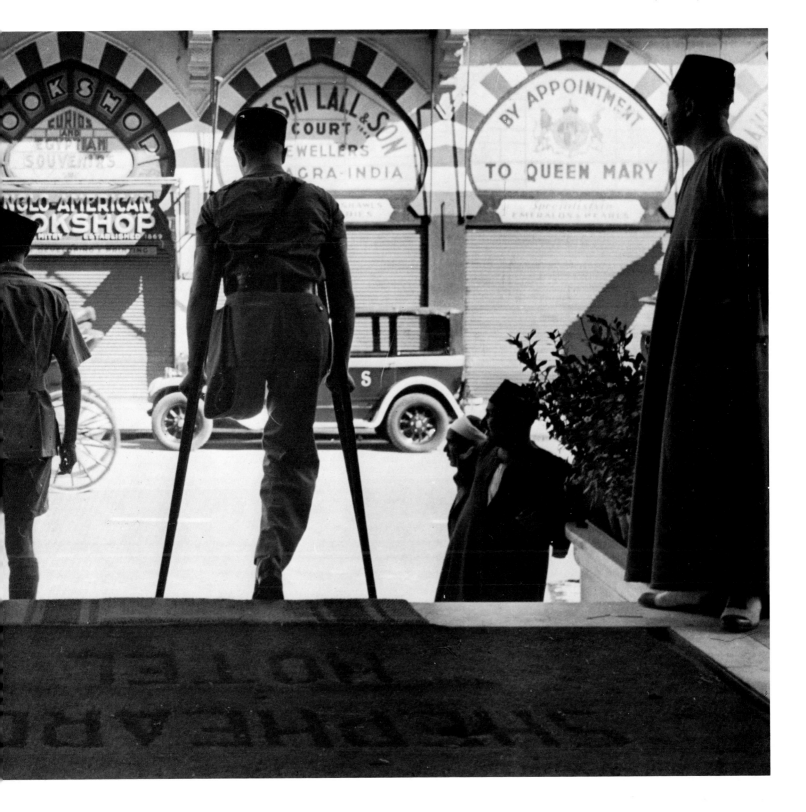

103

By the late summer of 1942 everyone sensed that the big push was coming. The question was: when? In the bars of Alexandria and in the Eighth Army's vast tented camp that had sprung up at El Alamein, 60 miles west of Alexandria, the British traded rumors endlessly. Only one thing was certain: the battle about to be joined would eclipse any the desert had seen before.

The Axis forces at El Alamein were dug in only a few thousand yards from the British lines, in a defensive position running from a rocky hummock on the coast to the Qattara Depression some 40 miles to the south. This position—the so-called Alamein line—could not be outflanked. If the British were to overrun it, they would have to do so by a massed frontal attack.

Day after day, from August to October, British reinforcements streamed to El Alamein: 41,000 men, 800 guns, more than 1,000 tanks, including 300 of the new 36-ton Shermans that Roosevelt had promised Churchill following Tobruk's fall. The tank commanders pinned their faith on the Shermans. With their 75mm guns, the Shermans could outshoot any Axis tanks except the Panzer IVs that had been fitted with new long-barreled guns—and of these Rommel now had no more than 30.

Despite the crushing reverses of the past seven months, and the formidable Axis defenses, few among the British were pessimistic. Within days of his arrival on August 13, Lieut. General Montgomery—already "Monty" to his troops—had instilled a new mood of confidence. Under his incisive leadership, the disillusioned men of the Eighth Army had swiftly grasped one salient truth: there would be no more retreating. To show that he meant business, Montgomery threw out Auchinleck's contingency plans for withdrawal to a secondary line of defense along the Nile Delta if Rommel broke through at El Alamein. "That's no plan," Montgomery growled. "By the time they have retired 10 yards," he said of his troops, "they will have lost half their fighting value." He announced that he was going to burn the plans. He took other convincing measures. He found a group of Tommies laboring on slit trenches to the rear and told them: "Stop digging there at once—you'll never need them." He sent the trucks on which any withdrawal from the front line would have depended lurching to the rear. Then, to all ranks he issued a blunt ultimatum: "From now

4

THE CRUCIBLE OF VICTORY

on the Eighth Army will not yield a yard of ground to the enemy. Troops will fight and die where they stand."

Montgomery was a stern disciplinarian who expected unquestioning compliance with his orders. "I want no belly-aching," he said. Moreover, he refused to tolerate sloppiness or low standards of discipline even in small matters. Staff officers soon learned to appear for meals spruce and on time in a brand-new mess tent fitted with laundered table linen and burnished cutlery. A slovenly army, in Montgomery's view, was an army halfway defeated.

Not all of his officers became Monty fans overnight. Some were irritated by the general's cocksureness and his mannerism of high-pitched repetition—"Bought it for the desert, bought it for the desert," he exclaimed of a new picnic basket. Deprecatory Monty jokes were heard here and there. In one a psychiatrist is summoned to heaven by St. Peter: "God's not feeling well. He thinks he's Monty." Someone later was to coin a heraldic motto for Montgomery: "In defeat, indomitable; in victory, insufferable." But the new desert general, borrowing a politician's techniques, scored resoundingly with the lower ranks. With his black Tank Corps beret ("worth two divisions," he said) and his cricket metaphors ("We've got to hit the enemy for six"), he proved to be a tonic for the bruised and bemused Eighth Army. Their job was to kill Germans, he told the troops, "Even the padres, one per weekday and two on Sundays."

But there was more to Montgomery's impact than salesmanship and wit. The quality that frontline troops most admire in their commanders is the ability to win battles. When Montgomery took over, the Eighth Army had endured a series of lackluster commanders who had repeatedly been outsmarted by Rommel. What they needed now was a demonstration that the new commander could lead the army to victory against the Axis forces. The opportunity was not long in coming.

On the night of August 30, Rommel launched his last attempt to smash the Eighth Army and break through to Cairo and Alexandria. The plan called for a large part of his forces, including four armored divisions, to attack in the south near the Qattara Depression, then to veer and cut off the Eighth Army from its bases by lunging north to the sea.

The operation depended on speed for its success. But the British had heavily mined the area where the assault was launched, and Rommel's troops spent the entire night clearing a way through the minefields. When they finally broke out, Rommel changed his plan and aimed his attack at a dominating topographical feature to the northeast called the Alam el Halfa Ridge. There, having anticipated the shift, Montgomery had dug in his American Grant tanks. Rommel's tanks and trucks were mercilessly shot up by the British armor and heavily bombed for two days and nights by the RAF. By September 3, after he had lost 49 tanks, Rommel fell back.

The Eighth Army now knew that it had a leader who could hold his own with the Desert Fox. But it soon became apparent that Montgomery was to take his own good time in getting ready for a decisive encounter with the Axis forces. The slowness of his preparations exposed him to some high-level criticism in London. Prime Minister Winston Churchill was impatient for the start of the big battle. "My next trouble will be to stop Winston from fussing Alex and Monty and egging them on to attack before they are ready," noted General Alan Brooke, Chief of the Imperial General Staff. Brooke was right. Churchill was urging a September attack, stressing the need to defeat Rommel before the autumn. On November 8 a mass Anglo-American invasion, under the code name Operation *Torch*, was to take place in French Algeria and Morocco. Churchill felt a victory at El Alamein would ease the way for the invasion by obliging the Vichy French in North Africa to take a more cooperative view toward the Allied effort. Moreover, Churchill was extremely eager for the Eighth Army to relieve the pressure on the embattled island of Malta—now under intense aerial bombardment for its role in the War as a British air and naval base—by capturing Axis airfields to the west of El Alamein.

But Montgomery categorically refused to move before October. If Churchill ordered a September attack, he would have to find someone else to command it, the general made clear. "It was blackmail," he later admitted, but it worked: no more was heard about a September attack.

Montgomery had a good reason for not attacking sooner. Even though the desert war had been going on for two years, he felt that the Eighth Army was not ready for the climactic battle. There were too many new recruits and improperly trained soldiers in its ranks. Montgomery was determined to make the army over into a top-notch fighting force. He pulled units out of the line, dispatched them to the rear, drilled them in the fundamentals of desert warfare and put them through field exercises on ground exactly like the terrain around the Alamein line. Six new antitank ranges were set up along the coast; there rookies fired 6-pounders at dummy tanks mounted on a moving assembly line. Nearby, a minefield-clearance school was established, and teams from 56 different engineer units were trained in mine-removal techniques.

For his part, Montgomery concentrated on tactics. His plan was to strike in the north, at the Alamein line's most heavily defended sector. To ensure complete surprise, one of the most elaborate plans of deception and concealment in British military history was adopted. Under Lieut. Colonel Charles Richardson, of Montgomery's planning staff, an elaborate bit of fakery was contrived to dupe the Germans into believing that the British intended to strike in the southern part of the line.

In order to deceive Axis air reconnaissance, three and a half dummy field regiments of heavy artillery were constructed from timber and canvas—and manned by dummy gunners. Dummy soldiers were even positioned squatting on dummy latrines. A dummy water pipeline, simulated by empty gasoline cans, was begun, running 20 miles south to a portion of desert dotted with 700 stacks of dummy supplies. The ongoing construction was deliberately calculated to suggest to the enemy that the attack would not come

Wearing a jump suit and toting a parasol against the blistering sun, British Prime Minister Winston Churchill tours the Egyptian desert near El Alamein in August 1942, accompanied by his leading commanders. The Prime Minister, who regularly pestered his officers with advice and queries from London, relished the trip. "Now for a short spell I became 'the man on the spot,'" he wrote. "Instead of sitting at home waiting for the news from the front I could send it myself. This was exhilarating."

until after the pipeline was finished. At last the British were learning from—and improving on—Rommel's own successful use of deception.

To the north, a massive calm appeared to prevail among the British forces. But under cover of darkness, almost 2,000 tons of gasoline were concealed in 100 slit trenches near Alamein Station, on the coastal rail line. Food supplies were trucked in and draped with camouflage nets. And on the eve of battle, tanks were moved from staging to assembly areas and disguised as trucks with detachable canvas covers. Before dawn, to conceal the transfer, Richardson's men replaced with 400 dummy vehicles the real tanks that had left the staging areas.

Montgomery picked the night of October 23 for the assault. The training of his troops would be completed by then, and there would be a full moon, which would help the sappers clear paths through the enormous minefields that Rommel had laid in front of his position. Between the British front line and the Axis' rear headquarters the minefields stretched five miles deep and 40 miles long—500,000 deadly mines arranged in horseshoe patterns that Rommel called "The Devil's Gardens." In the eight hours before dawn the sappers were supposed to neutralize the mines, and the infantry and armor to push on through the fields.

As the zero hour approached, the Eighth Army could count on a 2 to 1 superiority over its panzer army opponent in almost every respect. Its troops outnumbered the Axis forces by 195,000 to 104,000, its medium tanks by 1,029 to 496. The British could also claim an almost 2 to 1 superiority in antitank guns and artillery. And the Eighth Army was well supplied. The Axis forces, by contrast, were suffering from critical shortages. Rommel's supplies had to be transported long distances from Axis-held ports—300 miles from Tobruk, 600 from Benghazi, 1,200 from Tripoli—making them vulnerable to air attack all along the way. In three short months, British submarines and bombers had cost the Germans and Italians 20 supply ships. Against the monthly 30,000 tons of supplies Rommel had demanded as a minimum, he had received no more than 6,000 tons.

To further compound the problems besetting the Axis, the Desert Fox had fallen ill. Throughout the summer Rommel had been driving himself to the edge of endurance. At last, on September 23, he could hold out no longer. Stricken by chronic stomach and intestinal catarrh, in addition to circulatory troubles and nasal diphtheria, he was forced to quit the front to undergo treatment 1,500 miles away in Semmering, Austria. General Georg Stumme, a paunchy veteran of the Russian campaigns, afflicted by acute high blood pressure, had taken his place.

Still, no one among the British saw the coming fight as an easy one—and the details of Montgomery's plan made all too plain how brutally difficult it was going to be. Under cover of a massive artillery bombardment, four infantry divisions of Lieut. General Oliver Leese's XXX Corps would move through the minefields, rooting out enemy machine-gun and infantry positions. Sappers would then clear lanes for the tanks of Lieut. General Herbert Lumsden's X Corps, which would then pass through and smash the Axis defenses. A secondary attack in the south by Lieut. General Brian Horrocks' XIII Corps would pin down German panzers in that sector to confuse the enemy further as to the Eighth Army's true objective. Meanwhile, British and American planes would bomb enemy positions and attack forward airfields in the Western Desert to prevent Axis planes from interfering with the Eighth Army's advance.

By the night of October 23 everything was in readiness. A skilled stage manager, Montgomery had overlooked few details. To the rear, 2,000 military policemen, in white gloves and red caps, stood by to shepherd the tanks to their objectives along six separate routes—and to direct the forward movement of water carts that would sprinkle the sand and hold down the dust. Medics double-checked their supplies of bottled blood and plasma inside refrigerated trucks, which were identified by the sign of a giant vampire bat. Sappers assembled their cumbersome paraphernalia: 500 long-handled mine detectors, like flat disk-shaped vacuum cleaners, 88,000 lamps to mark the minefield gaps for the advancing armor and 120 miles of marker tape to delineate cleared paths.

It was an unsettlingly quiet night, the silence broken only by the eerie call of night birds. The wide, golden moon, hanging low over the desert, was so bright that noncombatants to the rear, courting sleep, tugged blankets over their heads in order to blot out the light. Among the men who would soon be chancing death, reactions varied. Lieut. Col-

THE EIGHTH ARMY'S INTREPID DESERT COMMANDOS

In the fall of 1942, during the lull preceding the Battle of El Alamein, a handful of Eighth Army soldiers were waging a very different kind of war with the enemy. They were members of the Long Range Desert Group and the Special Air Service, two small bands of trained desert commandos.

The Long Range Desert Group was a reconnaissance force based deep in the Sahara, far behind enemy lines. Like a tribe of Bedouin nomads in British uniforms, its members had learned to survive in the desert—often on only half a pint of water a day—and to navigate the trackless wilderness with instinctive precision.

Such skills made these men invaluable as guides for the Special Air Service (SAS), a ground-based force that was so named because it originally was composed of paratroopers. SAS men were daredevils who wreaked havoc in lightning raids on Axis depots and airfields. They slipped into enemy strongholds by night, blowing up equipment and killing personnel, and then faded into the desert like a mirage when they were pursued. With help from the Long Range Desert Group's expert navigators, they made seemingly impossible treks hundreds of miles to and from their camps with remarkable ease.

Joint teams of Desert Group guides and Special Air Service commandos harassed the Axis unmercifully. They destroyed enemy aircraft, sometimes entering airfields on foot, sometimes donning German uniforms and boldly speeding past sentries in trucks with German markings. They apparently enjoyed their work and spread terror with cheerful liberality. One SAS officer recalled with relish tossing a bomb through the window of a German staff office as he shouted to the officer inside, "Here, catch this."

But their love of the theatrical did not impair their effectiveness. By the end of 1942 their relentless harassment had made such a dent in Axis supplies and morale that they received a kind of tribute from General Rommel himself, who in his diary said they "caused us more damage than any other British unit of equal strength."

A patrol of Special Air Service raiders, looking stern behind their machine guns, returns from a three-month sortie into enemy territory in September 1942.

onel Jack Archer-Shee and the officers of the 10th Hussars changed into formal dress for dinner, then proposed a toast to King George's health with vintage wine. The elegant Lieut. Colonel E. O. Kellett, of the Nottinghamshire Yeomanry—"Flash" to his men—set his servant to pressing and starching his best pair of breeches. If he was to be killed in battle, at least he would die looking his finest. Almost everyone wrote a letter home or made entries in a diary. Major-General Leslie Morshead, commander of the 9th Australian Division, warned his wife: "A hard fight is expected, and it will no doubt last a long time. We have no delusions about that. But we shall win out and, I trust, put an end to this running forward and backward."

Montgomery retired early to bed in his trailer. On the wall was a portrait of Rommel, beside which he had pinned a quote from Shakespeare's *Henry V*: "O God of battles! Steel my soldiers' hearts."

Five miles across the minefields, Stumme had no idea that the battle was at hand. Montgomery's ruses had worked. The Germans expected the attack to come in the south—and not until early November, after the water pipe the British were so busily laying was completed. The notion must have given Stumme some relief. He lacked gasoline for the 500 tanks that were supposed to support his infantry along the 40-mile Alamein line, and without sufficient fuel he could ill afford to shift his panzers back and forth to contain a British attack.

At 9:30 p.m., from far overhead came a faint throbbing: British bombers were moving up from the east to strike enemy positions and airfields. Then, briefly, there was silence. On the ground, all along the British front, gun commanders checked the snail-paced hands of their watches.

At 9:40 p.m., all along the line, the order was given: "Troop, fire!" Nine hundred guns spoke with an earsplitting, earth-shaking roar, and the entire front erupted in flame. The barrage—unequaled since World War I—poured a storm of fire onto the Axis positions; the explosions could be heard in Alexandria 60 miles away. Soon the British gunners were deaf from the thunder, and their thick gloves were burned through by the red-hot gun barrels. One Anzac officer reported feeling the ground vibrating under his feet "like the skin of a kettle drum." New Zealander Pe-

ter Llewellyn, who was a supply-corps driver, conceived a weird fancy—"giants were striking matches as big as pine trees on the rough desert, and a roaring wind was blowing out the flames."

Confusion reigned along the entire Axis line. The officers of the German 164th Division had been drinking with their commander, General Karl Lungershausen, in the huge dugout that served as tactical headquarters. With the first explosions a soda siphon rolled to the floor with a crash. One of the staff officers lunged forward to save a teetering bottle of wine. Peering through the slits of the dugout, Lungershausen could see the sky lit with brilliant flashes. He said incredulously, "The attack has started."

As the shells burst among the Axis strong points, acres of mines went skyward, spewing geysers of rocky sand and jagged lengths of barbed wire. Under the murderous roar of 900 rounds a minute, blockhouses crumbled and dugouts caved in; German and Italian soldiers dropped dead from the concussion of the exploding shells, with not a mark on their bodies.

Few men were more confused than Stumme. Within seconds of the start of the barrage, shells had torn his communications to ribbons. Stumme was cut off from every division, every regiment. He determined to head for the front line. Along with a staff officer, Colonel Büchting, and a driver, he set off for the battlefront early the next morning.

Jouncing through shellbursts, Stumme's staff car suddenly came under a hail of fire from Australian machine gunners. Büchting, mortally wounded, slumped forward. Now the driver reversed the car furiously—too intent on evasive action to see that Stumme was groping from his seat, fighting for breath, his face gray and mottled, pain gripping his breast. Stricken by a fatal coronary, he vainly tried to scramble from the car, then crumpled and fell.

The Axis forces were temporarily leaderless—and the battle was only a few hours old.

Montgomery's infantry had started moving up soon after the barrage began. One man who watched them, Captain Grant Murray, of the Seaforth Highlanders patrolling the line of departure, was never to forget it—"line upon line of steel-helmeted figures, with rifles at the high port, bayonets catching in the moonlight . . . gave us the thumbs-up sign. We watched them plod on towards the enemy lines which were by this time shrouded in smoke." They moved as they had been taught to move, three yards between men, covering a steady 50 yards a minute. In the Highland Division, in the northern sector of the line, each infantryman carried not only his small pack, two grenades, 50 rounds of ammunition, a day's rations and a full water bottle, but also a pick or shovel for digging slit trenches and four empty bags to fill with sand for protection. Each backpack was marked with a white St. Andrew's cross to orient those following.

Ahead of each battalion moved the navigating officers, compasses in hand, counting the paces, until the wire girdling the first minefields loomed into view. As one battalion of the Black Watch Highland regiment neared the wire, a voice called out to a company barber, who had charge of the wire cutters. "Get a bloody move on, Jock," it said. "You're no' cuttin' hair now."

From the first, the sappers faced a nightmare task. Although thousands of mines had already been exploded by the barrage, to clear all the mines was an impossible feat, and they did not attempt it. Instead, they tried to clear several lanes of up to 24 feet in width to allow the tanks to advance two abreast. They "deloused" antitank mines by feeling for and removing the igniters. Deadly S-mines, which were no larger than a can of beans and fired a lethal spray of shrapnel when stepped on, were disarmed by inserting nails into the small holes that had housed the safety pins before the mines were laid. Finally each gap, when cleared, was marked by white tape and orange and green pin-point lights—a signal that tanks and trucks could move up. Using detectors that reacted to metal objects underground with a sharp "ping" in the earphones, the sappers could clear up to 200 yards an hour.

Despite these heroic efforts, in the hours before dawn thousands of booby traps and mines took a gruesome toll. One section officer, forging ahead, had three trucks blown from under him in eight minutes. Miraculously he survived, but other men lay where they had fallen, torn apart by S-mines and fat, black Teller mines. A murderous 250-pound aerial bomb planted as a mine ripped a platoon of 30 men into bloody fragments. In one Black Watch battalion, mines killed or maimed seven navigating officers before dawn.

Yet a savage determination prevailed. Lieutenant Bruce Rae of the Gordon Highlanders, coming under fire, felt "as though I had had a couple of bottles of champagne." Lieut. Colonel Reg Romans, of the 5th New Zealand Brigade, somehow finding himself three quarters of a mile inside enemy territory with no enemy in sight, called out to his adjutant, "We can't stop here—we haven't fought yet!" He stumbled on until shellfire forced him to take cover.

Out of the maelstrom, men would carry with them scenes of surreal horror: a dead German signals officer with a telephone still cupped to his ear; another with a cigarette clutched in one hand, matches in the other; a severed white hand in the moonlight; blood seeping from the tight-shut door of an ambulance. Alaric Jacob, a war correspondent of long experience, could take no more than a few minutes at Dressing Station 86 of the 11th Australian Field Ambulance. "In one cubbyhole a doctor was amputating an arm, in another men lay gasping on trestle tables having fresh blood pumped into them. . . . Men with faces like soiled cardboard were slopped on a bench. The doctors worked like overworked butchers on a Saturday night."

Now a shortage of mine detectors slowed the advance literally to a crawl. Many of the detectors had proved defective, and others had been broken or destroyed in battle. The sappers had to prod the sand with bayonets; the rate of progress became that of a man on his hands and knees, listening, peering, probing. Anxiety spread from sector to sector. Could the mines be lifted fast enough for the oncoming armor to achieve its goal—a salient 10 miles wide, five miles deep—by dawn?

The answer was all too obvious. Struggling through the minefields, the advancing army was pinned down by Axis fire. In spite of the intensive artillery barrage and the efforts of the infantry, most of the Axis defensive positions remained intact. At dawn, in the north, British tanks unable to move forward were jammed together behind the infantry, motors running, radiators boiling. One man described the scene as resembling "a badly organized car park at an immense race meeting held in a dust bowl."

For all the fighting spirit of his troops, Montgomery had demanded too much of them.

All through the morning of October 24, as the sappers advanced yard by painful yard, with the armor stalled behind them, Montgomery, chafing in his headquarters, grew increasingly skeptical of their valor. "The X Corps Commander was not displaying the drive and determination so necessary when things begin to go wrong," he said later. He ordered the armor to push ahead regardless of whether the way had been cleared.

The top armor commanders were fearful that such an advance would mean heavy tank losses, not simply from the undetected mines, but from German antitank guns as well. Lieut. General Lumsden was appalled by the concept. One had to understand how to fight with armor, he said. "If you don't take your time you will get run through the guts. It is not for tanks to take on guns."

On the night of the 24th-25th what Montgomery was later to call "the real crisis of the battle" occurred. The tanks,

under Montgomery's orders, once more inched forward under cover of darkness. At about 10 p.m. a cluster of Luftwaffe bombs struck several supply trucks of the Nottinghamshire Yeomanry. In the tight column, truck after truck caught fire, and soon a wavering orange curtain of flame from 25 blazing trucks lighted up the night. Using the flames as a ranging point, field artillery, antitank guns, even lone bombers, loosed a rain of death on the tanks.

One regiment, the Staffordshire Yeomanry—sturdy brewers recruited from the Bass Brewery at Burton-on-Trent—came under the blowtorch fire of 88mm guns. An eyewitness, Major John Lakin, watched 27 tanks "go up in sheets of flame, one by one, just as if someone had lit the candles on a birthday cake." The Staffordshire's commanding

Mediterranean Sea

BRITISH FORCES

AXIS FORCES

MINEFIELDS

0   5

Scale of Miles

Sidi Abd Rahman

Rahman Track

El Alamein

Miteirya Ridge

Alam el Halfa Ridge

The Battle of El Alamein began on the night of October 23 with a British assault (black arrows) all along the front. Forcing their way through the enemy's minefields (shaded area), the British made moderate gains in spite of intensifying Axis resistance (red arrows). On October 31, British troops reached the coast, but the turning point of the battle did not come until November 2, when British armor, battering Axis defenses along the Rahman Track about 10 miles south of the coast, forced Rommel to break off and withdraw to the west.

officer, Lieut. Colonel James Eadie, broke down and wept.

Lumsden sent an urgent message to Montgomery's chief of staff, Brigadier Francis de Guingand: it was time to call off the attack. De Guingand acted swiftly. Despite Montgomery's deeply rooted aversion to being awakened at night, de Guingand, after first summoning Lumsden and Leese, commanders of the X and XXX corps, to a small-hours conference, aroused Montgomery to tell him.

At 3:30 a.m. on October 25, in Montgomery's trailer, the army commander listened in silence as Lumsden voiced his objections. The operation, Lumsden argued, should be abandoned; those few tanks that had already crossed Miteirya Ridge, a high strong point in the Axis line seven miles south of the coast, should be withdrawn before first light. Facing them just beyond the ridge, Lumsden warned, lay batteries of Axis artillery.

Montgomery shook his head. His plan must be followed through to the end: a withdrawal was out of the question. If Lumsden and his subordinates were unwilling to push ahead, others would be found to carry out the assignment.

Montgomery was giving his commanders a concept of warfare new to them. He reasoned with clinical logic that tanks, 900 of which were still operative, were expendable. But his infantry reserves were low; more than 6,000 men had fallen, dead or wounded, in the battle thus far.

Back to the raging fight on October 25 flew a weary Rommel. Although he knew that "there were no more laurels to be earned in Africa," he had been urged to return from his sickbed by an alarmed Hitler, who was still in the dark as to why Stumme had vanished. (In the heat of battle Stumme's disappearance had been reported but not his death.) Arriving at his headquarters just before nightfall Rommel now learned the worst from General Ritter von Thoma, commander of the Afrika Korps, who had taken temporary charge of Panzer Army Africa. Barely enough gasoline remained on the Axis side for three days' all-out fighting.

Rommel, who had distrusted the Army High Command but had retained his faith in Hitler's word, now realized for the first time the emptiness of the promises of the Führer. As recently as the end of September at his headquarters in Rastenburg, East Prussia, Hitler had assured Rommel, "Never fear, we are going to get Alexandria, all right." He had expanded, weaving a web of military fantasy: a fleet of shallow-depth ferries, already in mass production, would rush gasoline across the Mediterranean by night and solve the supply problem; a brigade of new Nebelwerfer multibarreled rocket launchers and 40 Tiger tanks, also in production, would be flown to Africa.

The reality was something else again. Not only were Rommel's fuel and ammunition supplies dangerously low; promised weapons had not appeared. The fighting in the desert had boiled down to a struggle of attrition, the kind of battle that the outnumbered Germans could not hope to win. Men fought with insane tenacity for a stony hill, for a hole in the ground, for a length of barbed wire. "Rivers of blood were poured out over miserable strips of land which, in normal times, not even the poorest Arab would have bothered his head over," Rommel later said.

During the first hours of fighting the Axis had managed to prevent a decisive breakthrough, but Montgomery was wearing down Rommel's forces piecemeal. The 15th Panzer Division, which had taken the brunt of the offensive in the north, had lost all but 31 of its 119 tanks. Rommel made desperate attempts to restore the old Axis line by counterattacks; they failed. The morale of the Germans and Italians alike had plunged. Rommel himself was feeling the pressure. "A very hard struggle," he wrote to his wife on October 27. "No one can conceive the burden that lies on me."

Montgomery was not one to admit to such doubts—but he too had reason for concern. His plan had been designed to achieve a dramatic victory over Rommel. But by October 26, the third day of the battle, most of his forces were still short of the objectives that he had originally expected them to reach in eight hours' fighting. Unless a new thrust could be developed and the stalemate broken, he realized, the British might well lose their momentum and their will to win. He spent most of the day closeted in his trailer—and emerged with the outline of a new plan.

Monty's best progress thus far had been made in the north, where the 9th Australian Division had penetrated most of the five-mile minefield and defense zone, and was now moving northwestward toward the coast. On the way it captured a piece of high ground that afforded a good view of the coastal road and railway. Montgomery now considered assembling a huge assault force to exploit the Austra-

SURVIVAL OF THE FITTEST IN ARMORED WARFARE

"The armor is the core of the motorized army," said Rommel, "everything turns on it." And the desert, with its flat, open terrain, provided the setting for armored warfare in its classic form. The result was a technological race between the protagonists to equip their armies with tanks that could outshoot, outmaneuver and outlast those of the foe. The tanks—some of the most widely used of which are displayed here—ranged from fast, light models for reconnaissance to heavily armored types for assaults on fortified positions.

At the start of the war, British armor, including the "Matilda," crushed the flimsy Italian M 13/40. But the balance shifted when Rommel arrived in early 1941 with his Panzer IIIs and IVs, two mobile tanks with excellent firepower. The panzers later were fitted with thicker armor and longer-barreled, more powerful versions of their already formidable guns.

The British were outgunned until they received American-built M3 Grants in May 1942. It was said that British crews manning the Grants shed tears of joy when they first found themselves overpowering panzers. The Grant's successor, the rubber-tracked Sherman, a rugged fighting machine that was possibly the finest all-round tank in the North African war, arrived in time to be a key factor in Montgomery's victory at El Alamein.

The unreliable Italian M 13/40 was dubbed the "mobile coffin" by the Axis forces because its armor plate was weak and it kept breaking down.

The 30-ton British Matilda, with a 2-pounder turret gun and a top speed of 15 mph, could withstand heavy fire because of its 78mm-thick armor.

The Panzer III, speedy and maneuverable, was highly effective in tank duels. Plated with 30mm armor, the 22-ton tank carried a 50mm gun.

The Grant tank boasted both a 37mm turret gun and a 75mm gun, but the larger weapon was mounted on the hull, which restricted its arc of fire.

The 25-ton Panzer IV, a general-purpose medium tank, took on machine-gun nests, tanks, infantry and antitank guns with its 75mm turret gun.

Although the Sherman tank had 62mm armor and weighed 36 tons, it could reach speeds of 25 mph and had a 75mm gun in a power-driven turret.

lians' gains; if the coastal road could be seized, Rommel's supplies would be completely cut off. He began to pull the weary New Zealanders out of the line for rest and refitting: they would head up the new offensive.

Rommel, well aware of the dramatic Australian gains, brought his 90th Light Division in from reserve, and the 21st Panzers were moved some 30 miles from the south to the northernmost sector of his line. It was an irrevocable decision: he knew the gasoline shortage would not allow him to move the panzers south again if the necessity arose. But he could not afford to worry about that possibility; he must stop the British drive in the north.

In London, Churchill was puzzled. He feared that Montgomery might be giving up the attack when he pulled his troops from the line. "What is your Monty doing now, allowing the battle to peter out?" he demanded of Brooke. From Cairo, Richard Casey, Churchill's Minister of State in the Middle East, was sped to Montgomery's headquarters to investigate. He spoke to de Guingand, Montgomery's chief of staff. If Montgomery was to break off the attack, Casey suggested, perhaps a message should be sent to Churchill preparing him for the worst. "If you send that signal," declared the outraged de Guingand, "I will see that you are hounded out of political life!"

In actuality, Montgomery was hardening his battle plan. When he learned that Rommel was shifting his elite German troops to the north he decided to switch his main effort about five miles farther south. The Australians would continue to mount their attacks in the north. But the big push would be made through the vulnerable juncture where the German defenses abutted on the Italian part of the line. The initial objective, some four miles beyond, would be a powerful concentration of Axis field artillery along a section of undeveloped road known as the Rahman Track. The XXX Corps would carry out the attack, led by part of the highly respected 2nd New Zealand Division under Lieut. General Bernard Freyberg, a battle-scarred veteran of Gallipoli, the Somme and, more recently, Greece and Crete. The New Zealanders would be augmented by two British infantry brigades. Preceded by a thunderous artillery barrage, the infantry would attack to within 2,000 yards of the Rahman Track. Then the 9th Armored Brigade and the 1st Armored Division would pass through the infantry, overrun the Axis artillery positions along the track and break out into the clear. Rommel's panzer army would finally be destroyed—or so it was hoped.

The operation—under the code name of *Supercharge*—inevitably would surpass in its ferocity any action the men had seen so far in the battle, a fact that the British commanders, following Montgomery's stern rebuke of Lumsden, somberly accepted. At a conference before the battle, Brigadier John Currie, in command of the 9th Armored, noted that his brigade's task might mean 50 per cent losses. Freyberg replied quietly, "It may well be more than that. The Army Commander has said that he is prepared to accept 100 per cent."

At 1 a.m. on the 2nd of November, 360 guns opened fire simultaneously on the minefields beyond Miteirya Ridge, and the cold, blue desert night seemed to split apart. Like a steel shield advancing 100 yards every three minutes, the barrage poured a creeping cataract of fire upon mines and trip wires. It was so dense and so accurate, one officer later remarked, that his men "could have leaned on it." Indeed, some trod so close in the wake of the bursting shells that the first casualties turned out to be men suffering extreme dizziness from the bitter fumes of high explosives.

The infantry reached their objectives by 5:30 a.m. The tanks then passed through the infantry, but they had fallen a crucial half hour behind schedule, having been held up by mines and blinding dust. Forewarned by the bombardment, Rommel had time to set up a screen of antitank guns, even more murderous than the field artillery the British expected to face. The sky was beginning to brighten to the east, and the black silhouettes of the 9th Armored's lead tanks were plainly visible to the Axis troops manning the heavy guns on the other side of the Rahman Track. Tank after tank was hit and burst into flame, the crews bailing out through inky torrents of smoke and rolling frenziedly through the sand to stifle the flames that licked at their clothing.

But some tanks broke through to the gun pits, and as they lumbered forward the German gun crews were crushed under the tanks' treads or slaughtered by machine-gun fire. Some of the defenders turned and ran, others stood and fought, and died in the sand. A few Germans, like Lieutenant Ralph Ringler of the 104th Panzer Grenadiers, even tried to tackle the tanks singlehandedly. Ringler lobbed a hand grenade at a Sherman's turret and saw it bounce off harmlessly. Standing in the turret, the British tank commander called out, "Near miss!"

The toll mounted heavily on both sides. Within an hour, 70 British tanks were knocked out. Although Currie's 9th Armored never made it all the way through the enemy positions, a dent had been made, and now the tanks of the 1st Armored Division's 2nd and 8th brigades took up the assault. A furious counterattack ensued, as Rommel's 21st and 15th panzer divisions desperately tried to wipe out the British advance by hitting it from both sides.

The battle raged through most of the day. By evening Rommel was down to 35 German tanks. Almost 100 Italian tanks remained, but they had proved ineffective in the battle. A grim but inescapable fact was staring Rommel in the face: His panzer army had been decisively defeated. Rommel ordered gradual disengagement and withdrawal 60 miles to the west.

But the next day an order arrived from Hitler. "In the situation in which you find yourself," the Führer said, "there can be no other thought but to stand fast, yield not a yard of room and throw every gun and man into battle. . . . It would not be the first time in history that a strong will has triumphed over the bigger battalions. As to your troops, you can show them no other road than that to victory or death."

Rommel instructed his troops to stop their withdrawal, but he was aghast. "This crazy order has come like a bombshell!" he exclaimed to Field Marshal Albert Kesselring, who arrived to visit the front on the morning of November 4. Rommel, schooled in implicit obedience, was extremely reluctant to disobey the Führer's order. But throughout November 4 he saw more and more of his forces being destroyed, and finally decided he had no alternative. The Afrika Korps' Thoma put it even more strongly. "This order is a piece of unparalleled madness," he said. "I can't go along with this any longer." Sadly, Rommel ordered the withdrawal to the west to resume, "to save what still can be saved." He had lost an estimated 32,000 men, more than 1,000 guns, at least 450 tanks. A day later, Hitler authorized the withdrawal.

Now, as Rommel's shattered forces fled, an unnatural quiet descended upon the battlefield. For mile upon mile the sand was strewn with smouldering, gutted tanks. All around were gray-white Afrika Korps caps, empty shell cases, tar barrels, barbed wire and—incongruously—postcards. The dead, already blackening with decay, were surrounded by the last letters of loved ones. "We are so glad you have left that awful desert and are now in beautiful Egypt," read a message from a German mother. Scrawled in an Italian woman's handwriting were the words: "Always be a brave soldier, my dearest, and may Saint Dominic protect you."

Many British commanders were bitter over the cost: in 12 days, 13,500 troops killed, missing or wounded. The 51st's Major-General Douglas Wimberley, watching as the bodies of his Highlanders were carried from the field, swore, "Never again!" The 9th Armored Brigade's John Currie, asked where his armored regiments were, pointed grimly at the 12 tanks left to him: "There are my armored regiments."

Montgomery, however, was elated. Attired in a gray knit sweater and khaki pants, a silk scarf knotted at his throat, he told the war correspondents grouped around him, "It was a fine battle. Complete and absolute victory." Then, using the old World War I term for the Germans, he added, "Boches are finished—finished!"

It was almost—but not quite—true. In the driving rain that now engulfed the desert, Rommel was struggling to save the remnants of his army. But now there could be no real escape. As he retreated westward, his army's fate was already being sealed.

A BRUTAL POUNDING OF THE AXIS

The nighttime blaze of a 900-gun barrage on Axis positions at El Alamein silhouettes British infantry troops who are waiting to charge following the rain of shells.

BLOODY EL ALAMEIN: THE TURNING POINT

As a golden strip of fire flashed into the night over the El Alamein line on October 23, 1942, Field Marshal Erwin Rommel's Panzer Army Africa was taken by surprise. The artillery fire signaled the start of the biggest British attack of the desert war. In the days ahead, Lieut. General Bernard Law Montgomery threw in everything he had to crush the German-Italian army once and for all.

Although outnumbered almost 2 to 1 in men, guns and tanks, the Axis forces clung bitterly to their battered lines and faced some of the worst combat of the war. Lieutenant Ralph Ringler, in command of a company of panzer grenadiers, described a British tank assault he witnessed: "The first tank had reached the machine-gun position. It drove over the position and came to a stop with a squeaking of its tracks. It turned and buried the crew alive." Rommel himself described the fate of the Italian Armored Corps: "Tank after tank split asunder or burned out, while all the time a tremendous British barrage lay over the Italian infantry and artillery positions." After 12 days, Rommel had lost some 90 per cent of the 500 tanks with which he had begun the battle.

Facing annihilation, the Desert Fox had no choice but to order a complete withdrawal on November 4. His immediate goal was the Sollum and Halfaya passes on the coast near the Libyan frontier some 270 miles west of El Alamein. If he got there before the British did, he could block the passes with rear guards, whose staging action would enable him to escape with the rest of his army over the high plateau and along the coastal road west of them. In a race against time, the once-proud Afrika Korps and the remnants of Rommel's other units began their retreat. Along the coastal road, the tattered column stretched 40 miles long.

The fleeing army left behind more than 30,000 soldiers— captured and marched off to barbed-wire stockades around Alexandria. But Rommel's survivors did beat the British to the vital passes. With Montgomery's Eighth Army snapping at its heels, Panzer Army Africa fled 1,400 miles across Libya, reaching the sanctuary of Tunisia's hills in January 1943.

A line of British Crusader tanks rushes into the desert to hound Rommel's defeated Axis army from El Alamein westward across Egypt and Libya.

Tough Australian infantry troops, with their bayonets fixed for hand-to-hand combat, sneak over the smoke-filled battlefield to storm a German strong point.

A near-miss explodes into a column of sand and smoke, jarring a British heavy tank as it advances on Axis positions through a hailstorm of artillery fire and antitank shells.

Under an enemy artillery barrage on the front line, British soldiers of the Middlesex Regiment—automatic-weapons experts—man their machine gun during the El Alamein assault.

British soldiers, threatened by shellfire as they pursue the enemy across the open desert, crouch behind a German tank, hit and abandoned in the earlier fighting.

After the battle, German soldiers shoulder a stretcher carrying one of their wounded. The British estimated that 10,000 Axis troops were killed and another 15,000 were wounded.

LIMPING AWAY TO SAFETY IN HILLS TO THE WEST

Carrying as many of their wounded with them as they could, the beaten Axis army offered the British a chance to deliver the final blow as it crawled painfully westward along the coastal road northwest of El Alamein. At 2:45 a.m. on November 6—the retreat's second day—pilots of the British Desert Air Force reported a solid mass of enemy vehicles on the coastal road. Since the British commanded the skies, this appeared the perfect opportunity to cut up Rommel's forces.

But, to the pilots' complete surprise, the Eighth Army—whose coordination with its air force was suffering from the confusion of battle—called for air strikes only five times on that crucial day. In the following days the retreating column was bombarded intensely. But the British pilots lacked the strafing ability that they would develop later in the War, and thus a larger number of men and vehicles survived than might have. The opportunity was lost completely by November 12, when the only German or Italian soldiers left in Egypt were prisoners of war.

Australian troops, emerging from a dust cloud on the debris-strewn El Alamein battlefield, help a wounded German soldier who was captured during the fight.

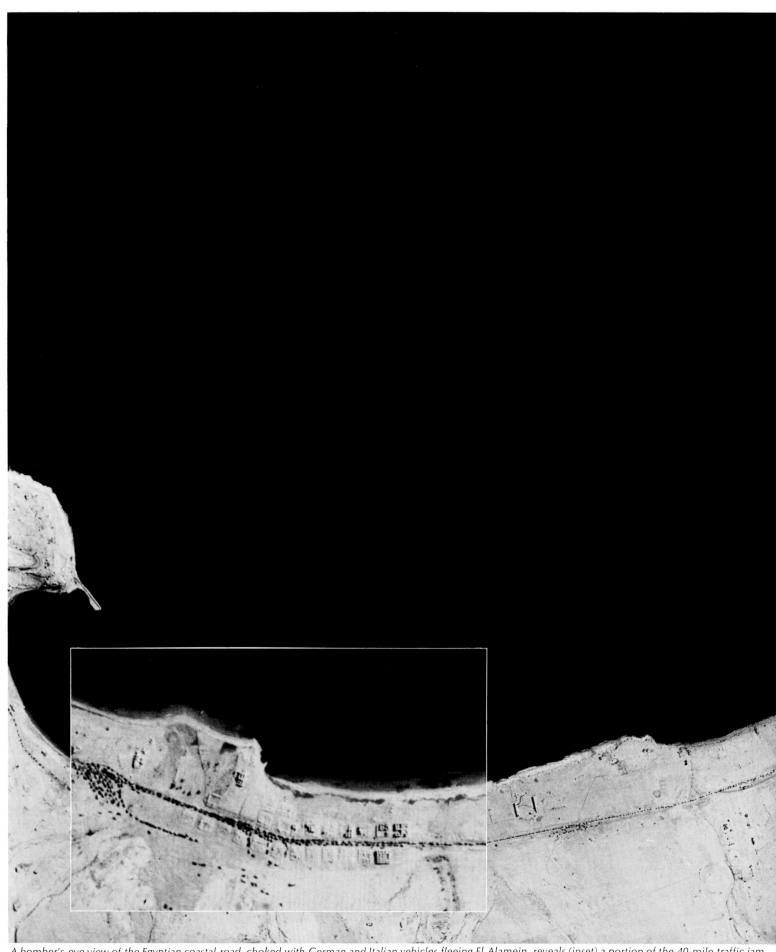

A bomber's-eye view of the Egyptian coastal road, choked with German and Italian vehicles fleeing El Alamein, reveals (inset) a portion of the 40-mile traffic jam

nearing the Halfaya and Sollum passes. The British dropped 170 tons of bombs on the road in just two nights, but relatively few of the vehicles were destroyed.

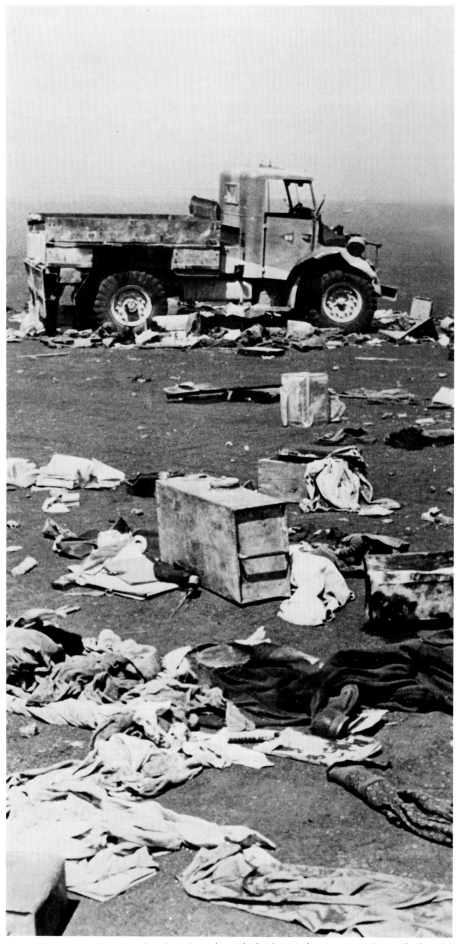

Discarded clothing and an abandoned truck mark the frenzied Axis retreat from El Alamein.

Having survived the bloody battle at El Alamein, this

German soldier was riding his bicycle westward, in an attempt to catch up to the retreat along the coastal road, when he was spotted and killed by a British sniper.

MONTY AT THE HELM

Primed for his first encounter with Rommel, Lieut. General Montgomery (center) discusses tactics with officers of the Eighth Army on the 15th of August, 1942.

A MAN TO TURN THE TIDE

Bernard L. Montgomery, the Eighth Army's commander at the Battle of El Alamein, was a paradox. Brusque, overbearing and rigidly uncompromising, he was almost everything the British people instinctively dislike. Yet he commanded not only the respect of his men in the field but the adoration of millions at home.

The Bible-reading, teetotaling son of a bishop, Monty—as his men liked to call him—was a natural leader who hated to be a follower. His childhood was a prolonged contest of wills with his mother and her iron Victorian discipline. At school he excelled at sports but refused to play unless he was made captain of the team. In the Army he gained promotion because of his single-minded devotion to soldiering. The senior officers who recommended him for advancement always groused that he was a bit too erratic and opinionated, and Montgomery himself admitted that he was a hard man to get along with. "One has to be a bit of a cad to succeed in the Army," he said early in his career. "I am a bit of a cad."

But Monty was more than a cantankerous eccentric. Beneath the flamboyant façade was a dedicated professional with a keen understanding of how to inspire combat soldiers. To the bedraggled force in the desert that had been outwitted and badgered by Rommel for more than a year, he was a refreshing change. Small and wiry, with searing blue eyes, he rode around dressed in a pull-over sweater and khaki pants, waving to his men instead of saluting, and tossing cigarettes to them as he passed.

He made a point of visiting frontline units, gave pep talks to the troops, instituted a rigorous new training program and let it be known that henceforth the Eighth Army would move only forward.

Everywhere he went, this brisk, decisive, relentlessly exacting general left the air charged with self-confidence. God and right were on his side, and victory was just around the corner. "We will finish with Rommel once and for all," he promised his men, and he never doubted that his prophecy would be fulfilled.

Wearing short pants, Montgomery at the age of 14 aims a gun while hunting rabbits in Tasmania, where his father served as bishop for 12 years.

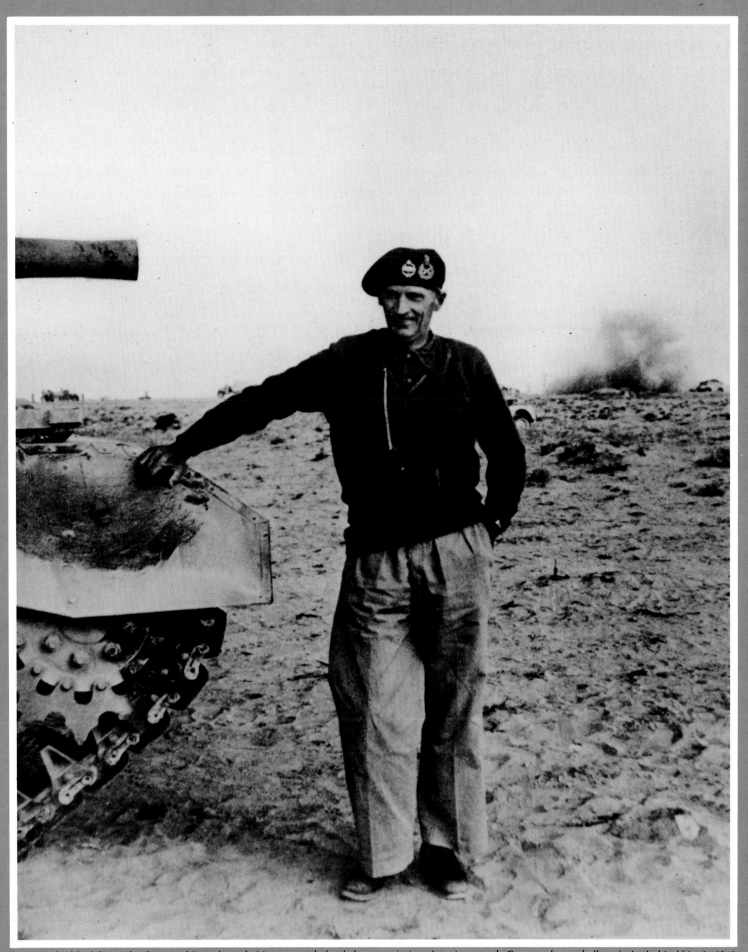

Sporting the black beret that became his trademark, Monty nonchalantly leans against an American-made Grant tank as a shell explodes behind him in 1942.

Montgomery takes a jump using the backward-seat technique fashionable during his days as a gentleman cadet at the Royal Military College at Sandhurst. The fractious Montgomery got into trouble with authorities there when he set another cadet's shirt on fire as a prank, but he still managed to graduate in 1908.

Boots muddied from a tour of the trenches in France, Brigade-Major Montgomery (at right) and his commanding officer lean on their canes near the Arras front in 1916. Fourteen months earlier Montgomery had been wounded and almost left for dead on the battlefield.

Major Montgomery was 39 when he married Betty Carver (above left). She was a gentle pacifist and appeared an unlikely match for the proud career soldier, but Monty was devoted to her. Ten years after their marriage Betty died of an infection caused by an insect bite; Montgomery, plunged into despair, vowed that he would never remarry.

Four years after his wife's death, Montgomery visits his son, David, a schoolboy of 13 in 1941. Monty was a dedicated father; to make sure David had a home while he was away he asked the headmaster of the boy's school to raise David as a member of his own family.

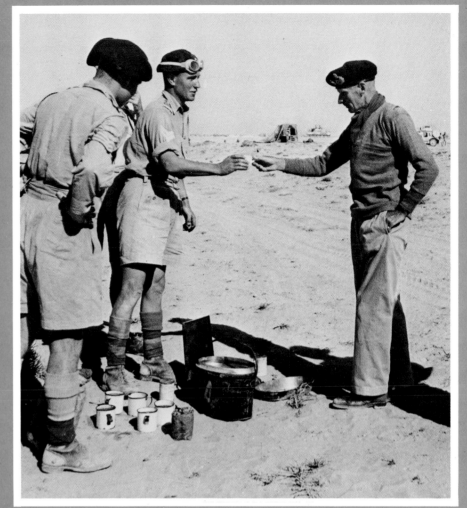

Monty takes tea with tank men of the 6th Royal Tank Regiment during a brief pause in their pursuit of Rommel across the desert after the victory at El Alamein. He let himself be known to his men and regularly stopped to talk tactics with the lowliest foot soldiers.

At an informal conference, Monty congratulates New Zealand and English armored troops who participated in the swift outflanking movement that forced Rommel to abandon the Mareth Line in southern Tunisia. By then, Monty and his men were a highly successful team, full of pride and mutual respect.

The dust-covered commander of the Afrika
Korps, General Ritter von Thoma, salutes
Montgomery after being captured during the
final day of fighting at El Alamein. Cordial
but professional, Monty invited the general to
dinner, verbally refought the battle with
him and made a tape of their conversation.

From the turret of his Grant tank, Montgomery beholds the outskirts of Tripoli, the last unconquered Italian port in North Africa. Tripoli fell to him on January 23,

1943, adding to his unbroken string of successes: in the three months following El Alamein he pushed the Axis forces back across 1,400 miles of North Africa.

5

Six miles off the coast of French North Africa, the ships rode quietly at anchor under a new moon. Only muffled sounds broke the stillness of the night: the muted squeal of winches as boats were lowered, the muttered curses of fighting men, each laden with 60 pounds of equipment, as they grappled down rope ladders into bobbing landing craft. Soon the first of the craft, their screws churning the water to a silvery froth, were gliding shoreward.

The time was shortly before 1 a.m., November 8, 1942—just four days after Montgomery's defeat of Rommel in the desert at El Alamein. Now, at diverse points along a greener and more populous stretch of coastline far to the west of Egypt, a new hammer blow at the German forces in North Africa was in the making, beginning with an amphibious operation on a scale never before attempted.

More than 107,000 troops—three fourths of them American, the rest British—were to go ashore on a mission of unique complexity. First they were to secure a foothold at nine key coastal points spread over a distance of some 900 miles. Next they were to take control of three of French North Africa's biggest port cities: Casablanca in Morocco, Oran and Algiers in Algeria. Then they were to speed eastward into Tunisia to seize Tunis and Bizerte before these major ports, the closest to the enemy's bases in southern Europe, fell into Axis hands.

The sheer magnitude of this venture—which was the first major joint Anglo-American operation of World War II—was daunting, but it was off to a good start. Astonishingly, the armada of more than 500 American and British ships, setting out from harbors as far apart as Portland, Maine, and Loch Ewe in Scotland, had traveled over the Atlantic unmolested by German submarines. Not until noon on November 7, less than 13 hours before the first landing craft were supposed to head for shore, did the Germans conclude that a massive enemy movement was under way—and even then they mistook its destination.

Because of the distances separating the three focal points of the landings—600 miles from Casablanca to Oran, 250 miles from Oran to Algiers—the Allied armada had been organized into three task forces: Western, Central and Eastern. Casablanca, objective of the Western force, lay on Morocco's Atlantic seaboard, directly accessible from the ocean. But in order to reach the Mediterranean ports of

AN ALLY JOINS THE WAR

Oran and Algiers, respectively the goals of the Central and Eastern forces, the transports had to travel through the Strait of Gibraltar.

German agents on the Spanish side of Gibraltar had reported an unusual number of Allied ships offshore as early as November 3. At that moment, however, Hitler had other things to worry about: not only Rommel's imminent disaster at El Alamein, but also the monumental battle in which German forces were locked with the Russians at Stalingrad. The enemy ships in the western Mediterranean, the Führer decided, were no more than a heavily guarded convoy bound for the island of Malta. By November 7, with Rommel retreating toward Libya, Hitler changed his mind. The Allied ships, he concluded, were indeed bent on invading the African coast—probably at the Libyan ports of Benghazi and Tripoli.

A deliberate feint by the Allies had encouraged both of Hitler's conjectures. Steaming due eastward, the Central and Eastern task forces had in fact appeared to be bound for Malta or beyond it for Libya. But sometime after dusk on November 7 both forces wheeled south and under cover of darkness took up stations off Oran and Algiers, even as the Western Task Force arrived off Casablanca.

Operation *Torch*—a code name suggested by Winston Churchill to replace the earlier, less lyrical choice of Operation *Super Gymnast*—was about to face its first critical test.

Aboard the transports, men waiting their turn to climb over the side squinted under dim red lighting designed to adjust their eyes to night vision and tried not to dwell on the dangers ahead. For most of the Americans, this would be their first taste of combat. Some shored up their courage with flippancy, others affected nonchalance. On the H.M.S. *Royal Ulsterman* off Oran, Sergeant Walter S. Sieg of the U.S. 1st Ranger Battalion devoured a last-minute hamburger, quipping: "At least we get something American in our stomachs before we die." Sergeant Gene K. Elzas listened intently to a short-wave broadcast from home of the Army-Notre Dame football game. Aboard the cruiser U.S.S *Augusta*, Major General George S. Patton Jr., commander of the Western Task Force, was deep in a paperback whodunit, *The Cairo Garter Murders*.

Other commanders were moved to exhortation. Major General Charles W. Ryder, in charge of the Eastern Task

Force off Algiers, offered dubious comfort to his men: "Some of you will not make the beaches—but you will be immortal!" An infantry colonel from Minnesota struck an earthier note, counseling his troops to "light out like stripey-assed baboons up the wharf until you can get some cover—then fight like hell."

For the men who were already nearing the shore in the first wave of assault craft, the time for exhortation was past. Instead, they heard only their own loudspeakers repeatedly booming shoreward over the dark waters: "*Ne tirez pas. Ne tirez pas. Nous sommes vos amis. Nous sommes Américains.*" ("Don't shoot. Don't shoot. We are your friends. We are Americans.") Then, in sudden response, the horizon ahead was marked by what looked like sheets of lightning—the flashes of 75mm coastal guns, manned by French crews. The word spread: "They're fighting."

The planners of Operation *Torch* had known that its first big hurdle would be of French rather than German making. Though defeated at home, the French still controlled their overseas empire. The men in charge in the colonies differed widely in their sympathies toward the Allied cause. Some fervently favored it; some were pro-American but implacably anti-British; others, swayed by the smashing German triumph over the French homeland, regarded any aid to Germany's foes as both foolhardy and futile.

Whatever their personal views, French North Africa's administrators were officially answerable to their superiors at Vichy, seat of the government that had been formed after the fall of France to rule the part of the country not occupied by the German victors. In turn, the Vichy regime was answerable to Berlin. Hitler had exacted a price for allowing the French to retain control of their African possessions: Vichy had pledged that the French themselves would defend these territories in the event of an Allied invasion.

How stubborn the defense would be was a question that had occupied the planners of *Torch* during months of inconclusive probing. Because Vichy had severed ties with Britain, the task of sounding out the French had fallen mostly to the Americans—who still maintained relations with Vichy—and to one American in particular: a craggy, affable career diplomat named Robert D. Murphy. As counselor of the American Embassy in Paris and more recently in

Vichy, Murphy had acquired a host of French friends and a feel for the intricacies of Gallic thinking.

Secretly assigned by President Roosevelt as his personal representative in North Africa, Murphy shuttled about the area discreetly ascertaining the private sentiments of military officials and influential civilians, gauging the potential worth to the Allies of various anti-Vichy and anti-Nazi underground groups, appraising the help or hindrance that might come from Arab nationalists who hoped in time to rid their lands of all Western rule.

One of Murphy's myriad assignments involved a carefully concealed trip to England two months before the invasion to brief the man who was to direct the Allied Expeditionary Force, an American then so little known to his countrymen that some newspapers back home had at first spelled his name wrong. He was Lieut. General Dwight D. Eisenhower.

As Murphy recalled: "From questions asked I could see that Eisenhower and some of his officers had mental pictures of primitive country, collections of mud huts set deep in jungles. I assured them that French North Africa was more like California than a tropical wilderness, and I described briefly the creature comforts of Algiers and Casablanca. Eisenhower then prudently inquired whether winter underwear would be necessary, and I told him it was, especially on the high plateau in eastern Algeria. Thousands of American soldiers appreciated that the following winter."

To the key question—the sort of reception that would greet the landings—Murphy offered two possible answers. If the French perceived *Torch* as an American operation, they would be less inclined to resist, for the tradition of Franco-American friendship died hard. But if they perceived *Torch* as a British affair, they would fight bitterly.

Still rankling the French were two instances of what they regarded as their former ally's perfidy. In an attempt to keep the French fleet from Hitler's grasp after the fall of France, the Royal Navy had shelled and sunk or disabled four French warships at Mers el Kebir, near Oran, killing more than 1,200 sailors. To cap matters, the British had given haven to a "Free French" government-in-exile led by an arrogant general, Charles de Gaulle, whom many of his compatriots viewed as a traitor.

But there were two other Frenchmen whose support, if won by the Allies, could lessen if not eliminate resistance to the landings. One was General Henri Giraud, a North African expert and brilliant soldier in both world wars, held in high esteem in the French Army. Though he had found sanctuary in Vichy after escaping from German captivity, he had not—unlike other top-ranking French officers—sworn an oath of allegiance to Vichy's aged chief of state, Marshal Henri Philippe Pétain.

The second, if fainter, hope of the Allies rested on a five-star admiral, Jean François Darlan, who served Vichy as commander in chief of all French forces—naval, land and air. A sometime admirer of the German war machine, Darlan had given recent signs of a change of heart, hinting to Murphy that North Africa would take up arms against the Axis—if given the help of 500,000 American troops.

Just 16 days before the landings were to begin—some convoys had already sailed from the United States—a secret parley took place in an isolated villa on the Algerian coast. Arranged by Murphy at Eisenhower's request, the meeting brought together three American officers led by Major General Mark W. Clark, Eisenhower's deputy commander, and a group of French officers led by the ardently pro-American Major General Charles Emmanuel Mast, deputy commander of French ground forces in Algiers and a staunch supporter of General Giraud. Little was accomplished except a vague

During Operation Torch, gunners aboard the U.S.S. Augusta watch the splash of salvos fired by the French battleship Jean Bart from her moorings about 12 miles away in Casablanca harbor. (The smoke on the horizon is a screen laid by two French corvettes.) Soon thereafter U.S. bombers hit the Jean Bart (far right) and opened a 75-foot gash in her hull.

promise—never kept—to put Giraud, eventually, in charge of the Allied forces. Because the Americans were under orders not to mention the British role in *Torch* or to reveal the impending date of the landings, the French got the impression that *Torch* was months away, giving them time to prepare to help it succeed.

The meeting had unexpected elements of slapstick. Local Arabs, noting the unusual stir at the villa, suspected smugglers; hoping for a reward, they notified police, whose arrival forced the American officers to hide in the wine cellar while Murphy, upstairs, feigned a drunken stupor. Clark, too, had his moment of discomfiture; en route back to the British submarine that had stealthily deposited him on Africa's shore, he somehow managed to lose his trousers.

The invasion planners' concern with secrecy was to lead to more serious problems. Murphy was forbidden to alert the pro-Allied French underground until four days before the landings, thus reducing the chances for concerted action with the one source of French support on which the Allies could absolutely rely. More than 20 tons of small arms and walkie-talkies intended for these clandestine groups, and due to be landed by British submarine, never did arrive—largely, Murphy suspected, because the British doubted the ability of either the French or the Americans to keep a tight lip. Forced to depend on such antiquated weapons as were at hand, the Allies' strongest sympathizers were to prove no match for the well-equipped Vichy loyalists.

In Algiers, the indefatigable Murphy made one last effort to ensure that the fighting would be minimal. Word of the start of the landings had reached him over a small radio receiver-transmitter flown from Washington by way of Lisbon in a sealed diplomatic pouch; the code message, contained in a BBC broadcast in French from London, said simply: "*Allo Robert. Franklin arrivé.*" At once Murphy sped

to the suburban villa of his good friend General Alphonse Pierre Juin, commander in chief of all of French North Africa's ground forces. Roused from bed, sleepy and rumpled in pink-striped pajamas, Juin reacted to the news of the landings with shock. Although he was bitterly anti-German, his only concern now was that French lives lay in jeopardy. But as Murphy pleaded with him to order his troops not to fight, Juin shook his head. Any such order, he pointed out, could be countermanded by Admiral Darlan, who outranked him.

By pure chance, Darlan was in Algiers, summoned from Vichy to the hospital bedside of a son who had been stricken with polio. At Murphy's urging, Juin telephoned Darlan. In less than 20 minutes the admiral appeared—only to turn purple and explode as Murphy broke the news. "I have known for a long time that the British are stupid," Darlan shouted, "but I always believed Americans were more intelligent. Apparently you have the same genius as the British for making massive blunders!" The invasion, he went on, was "premature," and "not at all what we have been hoping for."

Murphy retorted: "It is your responsibility to arrange that no French blood will be shed by senseless resistance to the American landings already in progress."

Pacing the room and puffing furiously on a pipe, Darlan seemed torn by indecision. "I have given my oath to Pétain and preserved allegiance to the Marshal for two years," he said. "I cannot revoke that now." Murphy kept talking and kept pace, tactfully adjusting his long stride to the pint-sized Darlan's shorter steps. Finally, Murphy asked if the admiral would cooperate if so authorized by Pétain. Darlan agreed, and drafted a message to the Marshal.

But in the message, reporting the situation as Murphy had outlined it, Darlan also took pains to note—as if to signal

Vichy that he had not forgotten—that the 1940 armistice terms with Germany required the French to defend their territories. The admiral was cannily hedging his bets, waiting to assess the strength and mettle of the invasion force.

The answer to that question was even then being spelled out on beaches and airfields, docks and streets throughout Darlan's sphere of command.

The Allies' tactical plan called for each of their three main objectives to be taken the same way: by landing troops at points on both sides of the objective, then encircling it. In addition, the inner harbors of Algiers and Oran were to be seized by special detachments to head off sabotage of the port installations by the defenders; the shipping facilities of these cities, much closer than Casablanca to the Allies'

ultimate goal, Tunisia, would prove invaluable in the Allied drive eastward.

Algiers was the first objective to be taken, though the assault on the port itself failed dismally. Nearing the Bay of Algiers in the predawn darkness, the British destroyers *Malcolm* and *Broke,* packed with more than 600 American infantrymen, made several passes before finding the harbor entrance. Then, caught in the searchlights, the two ships came under withering shellfire from the heights above the bay—from batteries equipped with infrared thermal detectors and range finders. The *Malcolm,* badly hit, had to withdraw. The *Broke* managed to slice through the barrier booms, berth at a quay and unload 250 men. But on her way out in the early morning light she was so heavily pounded that she later sank. Though the members of the landing

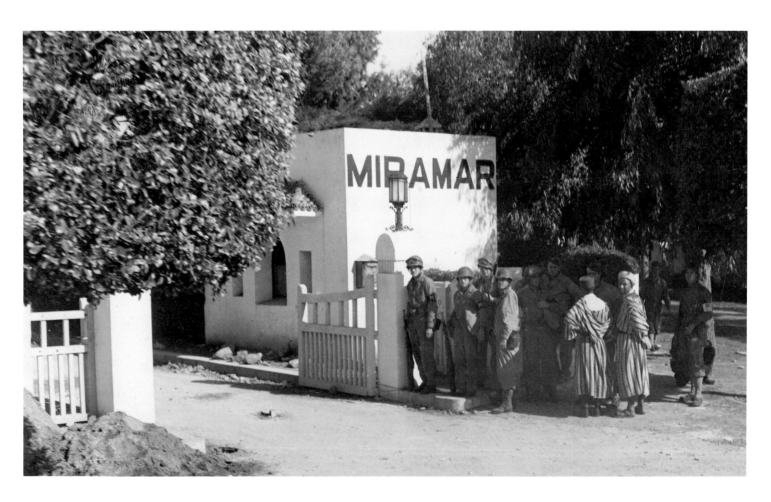

GIs wearing combat garb and Moroccans dressed in djellabahs mingle at the gatehouse of the Hotel Miramar on the outskirts of Casablanca, where Major General George S. Patton set up his headquarters on the second day of Operation Torch. "Very nice," commented Patton of the Miramar, "but it had been hit several times so there was no water nor light and only cheese and fish to eat and champagne to drink."

party secured a power station and oil storage tanks, they were soon pinned down by machine-gun fire and captured.

Behind the harbor another key move went awry. General Mast, despite the ambiguous answers he had been given by General Clark at their secret meeting two weeks earlier, had irrevocably thrown in his lot with the Allies. At his direction, anti-Vichy groups seized police stations and Radio Algiers. But as morning came and American troops did not appear, Mast's people were overpowered by Vichy loyalists.

Mast's efforts proved more effective among friendly fellow officers at military installations outside the city. The landings were virtually unopposed; Fort Sidi Ferruch, on the coast 12 miles west of Algiers, surrendered without a shot. From three sets of beaches designated as Apples, Beer and Charlie, men and tanks and armored cars moved on past fishing hamlets and seaside resorts, through olive groves and vineyards, meeting only minor pockets of resistance.

Inland, Algiers' main airfields, Maison Blanche and Blida, yielded quickly. Patrolling over Blida, the leader of a flight of planes off the British carrier *Victorious* noticed white handkerchiefs fluttering on the field; he landed and got the French commander's written permission for Allied planes to fly in. American ground troops reinforced by British commandos took Maison Blanche, soon followed by two squadrons of Hurricanes from Gibraltar; though they had no way of knowing when taking off that the field would be in American hands, the RAF pilots had risked making the flight from the Rock without enough fuel to get back.

By mid-afternoon, Allied forces were on the high ground overlooking Algiers and a cease-fire was being arranged by General Juin—with Admiral Darlan's approval. At 7 p.m. on November 8, less than 20 hours after the landings began, American troops moved in to occupy the city.

Oran held out longer and fought harder; memories of Great Britain's devastation of French warships and crews at nearby Mers el Kebir were still fresh, and General Robert Boissau, the area commander, ordered that a stern resistance be shown to the invaders.

The element of surprise was also lost. As some of the ships of the Central Task Force prepared to lower boats for a run to a beach west of Oran, their path was crossed by a small French convoy inward bound. By the time of the Allied frontal assault on the inner harbor of Oran, sirens had sounded a general alarm throughout the city and a blackout was in effect. Attempting to land troops and antisabotage personnel, the U.S. Coast Guard cutters *Walney* and *Hartland*—transferred to the Royal Navy under Lend-Lease, but flying the American flag—met a rain of fire both from shore batteries and from French destroyers and submarines in port. The *Walney*, raked by broadsides, was soon a blazing hulk; drifting helplessly, she eventually rolled over and sank. The *Hartland* was blasted by a shore battery that wiped out her gun crew. Then she was hit at point-blank range by a French destroyer; the shells burst in her engine room and amid troops massed to land. The dead were heaped so thickly on deck that the survivors could not get at the hoses to fight the fires. As the *Hartland* drifted about the harbor, all power gone, flames funnel-high, her captain, blinded by a shell fragment, gave the order to abandon ship. More than half of the 600 men on the two cutters were lost; most of the rest were taken prisoner.

Calamity also attended the initial attempts to take the key airfields at La Senia and Tafaraoui, south of Oran. Troops moving inland from the beaches were to have been joined by paratroops flown directly from Cornwall, on England's Channel coast. Storm and fog en route broke up the formation of 39 planes. Seven of them never made it to Algeria; 12 planes dropped their troops more than a day's march from the objectives; the remaining 20, short of fuel, landed close enough to take part in the action, but four were seized on the ground by the French.

It took a concerted attack by American armor and infantry, finally converging on Oran after having to fight most of the way, to force the city to surrender. Major General Lloyd R. Fredendall, Commander of the Central Task Force, received the formal capitulation shortly after noon on November 10—more than 48 hours after the first of some 39,000 troops had come ashore.

Yet despite the tenacity of the defense, scores of Allied units had learned at first hand that the French front against them was less than solid. U.S. Rangers, scaling one of the steep bluffs near Oran like mountain goats, had found the gunners of the French Foreign Legion garrison at Fort du Nord distinctly disinclined to shoot; after the Rangers' leader, Lieut. Colonel William O. Darby, agreed to an offer of "token resistance"—the firing of one rifle round skyward—the gunners came out with their hands up. During the battle in Oran harbor, Americans struggling in the water and trying to dodge the machine-gun fire from a circling French motor launch had watched other Frenchmen—in rowboats—braving the bullets in an effort to rescue them.

Similarly bewildering scenes had taken place all along the invasion coast. "The mix-up of French emotions was fantastic," wrote the American war correspondent Ernie Pyle. Even as some Frenchmen fought to the death, others—including many civilians—hailed the Allies as deliverers. American troops moving to seize the Cape Caxine lighthouse in Algiers had been intercepted by a joyful bistro keeper nearby, insistent on feting them first with champagne. Near Casablanca, one boatload of Americans, forced to take precipitately to the water after their craft had been ripped by a French destroyer's shells, were hauled ashore by dozens of sympathetic civilians, who wrapped the dripping soldiers in their own coats.

But the powerful French naval contingent at Casablanca was less kindly disposed. The most celebrated of the warships in the harbor was the 35,000-ton battleship *Jean Bart;* under construction at a base on the Bay of Biscay when France fell, she had been sent to North Africa to prevent her seizure by either the British or the Germans. Though still unfinished, and unable to leave her moorings, the *Jean Bart* was capable of wielding her four formidable 15-inch guns. In the first daylight hours of the invasion, she opened up on the covering warships of the Western Task Force, dueling with them at 12- to 17-mile range. It took eight hits from the battleship *Massachusetts* and strikes by U.S. bombers to put the *Jean Bart* out of action.

Meanwhile, under cover of a smoke screen, seven French destroyers and eight torpedo-bearing submarines, followed by the cruiser *Primauguet,* slipped out of Casablanca harbor on a bold mission of their own: to attack the American transports as they unloaded their landing craft off the small nearby port of Fedala. Of the three landing points in Morocco selected by the planners of Operation *Torch,* Fedala was the closest to Casablanca, only 14 miles away. The French attackers appeared, came under fire and withdrew. But they returned again and again—finally to encounter the heavy guns of the cruiser *Augusta* and other covering warships. All but one of the French ships were sunk or forced to beach.

The battles off Fedala and Casablanca cost the French Navy the lives of some 500 sailors. Among the fatalities were wounded men who had been lying helpless on the deck of the *Primauguet,* and who had been savaged by fear-crazed pigs broken loose from their pen in the ship's hold.

One grim-faced witness to the clash off Fedala was General Patton, on the *Augusta;* his diary that day was to record a landlubber's awe at the American ships "all firing and going like hell in big zig-zags and curves." When the French appeared, Patton and some of his staff had been about to take off for the Fedala beachhead; a landing craft had been stowed with his gear, including his cherished brace of ivory-handled pistols. The craft, still swinging from davits, was blown to bits by a muzzle blast from the *Augusta's* rear turret—but someone had thought to retrieve the general's pistols in time.

Patton had less reason to rejoice when, on the morning of November 9, he made a tour of the Fedala beaches. Confusion reigned. The planners of *Torch,* lacking any precedent for an amphibious operation of such magnitude, had overlooked many essential details. In the unloading of the supply ships, automotive transport had been given low priority; thus matériel brought in could not be moved inland, and lay heaped in the sand on the beaches. Army engineers, who should have been among the first ashore in order to organize exits from the beaches, had been unaccountably detained aboard their transports. Then mechanical failures beset some of the unloaded amphibious tractors, making it impossible to salvage many of the landing craft that had been swamped or stranded.

Similar mishaps had bedeviled the landings around Algiers and Oran, but Patton had two special problems to cope with. One was the pounding surf along the Atlantic shore, which made a mockery of unloading schedules. The other was the extent of the front assigned to the Western Task Force. It stretched almost 200 miles, from Safi, a small, deepwater port 125 miles southwest of Casablanca, to Mehdia, 70 miles northeast—the nearest approach to Port Lyautey, the site of French Morocco's best airfield.

Added to these complexities was another that Patton ran into only after he began roaming the Fedala beaches. A

High-ranking Allied officers and a guard of honor surround the coffin of Admiral Jean Francois Darlan, gunned down in his Algiers headquarters on Christmas Eve, 1942. The assassin was a young French Royalist named Bonnier de la Chapelle. Chapelle, summarily executed, apparently was enraged by the bargain that put Darlan in charge of civil affairs in French North Africa in return for his assistance during the Allied invasion.

warrior born, he was mortified to find men under his command who were plainly frightened by strafing French planes overhead. Under fire for the first time, they were more preoccupied with digging foxholes than with unloading supplies. Patton, short on patience and long on profanity, moved among the men cursing and exhorting, wading up to his waist in water as he guided in landing craft, dragging men from their foxholes, kicking the backside of any soldier who dared crouch down.

The final straw for Patton was a lack of adequate communications equipment, desperately needed to keep in touch with his far-flung subtask forces. By November 10, only one of the bulky SC-299 radio sets he had counted on had been brought ashore. Cipher machines had been landed far from the units that required them; vital items of signal equipment

lay buried beneath piles of supplies still aboard the ships. As one Patton biographer later noted: "For once, the United States Army's most loquacious general had lost his voice."

One message, however, did come through to Patton on November 10. It was from Eisenhower, saying: "The only tough nut left is in your hands. Crack it open quickly." The shooting had stopped in Algiers and Oran. The two outermost objectives in Morocco, Safi and Port Lyautey, had been subdued. Casablanca alone still held out. Patton, without consulting his commander in chief, decided there was only one quick route to victory: an air and naval bombardment of Casablanca at daybreak the next morning, followed by a ground attack, to force the city's surrender.

But at 6:48 a.m. on November 11, Colonel Elton F. Hammond, Patton's signal officer, heard his walkie-talkie crackle

HIGH-LEVEL MATCHMAKING AT CASABLANCA

In January of 1943, as the Allies were closing in on the Axis armies in Tunisia, a top-secret meeting was taking place in a Casablanca hotel surrounded by barbed wire and bristling guards. President Roosevelt and Prime Minister Churchill had traveled to North Africa, where their armies were fighting side by side, to map out a grand strategy for the rest of World War II and to agree on a new objective: the "unconditional surrender" of the Axis powers.

At the same time, the Allied leaders tried to force a "shotgun marriage"—as Roosevelt put it—on the two leading figures in the tangle of French politics that imperiled stability in North Africa. General Henri Giraud, who had been made High Commissioner of French North Africa with Allied approval, came face to face with the politically ambitious General Charles de Gaulle, leader of the Free French.

At the end of the talks, Roosevelt got the two tall, proud Frenchmen to shake hands for press cameras. Their first touch was so fleeting and feeble that some photographers complained that they had missed the shot. The generals got up and shook hands again (below), then exited. Roosevelt called after them, "Bon voyage." Five months afterward, de Gaulle ousted Giraud through political maneuvering and took control of French North Africa.

Roosevelt and Churchill watch Giraud (left) and de Gaulle clasp hands for the cameras in the garden of the President's Casablanca quarters.

into life. "Call it off," came Patton's staccato voice. The French had capitulated—only minutes before the American attack was to begin. "It was a near thing," Patton wrote later to his wife, "for the bombers were over the targets and the battleships were in position to fire. . . . These hours were the longest of my life so far."

Later that day—the 24th anniversary of the signing of the World War I armistice, and Patton's 57th birthday as well— the commanders of the French naval, air and ground forces in Morocco arrived at Patton's headquarters at the Hotel Miramar in Fedala. He complimented them on the fight they had put up, read them the armistice terms, then added one condition of his own: they would have to join him in a toast—to the liberation of France by their combined efforts.

What had brought the hostilities to a sudden end was a cease-fire order applicable to French troops everywhere in North Africa—an order issued on the morning of November 10 by Admiral Darlan. Presumably it was issued in the name of Marshal Pétain, but the Vichy regime no longer mattered in any event. By midnight on November 10, Axis troops—10 German and six Italian divisions—had swarmed into unoccupied France, taking over full control.

Darlan's reward from the Allies was his appointment as High Commissioner of French North Africa, in charge of civil administration, with General Giraud under him as commander of the French ground and air forces. In America and Britain a storm of protest arose over the so-called "Darlan deal." Critics bitterly assailed the role bestowed upon a former Axis collaborator. In justification, President Roosevelt reminded questioners at a White House press conference of an old Balkan proverb: "My children, it is permitted you in time of grave danger to walk with the devil until you have crossed the bridge."

Ironically, the furor about Darlan was soon to become moot; before the end of 1942 he was dead at the hands of an assassin—a compatriot. But even his short-lived cooperation with the Allies relieved them of a heavy burden. They lacked officers who were versed in French or Arabic, and enough troops to police the region; they were in no position both to govern North Africa and press the next phase of their campaign—the sweep into Tunisia. They needed the assistance Darlan gave them, and the help of the 200,000 French fighting men he brought over to the Allied cause.

Buoyed by the success of the landings, the Allies confidently expected to reach Tunis and Bizerte, their main objectives in Tunisia, in a 450-mile dash from Algiers that they figured would take about two weeks. Speed, they knew, was essential. By November's end, northern Tunisia—the area of their projected operations—would begin to turn into a sea of mud, pelted by winter rains that would not let up before March. Nor was weather the only spur to swift action: Tunis and Bizerte had to be won before Axis forces got there in overwhelming numbers.

The Axis build-up was already under way. Hitler's indifference toward the Mediterranean theater, long a source of anguish to Rommel and farseeing German strategists, had vanished overnight. Suddenly, it had occurred to the Führer that more than the entrapment of Rommel's forces was likely if the Allies took Tunis and Bizerte. These cities, equipped with good port and airfield facilities and situated on the Mediterranean at its narrowest point east of Gibraltar, would serve as the best staging ground for an Allied move to breach Hitler's Fortress Europe where it was weakest, along its southern ramparts.

The vanguard of the Axis forces, 24 Stuka dive bombers and 27 Focke-Wulf and Messerschmitt fighters, landed at El Aouina airfield in Tunis on November 9, while the Allies were still fighting to take Oran and Casablanca. Scores more planes quickly followed; then came German ground forces, ferried in by air and sea at the rate of 750 per day. By the end of the month they would number some 15,000. Rommel, his own forces now wearily retreating toward Libya's border with Tunisia in a 40-mile-long column, was predictably bitter when he found out that some of the fresh troops in Tunisia had been drawn from reserves previously promised to him.

Only a few thousand men were initially available to the Allies for the drive toward Tunisia. As Eisenhower later explained it: "There still existed the fear that the Germans might thrust air forces down across the Pyrenees into Spain, to attack us from the rear." With the Western and Central task forces required for rear-guard duty, the responsibility for the Tunisian campaign fell primarily to British and American armor and to infantry of the Eastern Task Force, now renamed the British First Army under a new commander: Lieut. General Kenneth Anderson, a dour, unsmiling Scot nicknamed "Sunshine."

The troops left Algiers by sea, land and air on the evening of November 10, less than 72 hours after they had arrived there, and sped eastward. In accord with Anderson's plan, based on the need to shorten his supply lines, they took the eastern Algerian ports of Bougie, Djidjelli, Philippeville and Bône and swept inland to secure the highway towns of Sétif and Constantine before moving over the border into Tunisia. By November 16 they were at Souk el Arba, a railhead 80 miles southwest of Tunis.

Anderson had little to please him on his entry into Tunisia. In taking on his assignment, he had wondered aloud whether he should consider himself "an able general or an outright lunatic," and his forebodings now seemed justified. His hopes of expediting supplies by rail were dampened by the discovery that some of the railway lines were standard gauge, others meter gauge, creating delays in the transport of freight. Locomotives and rolling stock were old and inadequate, and there were no freight cars capable of accommodating medium tanks.

Even more discouraging was the terrain. Except for the coastal flatlands around Tunis and Bizerte, the northern part of the country was mostly mountainous, the eastern end of the great Atlas chain. For lovers of scenery, there was much to admire: red rock ranges ribbed by winding valleys and rivers, scattered with cork forests and with vineyards dappled in the scarlet and gold foliage of autumn. But military eyes noticed the narrow defiles through which tanks and troops would have to squeeze, the heights from which the enemy could observe their movements, the dense hillside shrubbery in which he could conceal his mortars.

For a time, however, Anderson's troops advanced largely uncontested; his opposite number, General Walther Nehring, had chosen to concentrate on his Tunis and Bizerte beachheads, steadily enlarging their perimeters against the Allied approach. On November 25, Nehring braced for a confrontation with the enemy. Word reached him that Allied tanks were within nine miles of Tunis. The report was false. What had happened, in fact, was one of the war's most extraordinary episodes: the triumph of tanks over grounded aircraft.

During a brush with the German garrison at Tebourba, 20 miles west of Tunis, Lieut. Colonel John K. Waters, commander of an American tank battalion—and Patton's son-in-law—had sent one of his companies to reconnoiter ahead. The tanks reached a low ridge above a newly established German airfield at a place called Djedeida. Carelessly guarded, it proved fair game for the 17 tanks of Company C. They rushed the field, destroyed 20 planes, shot up personnel and installations, and departed into the dusk.

Waters' satisfaction was short-lived. Next day, a few miles from Djedeida, his battalion took up positions on the slopes above a pass near the village of Chouigui. Then the whole countryside blew up. From what seemed at first to be some German mobile derrick equipment, near a farm about a mile to the north on a dirt road, shells came screaming in. The vehicles were the Germans' deadly Panzer IVs—13 of them. What had appeared to be boom spars were long-barreled 75mm guns.

In the battle that ensued—the first between German and American armor in World War II—the Americans learned that their lightweight M3 tanks, so efficient and responsive in field maneuvers, simply could not match the brutal power of the panzers. A young second lieutenant, Freeland A. Daubin Jr., saw the shells from his 37mm cannon bouncing fruitlessly off a Panzer IV's 50mm plates. The panzer came on, closing from 150 yards to 75, while Daubin vainly pumped 18 more rounds at it. At 30 yards, the panzer launched a round that buckled the M3's front like tin plate and killed the driver. Daubin was blown from his turret by the concussion and hurled to earth, still stunned and uncomprehending as medics carried him off the field.

By the time the battle was over, five more M3s had been destroyed. The best the Americans were able to do was to put six Panzer IVs temporarily out of commission—not by penetrating them with direct hits but by chipping away at the engine doors and shooting at the tanks' tracks.

But the Americans could draw no comfort from this feat; the real implications of the battle were appalling. A Panzer

IV could totally wreck an M3; an M3 could merely disable a Panzer IV, permitting it to fight again. Other U.S. tank battalions were equipped with the heavier General Lee, but in subsequent battles it too proved no match for the Panzer IV. If disaster was to be averted in Tunisia, the Americans there would need more powerful tanks.

On December 2, General Anderson informed headquarters that his troops were stretched thin, his communications imperiled, forward reserve supplies nonexistent and air cover wholly inadequate against relentless streams of German planes that were within quick striking distance from airfields in Tunis and Bizerte. General Eisenhower agreed to a breathing spell.

Two days later, the German army in Tunisia also paused—to receive a new commander far more aggressive than Nehring. The replacement was Colonel General Jürgen von Arnim, plucked by Hitler from the Russian front, where he had been commanding a corps.

The Allies' breathing spell, which was prolonged by worsening weather, ended a few days before Christmas. A thrust at Tunis was to be made by troops of the British 6th Armored Division; other troops were to protect their left flank by taking a number of positions in the hills above the valley of the River Medjerda. One position above all was prized: a hill two miles long and 800 feet high, known to the Arabs as Djebel Ahmera and to the Allies as Longstop Hill. Whoever held Longstop commanded the whole of the valley, which stretched all the way to Tunis, 25 miles distant.

At dusk on December 22, in a merciless rain, Lieut. Colonel W. S. Stewart-Brown's 2nd Battalion of the Coldstream Guards waded across sodden meadows to the slopes of Longstop. Clinging to saplings and bushes, they struggled upward. Then glittering sprays of tracer ammunition arched from the hillside above. Soon Britons and Germans were grappling in hand-to-hand combat across the rocky slopes, biting, gouging, kicking. But by 10 p.m. the Germans had melted into the night, and the Coldstream dug in.

Just before dawn on December 23 they were relieved by men from Colonel Frank Greer's 1st Battalion, 18th U.S. Infantry, and slogged the 12 miles back to base. At five that afternoon the Coldstream began slogging out to Longstop again: the Americans were in deep trouble. Unknown to the Allies, Longstop was a double peak. Beyond a gully on the far side loomed the second peak, almost 800 feet high—and in German hands. A surprise rush by the Germans had sent the Americans back down Longstop's slopes.

As the Coldstream Guards returned, the rains redoubled. The mud was now like some brute force, wrenching the rubber boots off men's feet. It was so thick that no vehicle could get within a mile of Longstop. Every grenade, every clip of ammunition, had to be passed by hand.

Pinned down on the lower slopes by mortar and artillery fire, the Allied troops fought through Christmas Eve to regain Longstop's crest. By 10 a.m. on Christmas Day, with 356 Americans and 178 Britons lying dead or wounded, an order came to withdraw. Longstop was lost; its jubilant German captors quickly renamed it Christmas Hill.

The Allied withdrawal had the unhappy consent of Eisenhower himself. During a personal inspection of the surrounding countryside the day before, the general had seen the appalling difficulties posed for his troops by the combination of weather and terrain. The hopelessness of a winter thrust toward Tunis, he was later to recall, was borne in on him by one incident in particular: "About thirty feet off the road, in a field that appeared to be covered with winter wheat, a motorcycle had become stuck in the mud. Four soldiers were struggling to extricate it but in spite of their most strenuous efforts succeeded only in getting themselves mired into the sticky clay. They finally had to give up the attempt and left the motorcycle more deeply bogged down than when they started."

Eisenhower now knew at first hand what would happen to any tanks that tried to push on. That evening, at Allied headquarters in a farmhouse near Souk el Khemis, he informed his assembled commanders of a "bitter decision"—a postponement of the campaign. The Allies had lost the race for Tunis. What lay ahead, instead of a pell-mell dash for the coastal ports, was a slow, months-long process of building up reinforcements and supplies.

TIPPING THE BALANCE

American infantrymen come ashore near the Algerian port of Oran on the 8th of November, 1942, carrying the Stars and Stripes into the North African action.

TORCH: A MASSIVE INVASION OF AFRICA

"This is the largest landing operation that has ever taken place in the history of the world," Hitler remarked with awe and envy as he received intelligence reports about hundreds of Allied transports and warships approaching North Africa on November 7, 1942. Operation *Torch*, a massive bid by the Allies to end the desert war, was under way.

Anything that floated—from a converted refrigerator ship to an ex-passenger liner—had been enlisted to transport more than 107,000 British and American soldiers to the Vichy French colonies of Morocco and Algeria. The ships came laden with 11,000 tons of food, 10 million gallons of gasoline and no less than 500,000 pairs of shoes. Early on November 8 the troops hit the beaches, weapons in hand—and equipped with mosquito netting, dust masks, water purifiers, sun goggles and salt tablets. Hoping to be welcomed by the French, the U.S. soldiers wore small American flags on their left sleeves and carried booklets that told them how to behave in North Africa. But as they soon discovered, the French reception was in most places anything but friendly.

Because of its scale, Operation *Torch* had its problems. Vehicles fell overboard, troops were landed on the wrong beaches and some soldiers wearing heavy packs drowned when their boats crashed onto reefs. At one landing site, ammunition reserves lay buried beneath tons of rations. And in a bit of tragicomedy, when the ramp of a landing craft was lowered too soon, an officer drove a jeep into eight feet of water.

Torch also had its share of resourcefulness and heroism. Shallow water stopped a ship carrying tanks more than 360 feet from the beach, but engineers hurriedly set up a pontoon bridge to get the vehicles ashore. When one American transport was crippled by a U-boat torpedo in the Mediterranean, the 700 infantrymen aboard piled into 24 landing craft and headed for the coast of Algiers—155 miles distant. The landing craft—designed for very short voyages—soon broke down, but the soldiers crowded aboard an escorting corvette and got to the scene of the fighting.

Aboard the carrier U.S.S. Ranger, crewmen carefully load a 1,000-pound bomb onto a U.S. Navy SBD dive bomber supporting the Torch landing.

While British sailors help to steady his descent, an American soldier climbs down the side of his transport into an assault boat for the run to Algeria's shore.

A U.S. Army 2½-ton truck, heavily loaded with supplies, splashes onto the Algerian shore from a landing craft to battle its way across the soft sand of the beach.

The wreck of a jeep that slipped from a swamped landing craft lies overturned on Morocco's Atlantic coast, where huge waves made the landing difficult.

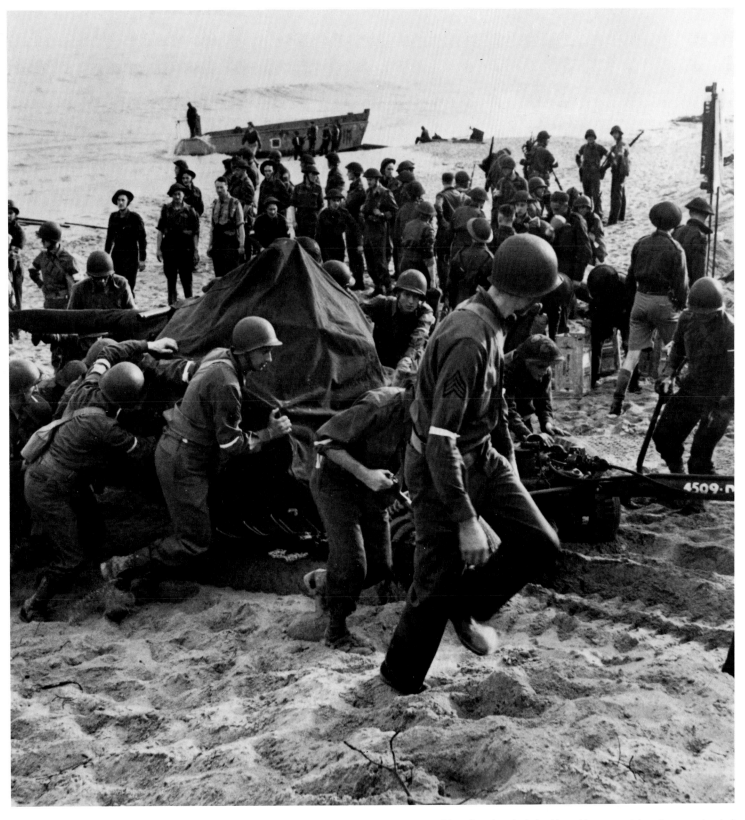

American soldiers bend to the job of beaching an antiaircraft gun unloaded in Algeria, while other United States and British troops wait for orders to advance. Although Vichy French planes strafed such landing sites, their infrequent attacks did not succeed in stopping the flow of men and matériel coming ashore. Ironically, some of the attacking planes were American-made P-36s that had been sent to France before its fall.

To search a building in Algeria, specially trained U.S. assault infantrymen called Rangers kick in a door while a buddy covers them with a submachinegun.

THE ENEMY THAT BECAME A FRIEND

"It felt just like going into hell and back out again," recalled U.S. Sergeant Ralph Gower, whose ship had come under point-blank fire from a French vessel in the harbor at Oran, Algeria. Many American soldiers got their first taste of combat from the French forces who opposed the landings. Although the French resistance crumbled within a short time, it involved several fights that were among the bloodiest in the North African campaign.

Because the landings were near major cities, some of the battles took on the air of spectator events. As both sides blazed away at each other, townspeople moved outside their homes to observe the action. During one encounter, milkmen continued making their deliveries, despite the chatter of machine-gun fire around them.

In the ensuing weeks, after the North African French switched their allegiance to the Allies, American troops got acquainted with their new comrades-in-arms and the local people. The GIs handed out literally tons of candy, gum and cigarettes. Some units donated one half of their milk ration to local children. Many GIs tried to learn French, causing a run on English-French dictionaries in stores. Others shared their recreation facilities with French soldiers, who joined the Americans in community sing-alongs. And, in a crowning irony, a U.S. infantry detachment met with French Zouaves, whom they had been fighting only two weeks before, to participate in a joint flag ceremony.

A French soldier is interrogated by his captors. French troops, many with only three bullets in their rifles, were ordered to hold out against the Allies as long as possible. Officers who had sworn allegiance to the Vichy government felt bound by honor to fight to the last.

159

After encountering the real enemy—the Axis forces—a wounded U.S. Army Air Corps sergeant stands grim-faced amid the wreckage of a camp hit by German bombers at Youks les Bains, Tunisia, in December 1942.

In Tunisia a few weeks after the Torch landings, grinning American troops —young, green, confident and as yet untested in battle—pause while loading their General Lee tank to cheerfully display the shells fired by its 75mm gun. Before too long the soldiers would be grimly struggling against panzers manned by veteran German tank men.

6

General Dwight D. Eisenhower spent the entire day of February 13, 1943, inspecting the American sector of the Tunisian front, and shortly after midnight he left his car for yet another briefing at a desert command post near an oasis village called Sidi Bou Zid *(map, page 166)*. The air was still and the moon shone brightly. The front was quiet. But despite the disarming tranquillity of the setting, Eisenhower—now commander in chief of all Allied forces in North Africa—was upset. In the distance, the lumpy mass of a mountain range loomed dark against the sky. Eisenhower feared an attack from the Axis forces on the far side of the range. That day he had visited the American troops defending the passes in those barren mountains. And what he had seen on his inspection tour gave him little confidence that the U.S. II Corps was ready to deal with an Axis onslaught.

Most of the U.S. troops had never tasted combat. Among the inexperienced officers he found a complacency that led—as he put it—to an "unconscionable delay" in preparing strong defensive positions. Infantrymen who had been in the area two days had not yet laid minefields, which Eisenhower knew the enemy would have prepared in less than two hours. He found that the II Corps' commander, Major General Lloyd R. Fredendall, had isolated his headquarters in a remote and nearly inaccessible ravine 80 miles behind the mountain range defended by his men and, still anxious that the enemy might find it, had engineers tunneling shelters for him and his staff. "I quietly asked whether the engineers had first assisted in preparing front-line defenses," Eisenhower later recalled, "but a young staff officer said 'Oh, the divisions have their own engineers for that!' It was the only time, during the war, that I ever saw a higher headquarters so concerned over its own safety that it dug itself underground shelters."

To add to Eisenhower's concerns, Fredendall, a loud and opinionated man, was not the sort of commander who inspired loyalty among his officers. He distrusted the ability of his principal subordinate, Major General Orlando Ward, commander of the II Corps' 1st Armored Division, to such an extent that he bypassed Ward entirely, giving orders directly to his subordinates. But it was Fredendall's distribution of his troops that most concerned Eisenhower. Instead of maintaining a strong, mobile reserve, ready to plug the mountain passes wherever the Germans might attack, Fre-

AMERICANS TASTE THE FIRE

dendall had scattered his units piecemeal along the front. The American line was dangerously thin, maintained more by bluff than military muscle.

Eisenhower had turned his attention to the southern flank of the forces under his command after the Allied drive in the north to capture the port cities of Bizerte and Tunis had bogged down in the icy mud of the Tunisian winter. The Allied front had solidified along a harsh mountain backbone called the Eastern Dorsal, which ran for 200 miles in a north-south direction, parallel to Tunisia's eastern seacoast and some 60 miles inland. In the northern sector of this line were the British, who waited for spring and good weather to renew their offensive. The center of the front was manned by poorly equipped troops of the French XIX Corps. Below them, defending the passes at the southern end of the mountain range, in what Eisenhower considered "the most dangerous area," was the U.S. II Corps.

To the east of the range, on the coastal plain between the mountains and the sea, there were now two Axis armies, each under the command of a formidable German general. Colonel General Jürgen von Arnim of the Fifth Panzer Army —the force that Hitler had rushed to Tunisia after the *Torch* landings—had proved his mettle by stopping the Allied drive toward Tunis in December. And now Arnim had been joined by Rommel and the Panzer Army Africa. The Desert Fox had arrived in Tunisia in January after his 1,400-mile retreat across Egypt and Libya with the British Eighth Army on his heels. Hugging the Mediterranean coastline, he had funneled his army through a narrow passageway formed by the sea and an impassable range of hills, 100 miles inside the Tunisian border. This easily defended natural corridor was spanned by a series of old French fortifications called the Mareth Line, and there Rommel had left a contingent to protect his rear against Montgomery's Eighth Army. Then he was ready to take the offensive again. His professed aim was to instill in the Americans in the Allied line "an inferiority complex of no mean order."

Eisenhower foresaw that the Axis forces might attempt to bull their way through the American-defended passes of the Eastern Dorsal, sweep across the wide plain west of the mountains, penetrate the passes of yet another range, the Western Dorsal, and then drive northward toward the Algerian coast. Along their path would lie rich prizes—Allied airfields and supply depots just across the Algerian border.

What Eisenhower had not realized until his inspection tour of February 13 was how ill prepared the Americans were to resist such an offensive. As he left Sidi Bou Zid and began the drive back to Fredendall's headquarters at Tebessa, he resolved to issue orders for new dispositions of the II Corps' defenses. It was too late. When he reached II Corps headquarters at 5:30 a.m., Eisenhower learned that the Axis had struck. The Germans had launched an attack on Sidi Bou Zid only two hours after Eisenhower had left.

Accompanied by a canopy of screeching Stukas that gave most of the GIs their first taste of dive-bombing, the 10th Panzer Division surged through the Eastern Dorsal via the Faid Pass. Under the cover of a sandstorm, the panzers rumbled toward the village of Sidi Bou Zid, where the Americans blocked a road leading west. At the same time the 21st Panzer Division pushed through the mountains south of Sidi Bou Zid and raced north toward the village.

By midmorning, U.S. troops stationed on two hills to the north and south of Sidi Bou Zid were surrounded by German tanks. Fredendall, who depended more on maps than visits to the front for information, had deployed forces on the hills, named Djebel Lessouda and Djebel Ksaira, to create islands of resistance. The men on the hills were supposed to support American tanks and troops in the plains below. But Fredendall had made a grave mistake. The forces on the two hills were not strong enough to affect the outcome of the battle on the plains and were too far apart to support each other. As the enemy tide lapped at the islands of resistance the GIs on the hills were marooned.

From the slopes of Djebel Ksaira, Colonel Thomas D. Drake watched the battle unfolding on the plain below him. He saw that artillery units supporting the American tanks were cracking, and troops were fleeing from the battlefield. He telephoned the Sidi Bou Zid command post—itself under attack—to report the rout.

"You don't know what you're saying," his shocked superior replied. "They're only shifting positions."

"Shifting positions, hell," Drake responded. "I know panic when I see it."

By dusk, the Americans had retreated from Sidi Bou Zid and the Germans held the town. But Fredendall ordered a counterattack the following day to retake the village and rescue the 2,500 Americans trapped on the two hills. Shortly after noon on February 15, Lieut. Colonel James D. Alger led his battalion of tanks in parade-ground precision across the level plains toward Sidi Bou Zid. The Germans were ready with a trap. They allowed Alger's tanks to near the Axis position virtually unopposed, and then opened an artillery barrage accompanied by a savage Stuka attack. In the confusion, the Americans noticed too late that panzers were boring in on their flanks. Alger's tank was hit, and he was captured. His entrapped armor fought valiantly, exchanging point-blank fire with the Panzer IVs, but only four of the American tanks managed to escape the German vise. Alger's battalion was annihilated, losing 15 officers, 298 enlisted men and 50 tanks.

Realizing the futility of another rescue mission, Fredendall had an airplane drop messages to the marooned GIs on the two hills telling them to try to break out on their own. At 10 p.m. on Tuesday, February 16, Colonel Drake led his 1,600 men down the slopes of Djebel Ksaira to the plain. All went well under the cover of darkness. Drake and his men marched through a panzer bivouac without a challenge. But as the sun rose, they were spotted and surrounded by trucks full of German infantry. Drake formed his men in a defensive perimeter, but their position was hopeless. He stood in the center and directed the fire. German tanks soon arrived—"huge monsters with yellow tigers painted on their sides," Drake recalled. One broke through the circle and bore down on Drake, its commander shouting: "Colonel, you surrender."

"You go to hell," Drake replied, and turned his back, waiting to be run down or shot. The tank swerved at the last second. Realizing they were beaten, the Americans stopped firing. They were rounded up and herded away.

On the other hill, Djebel Lessouda, Major Robert Moore ordered a breakout for the same night, February 16. He had led his 900 men only a mile into the plain when a German voice called out from a clump of trees. Moore ignored it and kept walking. But his bluff failed. The quiet night erupted suddenly with machine-gun fire. "Scatter!" Moore shouted to his men. As the darkness pulsed with the eerie light of tracers and bursting flares, Moore alternately crouched and sprinted as far as he could, then rolled on the ground and lay still. Gradually the din subsided. Moore regained his feet and spent the rest of the night walking nine miles west to the American lines. He and 300 of his men escaped; the other 600 were killed or captured.

Stunned by the extent of its losses—two battalions each of armor, artillery and infantry—in just two days of combat, the Allied high command ordered a withdrawal of the II Corps and part of the French XIX Corps from the Eastern Dorsal to the Western Dorsal, 50 miles away. The exhausted and discouraged Americans streamed over the hills and through the cactus patches of the plain, their withdrawal slowed maddeningly by traffic jams. By night, their way was marked by the flicker of exhaust flames. The moist air was heavy with the stench of gasoline.

The Americans fled across the waist of Tunisia, pursued and harassed by Axis armor and planes, until they reached the slopes of the Western Dorsal. Here the weary men of the II Corps turned to confront their pursuers. This time, an unyielding defense was crucial. One of the corridors through the mountains, Kasserine Pass, was a gateway to Algeria and the town of Tebessa, a vital Allied communications and supply base. From Tebessa, roads led north, and there were few natural obstacles to hinder Rommel if he chose to sweep to the Algerian coast. There seemed to be little reason to think that he would not: he could sever Allied supply lines, attack the British from the rear—and the Allies would be forced to withdraw or face disaster.

The odds were against the Americans holding Kasserine Pass. The II Corps was weary and distraught. The retreat across the plain had been disordered and tinged with panic. Many officers felt their troops slipping out of control. Units had lost their commanders; soldiers had been separated from their units. To add to the confusion, Fredendall was on worse terms than ever with General Ward, commander of the 1st Armored Division. The personality conflict between the strident commander and his calm, quiet subordinate had burgeoned into acrimony. Fredendall had frozen Ward out of the chain of command and overruled him constantly, thereby perplexing Ward's divisional officers.

To the Allies' good fortune, bungling caused by a new and curious arrangement of Axis dual command at this point created a two-day breathing spell. Rommel and Arnim

To the skirl of a bagpipe the Eighth Army's Gordon Highlanders cross the Libyan border into Tunisia in mid-February, 1943. From El Alamein to Tripoli, pipers of the Eighth Army's Highland Division punctuated momentous occasions of the British drive westward with strains of Scottish melody, an eerie intrusion on the sand-muffled silence of the desert.

were on equal footing, but it was a status that neither enjoyed. Their tenuous union was marked by rancor and jealousy. Each had his own strategy; both answered to Field Marshal Albert Kesselring in Rome, who was too far away to adequately coordinate their actions. As expected, Rommel wanted to exploit his success by striking quickly toward the Allied communications and supply base of Tebessa. Arnim argued that supplies were too low for an extended maneuver. Already he was shifting some of his troops away from the Kasserine area, intending to strike farther north. Rommel suspected Arnim of withholding forces "for a private show of his own." Field Marshal Kesselring flew in from Rome to settle the dispute. He gave Rommel the authority to attack, but even after Kesselring's decision Arnim withheld units he was ordered to transfer to Rommel. While the Germans bickered, the Allies gained valuable time—Rommel would remember with bitterness.

Fredendall did not know which one of five passes the Axis would choose for their main attack; he was compelled to parcel out his troops wherever there was an opening in the mountain range. Even after some French and British units were thrown in as reinforcements, none of the passes were strongly defended. By February 18, Axis reconnaissance patrols at Kasserine Pass made Fredendall suspect that an attack of some weight was intended there. Fredendall felt that only an experienced combat officer could be left in charge of Kasserine's meager defenses. He phoned Colonel Alexander Stark, whose 26th Infantry Regiment was covering a pass to the south. "I want you to go to Kasserine," Fredendall told Stark, "and pull a Stonewall Jackson."

With this vague instruction, Stark headed for the pass, arriving the next morning, February 19, just before the squat dark shapes of advancing panzers loomed through the mist in the plains below. A swift survey of his positions gave Stark little confidence that he could hold the pass. The only troops initially available to defend it were one battalion each of infantry, artillery and tank destroyers, and Colonel Anderson T. W. Moore's 19th Combat Engineer Regiment. The engineers had never been under fire.

The Americans chose to allow the enemy entrance to the pass, but not exit from it. The configuration of the pass dictated this tactic. At its narrowest point the rocky corridor was only 1,500 yards wide. In their advance, the Germans would be increasingly constricted, like sand flowing through an hourglass. The road that threaded the pass split near the exit and emerged into a wide basin; one branch went west to Tebessa, the other continued north to the town of Thala. The Americans set up their guns in the basin on both road branches. They would pound the Germans as they tried to funnel through the narrows of the pass.

On the afternoon of February 19, the Afrika Korps panzers of Brigadier General Karl Buelowius tried to storm through this natural bottleneck, only to be halted by a hail of artillery, antitank and small-arms fire. Then, as dusk fell, Buelowius resolved to seize by infiltration what he had failed to take by force. Afrika Korps infantry patrols worked their way up into the heights along the north sides of the pass, overran outposts on the ridges, then descended behind the defenders in the basin and took them by surprise. Some 100 Americans were captured on the Thala road.

On the Tebessa road, one company of Moore's engineers, unnerved by the phantom appearance of stealthy German night patrols, broke and ran. The panic became contagious. Several artillery forward observers, sent by Moore to direct fire on the Germans, abandoned their position after one announced: "This place is too hot." Though some troops were still holding out, others fled in fear and many were

missing. By midnight on the 19th, Kasserine's defenses were close to disintegration. Only the arrival later that night of reinforcements—another battalion of U.S. infantry and a small British force with only 11 tanks—kept the Germans bottled up in the pass.

As the Allies continued to hold on the next morning, February 20, Rommel grew increasingly impatient. His time was running out. For on that same morning, far behind him on the other side of Tunisia, the advance elements of Montgomery's Eighth Army began to probe the German rear guard that screened the approaches to the Mareth Line. Rommel anticipated a major battle there within a matter of days. A victory at Kasserine must come soon, before Montgomery forced the Desert Fox to backtrack to defend his rear at Mareth.

Rommel exhorted Buelowius to apply more pressure to uncork the bottleneck at Kasserine Pass, and the German attack on February 20 was unusually fierce. The pass echoed to the screams of rockets fired from six-barreled launchers called Nebelwerfers. In the wake of the massive artillery barrage, waves of Axis troops crashed through the drifts of

Mountainous Tunisia (map) was the last North African stronghold of the Axis. Through the Eastern and Western Dorsal ranges, Axis troops mounted their final major offensive early in 1943, sending the Allies reeling. General Sir Harold Alexander (above), who commanded the Allied ground forces in North Africa, regrouped his armies and countered with a drive that pushed the enemy into a bridgehead in the northeastern corner of the country. In recognition of his brilliant role in the ultimate Allied victory in Tunisia, Alexander was made a lord. His new title: the Earl of Tunis.

daisies and scarlet poppies growing on the floor of the basin. By midafternoon, the British force, which was defending the Thala road, lost its last tank. The American engineers on the Tebessa road fell back in disorder. Their commanding officer, Colonel Moore, barely escaped capture and appeared at Stark's headquarters to report that his 19th Engineers were faltering. Some 128 of them were dead, wounded or missing. The remaining troops withdrew down the road to set up another desperate defense.

At 4:30 that afternoon the Axis finally broke the bottleneck and Rommel watched the men of the Afrika Korps, the Italian Centauro Division and the 10th Panzers storm through the pass and pour into the basin. Italian tanks scouting along the road toward Tebessa reported no resistance. Nor did panzer reconnaissance troops find any opposition on the Thala road. Seeing the way clear for a drive deep into Allied territory, Rommel suddenly became cautious and halted the advance. He suspected that the Allies were planning a counterattack for the next day and he wanted his forces consolidated and well prepared. As Rommel paused, British and American reinforcements poured into the area to defend the roads to Tebessa and Thala.

When Rommel resumed his advance the next day, February 21, the newly strengthened American position held the Tebessa road but the vastly outgunned British force on the Thala road, pushed by the 10th Panzers under the command of Major General Fritz von Broich, gradually gave ground and finally dug into a ridge south of the village. Of all the reinforcements that fought in the battle for Thala, none played a more vital role than the three battalions of U.S. Brigadier General LeRoy Irwin's 9th Artillery Division. They arrived from western Algeria on the afternoon of February 21, after a feverish four-day march over muddy mountain roads. Irwin and his dead-tired soldiers spent the whole night getting their 48 howitzers into position. The impressive sight of the American guns heartened the small band of British holding out at Thala, and they abandoned their plans for an exodus. By dawn, Irwin was ready. As the morning mists rose from the valley on February 22, his artillerymen, although exhausted from their labors, pumped shells into the advancing panzers.

Irwin's first volley struck Broich's force as it was about to make its final assault on the village. The intensity of the bombardment startled the German commander; it convinced him that the Allies had been heavily reinforced during the night and that a strong counterattack was forthcoming. Halting the advance, Broich called Rommel and explained the situation. Rommel agreed that it would be wiser to assume a defensive stance and deal with the expected Allied thrust before proceeding with the assault on Thala. Broich waited all morning. The Allies were quiet. He informed Rommel that he would attack at 4 p.m.

The assault was never launched, for that morning Rommel's uncustomary caution mushroomed into grave doubt about the chances of his offensive succeeding. He had taken time out to examine captured U.S. war matériel: tanks, trucks, troop carriers and weapons. He had been amazed by the abundance of supplies and equipment, and the profusion of spare parts available to the Americans; he had been impressed no less by the speed with which Allied reinforcements had flowed into the Kasserine area. In contrast, his own forces were down to one day's ammunition and only six days' food. His vehicles had enough gasoline to travel only 120 miles.

On the verge of victory at Thala, Rommel came to the conclusion that the flow of Allied reinforcements was too great for his forces to check. If the Axis forces continued the drive, each day extending their already stretched supply line, they would surely be engulfed by the swelling tide of Allied strength. In addition, the Desert Fox was anxious to return his troops to the Mareth Line to stop the expected advance of the British Eighth Army, his old desert enemy.

Rommel's radical change of heart surprised his superior, Field Marshal Kesselring, who arrived at the front that afternoon brimming with optimism. "Nothing of his usual passionate will to command could be felt," Kesselring sadly observed later. In fact, Rommel was sunk in a pit of depression and suffering from jaundice and desert sores. On the next day, February 23, he pulled his troops back through the pass he had taken such pains to secure. He withdrew so discreetly that it was 24 hours before the Allies fully realized that he was gone.

Now the front shifted east again, back to the ridges of the Eastern Dorsal. Abandoning the towns and airfields between the mountain ranges they had taken during a week of fierce fighting, Rommel and his troops marched southeastward to a new arena of battle, the Mareth Line, to meet the Eighth Army.

The first major encounter between Axis forces and the Eighth Army since El Alamein, four months previously, came on March 6 near the town of Medenine, some 25 miles southeast of the Mareth Line. There, attempting to delay Montgomery's advance, Rommel launched a spoiling attack against the British. Warned of Rommel's advance by air reconnaissance, the British had time to superbly camouflage a line of antitank guns across his path. Cool British gunners held their fire until the panzers were within close range of the hidden emplacements, then loosed a holocaust of armor-piercing shells. One tank after another caught fire, their black-cross insignia disappearing in the flames. "Attack after attack was launched, but achieved no success," Rommel wrote later. The British used only one squadron of tanks at Medenine, but their antitank guns cost Rommel 52 of his panzers.

On that ignominious note, Rommel ended his two-year career in Africa. Three days after the battle he flew to Germany to try to persuade Hitler to abandon North Africa entirely and thereby save his soldiers from annihilation. Predictably, Hitler refused to listen to his argument, and then forbade the Desert Fox to return to his Tunisian command post. "Africa will be held," the Führer snapped, "and you must go on sick leave." General von Arnim would take charge of Army Group Africa, a newly designated command that included both his and Rommel's armies. Thus the Allies were rid of their once-formidable African adversary.

The departure of Rommel from the North African theater coincided with the arrival in southern Tunisia of a flamboyant American general whose aggressiveness matched that of the Desert Fox in his prime. The Allied high command had examined carefully the reasons behind the debacle that began with Sidi Bou Zid and continued through Kasserine. Many of the top brass—especially the British—attributed the failure to muddled leadership in the U.S. II Corps. Some suspected that Fredendall had lost control of his command, and they urged Eisenhower to replace him. Major General Ernest Harmon, who had seen Fredendall's performance firsthand, had counseled Eisenhower: "This is Rommel and

tank warfare at its latest—way above poor Fredendall's head." British General Sir Harold Alexander, commander of the Allied ground troops in Tunisia, expressed it more diplomatically: "I'm sure you must have better men than that."

The man whom Eisenhower chose arrived at II Corps headquarters in the little village near Tebessa amid a fanfare of screeching sirens. Arabs peering from the cover of doorways saw a convoy of armored scout cars and half-tracks bristling with machine guns, their fishpole radio antennas whipping in the wind, sweep into the dingy square. In the lead car, bolt upright like a Roman charioteer, stood Major General George S. Patton, a scowl on his face, his jaw straining against the web strap of his steel helmet.

Patton immediately cranked up an iron-fisted campaign of discipline to whip the discouraged men of the II Corps into fighting shape. Within days, one of his deputies recalled, "the II Corps staff was fighting mad—but at Patton, not at the Germans." A stickler for spit and polish, Patton quickly tightened uniform regulations. He wanted his men dressed by the book. Most had adopted the British Tommy's disregard for proper field dress; when not in combat, they removed their helmets and wore only the olive-drab liner beneath. To Patton, the helmet liner became the symbol of the II Corps' slovenliness. Coining a slogan, "Banish That Beanie," he levied fines—$50 for officers, $25 for enlisted men—on any soldier not impeccably clad in helmet, leggings and necktie. No one was immune. GIs musing in the latrine were rattled to be confronted by Patton yanking open the doors for a helmet check.

At 57, the volatile Patton was already a legend among the American soldiers. Fiercely proud of his warrior's reputation won in World War I, he sought to further it by practicing martial frowns in a mirror; on the other hand, his emotions often got the better of him—once he broke down weeping three times during the course of a staff conference. His oratory was flamboyant: "We won't just shoot the sonsabitches—we're going to cut out their living guts and use them to grease the treads of our tanks." Patton successfully used this combination of showmanship, bravado and severity to galvanize the sloppy Americans into a trim and effective fighting force.

He would soon get a chance to show the mettle of his revamped II Corps, which, in addition to its improved morale, now also had received some tanks that were a match for the Panzer IVs—new Shermans with 75mm guns. General Alexander still harbored doubts that the Americans were capable of mounting a major offensive against the Axis. So he gave the II Corps a secondary, though important task: to draw the Axis forces away from the Mareth Line while Montgomery tried to break through it. Patton was to probe the enemy's flank 90 miles northwest of Mareth through the oasis town of Gafsa and the mountain passes at El Guettar and Maknassy.

On the night of March 16, Patton assembled his staff for a last briefing in a dimly lit schoolroom that served as II Corps headquarters. Patton's apocalyptic message left his officers speechless. "Gentlemen," he said, "tomorrow we attack. If we are not victorious, let no man come back alive."

The advance began that same night. Initially, the ease of their progress deluded Patton's troops into dreams of imminent victory. Arriving at Gafsa, which had been abandoned by the Allies a month before during the retreat to the Western Dorsal, Major General Terry Allen's 1st Infantry Division met no opposition. The Italian garrison had pulled out and retreated into the hills beyond the date-palm oasis of El Guettar. "Jeez, General," a euphoric GI shouted to Allen, "aren't we doing swell?"

A few miles past El Guettar, the Americans had to pause. There, as they entered a vast green valley rimmed by ridges, the road leading east split in two; both branches disappeared through narrow passes in the high hills that blocked other exits from the valley. The Axis had converted these passes into fortified funnels sown with wide belts of mines backed up by aprons of barbed wire. The cliffs above them sprouted antitank and light and heavy machine guns.

The Americans recognized that a steep slope rising to the crest of the hill overlooking one of the passes might be climbed by a column of men moving in single file. A chain of gorges, crevices and saddles would serve as a rough path for their ascent. If they were able to gain the crest, they would be staring at the backs of the Italians whose guns were trained down on the pass.

On the night of March 20, a column spearheaded by 500 of Lieut. Colonel William O. Darby's U.S. Rangers set out over the path. They could not carry any sizable weapons;

the terrain was too difficult. The success of their mission would depend instead on stealth, surprise and shock. They marched in silence, picking their way painfully over a carpet of loose stone and struggling through crevices. The blue steel of their rifle barrels glistened in the light of a rising moon. At intervals, their progress slowed to a crawl as they scaled 20-foot cliffs, passing their equipment up from hand to hand. It was nearing dawn when at last the Rangers reached the rocky plateau that overlooked the Italian guns.

A bugle call signaled the attack, and skirmish lines of Rangers, their faces black with burnt cork, surged down on the sleepy Italians. The Rangers screamed as they bounded from rock to rock, terrifying some of the unsuspecting enemy troops into immediate surrender. Many of the defenders who resisted were bayoneted or shot. The morning sun rose on scores of Italian dead and 700 prisoners. The Rangers' exultant leader radioed his superior, the 1st Infantry Division commander, General Allen: "You can send in your troops. The pass is clear."

Clearing the enemy from the ridges and hills that loomed over the other exit from the valley—the pass on the road to Gabes and Mareth—proved more difficult for Patton's troops, and their advance was stalled for three days. Then, at dawn on March 23, with a panzer division diverted from the Mareth Line, the Axis struck back through this pass.

Fifty tanks of Broich's 10th Panzers rumbled through the defile and onto the dusty floor of the El Guettar valley, followed by mobile guns and troop carriers full of infantry. Messerschmitts swarmed out of the rising sun to strafe the 1st Infantry's foxholes and gun emplacements. Patton, watching from his nearby observation post, saw that the enemy attack was devastating. But his troops seemed determined to stand fast. General Allen set the keynote. Sighting two panzers trundling perilously close to command headquarters, one of Allen's staff officers suggested a change of scene. "I will like hell pull out," Allen answered, "and I'll shoot the first bastard who does."

The Germans overran a number of infantry positions and two field-artillery battalions, and it appeared that another Allied disaster was in the making. But then the panzers ran full tilt into a well-concealed minefield in a wadi that traversed the valley. As the surviving German tanks turned tail in confusion, the American artillery and antitank guns

DISARMING THE DEADLY MEMENTOS OF A RETREATING ARMY

Engineers—called sappers by the British—scan a taped-off sector of a minefield with metal detectors.

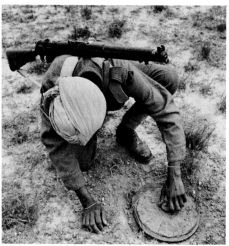

A turbaned Sikh sapper gingerly defuses a mine.

Sappers of the 4th Indian Division of the Eighth Army gently probe with bayonets for wooden or plastic mines that might have eluded metal detectors.

As the German Army retreated west, its engineers grew diabolically adept at the art of sowing the desert with mines. By 1943, the Allied engineers clearing German minefields in Tunisia faced a complex, nerve-shattering task. Their basic tool was an electric detector that buzzed when it was passed over buried metal. The engineers scoured the ground for a range of buried explosives—from heavy, saucepan-shaped Teller mines, whose blasts could turn tanks upside down, to small, cylindrical S-mines that, when set off by a footstep, sprang to shoulder height, then shot forth hundreds of tiny steel fragments.

Systematically, the engineers perfected intricate techniques for defusing delayed-action mines and carefully severing trip wires so that the unearthed mines would not explode in their hands. Among the most expert were the Indian engineers of Britain's Eighth Army, who became famous for the cool skill they brought to Tunisia's fields of hidden death.

covering the minefield blasted away at their targets. By 9 a.m. they had knocked out some 30 German tanks, and the rest of the enemy pulled back to reorganize.

At 4:45 that afternoon the Axis returned, this time in long skirmishing lines of infantry led by panzers. The American artillerymen had used the intervening hours to prepare well, and they coolly showered the incoming lines with shells. As the German infantry wavered and thinned, Patton, observing from a hillside, commented bluntly on the Axis commanders' use of their men. "They're murdering good infantry," he burst out. "What a hell of a way to waste good infantry troops."

As the Axis assault faltered, Lieutenant Heinz-Werner Schmidt, Rommel's former aide, detected a radical change in German will power. Three self-propelled assault guns, raked by fire from a squadron of Shermans that had moved onto the field, broke cover and sped by him toward the rear. As if to excuse his flight, the officer in charge called to Schmidt, "Tank attack! We must get back." Schmidt said to himself bitterly, "That would never have happened in Rommel's old Afrika Korps. We are facing defeat in Africa."

The bruised 10th Panzer Division retreated from the El Guettar valley and dug in to reinforce the Centauro Division in the mountains. Later the 21st Panzer Division, also dispatched from Mareth to meet the American threat, joined them. For three weeks Patton tried to hammer his way through the passes at El Guettar and farther north at Maknassy, but the Axis held fast in their mountain strongholds.

Yet, in a sense, Patton had already achieved his goal. He had revitalized the discouraged and bewildered II Corps. He had seen his novice troops acquit themselves well in tough battles—for the first time, at El Guettar, an American infantry division had taken on German tanks and won. Moreover, at a crucial hour, he had drawn two panzer divisions from the Mareth Line and diluted the opposition facing Montgomery and his Eighth Army.

Patton's jabs at the Axis from the west were timed to coincide with Montgomery's hammer blows from the south. On the same night—March 20—that Darby's Rangers assaulted the Italians at El Guettar, the Eighth Army attacked the Mareth Line south of Gabes.

Built by the French in 1939 to counter a possible Italian advance into Tunisia from Libya, the Mareth Line was a 25-mile chain of concrete blockhouses, gun emplacements, mines and barbed wire that was bounded by the sea on one side and the impassable Matmata hills on the other. Before they could take the fortifications, Montgomery's men would have to negotiate the Wadi Zigzaou, a ravine some 20 feet deep, running parallel to the line.

Montgomery had been planning his Mareth Line venture since early January, and he had concocted a maneuver to take the pressure off his frontal assault. In the second week of March he dispatched the 2nd New Zealand Division under Lieut. General Bernard Freyberg on an arduous 200-mile march that would take them up the western side of the Matmata hills. The New Zealanders then would drive through the Tebaga gap in the northern end of the range of hills and thrust at the Axis rear near the village of El Hamma, 30 miles behind the Mareth Line. Montgomery dubbed this flanking maneuver "my left hook."

Getting the left hook into position to strike took more than a week. The 25,600 New Zealanders first struggled through barren hills so riddled by wadis that their advance was often narrowed to a one-tank front. After several days the hills gave way to soft, powdery desert sand in which their trucks sank up to the axles. The long column crawled slowly northward, leaving a wake of billowing dust.

Once, Freyberg halted the advance after spotting German outposts on a spur of a mountain range that stood in his path to El Hamma. He summoned a Free French general in command of a unit providing cover for the New Zealanders, and asked him: "Do you think your chaps could clear the Germans off that mountain?" The French officer, a viscount whose name was Jacques Phillippe de Hautecloque but who used the name Leclerc, raised his eyebrows mildly and replied: "But of course—except that would it not be better to clear them off the whole range?" For the next two days, bayonet-wielding Senegalese troops led by French officers flushed the Germans from the crags and crevices of the mountain range, taking no prisoners. The path to El Hamma was again free of obstructions.

With his left hook ready to press through the Tebaga gap (and Patton's II Corps pushing from the west at El Guettar), Montgomery struck the Mareth Line with his right on the night of March 20. Under the cover of a British artillery barrage, sappers moved out to clear a path through the minefields for three divisions of infantry: the 50th Northumbrian leading, followed by the 4th Indian and the 51st Highland. From the beginning their attack was crippled. The noise of the artillery was so thunderous that the sappers could not hear the telltale "ping" in the earphones of their mine detectors, and the undiscovered mines claimed many victims among the infantry trying to rush the line.

Torrential spring rains had turned the Wadi Zigzaou in front of the line into a moat of muddy water, a tank trap. Engineers struggling to carpet the ravine with fascines—bundles of brushwood that would serve as crude roadbeds for the tanks—managed to create a single causeway over the wadi, but only four tanks were able to cross that night. The last to try smashed the fascines into the sodden floor of the ravine and sank up to its turret in muck and water, blocking the passage.

The infantry fared better than the armor in crossing the wadi. Using ladders, or forming human pyramids, British soldiers scaled the steep banks of the ravine and attacked the blockhouses with grenades. Despite heavy casualties—especially among the sappers—the infantrymen had won a bridgehead on the far bank by morning. But without armor and antitank guns it could not be held for long.

While the infantrymen broadened their bridgehead the next day, engineers worked feverishly to build a more substantial causeway across the ravine. This accomplished, the British commander made a costly error. Instead of sending antitank guns over first, he gave priority to lightly armed Valentine tanks. Forty-two made the crossing but churned up the causeway so badly it became impassable again.

And when the 15th Panzer Division counterattacked the next afternoon, March 22, the British infantry in the bridgehead on the other side of the wadi crumbled without antitank support. The British Valentine tanks were no match for the more powerfully gunned panzers and by dusk the bridgehead had all but disappeared. A few infantrymen clung to the sides of the wadi, making a feeble last stand.

The Allied command was stunned by this reversal, but Montgomery rallied with a new tactic. He decided to throw all of his weight behind his left hook. He sent Lieut. General Brian Horrocks and the British 1st Armored Division over Freyberg's long desert route to join the New Zealanders in their thrust through the Tebaga gap.

On March 26, as Freyberg's infantry and Horrocks' armor moved toward the entrance of the Tebaga gap, waves of 30 Allied bombers, paced 15 minutes apart, zeroed in on the Axis defenses in the valley passageway to El Hamma. The bombing and strafing lasted for three hours, and when at dusk silence again settled in the valley, Freyberg's New Zealanders, bayonets at the ready, poked into the gap. "If we punch the hole, will the tanks really go through?" Freyberg, who was skeptical of British armor, had asked. "Yes, they will," Horrocks assured him, "and I am going with them."

After the infantry led the way through the rim of the Axis defenses, it parted and let Horrocks' armor slide through and push on toward El Hamma in the moonlight. If the tanks did not clear the valley by dawn, however, they would be at the mercy of any German 88mm guns that might have survived the bombing of the hills rimming the gap.

As the 1,200 vehicles left the infantry behind and advanced on a single track, they passed almost unchallenged through the encampment where part of the 21st Panzer Division rested for the night. Crouched in the turret of his tank, Horrocks could see the occasional spatters of ill-aimed rifle fire. Even though the resistance was feeble, the progress of the gigantic column was agonizingly slow, impeded by frequent wadis. By dawn, the Germans had been able to scrape up enough 88mm guns to establish an antitank screen at the exit of the valley, three miles from El Hamma. They opened up on the 1st Armored Division and stopped its advance, keeping Horrocks at bay for two days.

But Montgomery's reinforced left hook had done its job. Fearing that Horrocks might break through at any moment and attack their rear in force, the Axis troops at the Mareth Line were compelled to retreat. They pulled out under cover of a sandstorm on March 26 and withdrew northward along the coast, settling finally for another fight at Wadi Akarit, 15 miles north of the port of Gabes.

Wadi Akarit was the last natural barrier that stood between the British and the Tunisian coastal plain. The Axis defensive line there bridged an 18-mile gap between the sea on the east and a range of ragged hills on the west. The wadi itself was a deep and formidable obstacle for only four miles of its length. Where it was shallow, the Axis had reinforced their line with a chain of minefields and antitank ditches.

Unlike the Mareth Line, Wadi Akarit lacked both concrete bunkers and pillboxes, and this absence of permanent fortifications contributed to the air of disillusionment among the Axis troops that had recently suffered defeat at Mareth. As they dug in at Akarit, a noncommissioned officer, intent on boosting the morale of his weary and bedraggled men, announced, "This is a much better line than Mareth." Private Giuseppe Berto, of the 6th Blackshirt Division, retorted sourly, "Then why didn't we come here in the first place?"

From the Allies' point of view, the most disturbing feature of the defense was the 900-foot-high Djebel Fatnassa that commanded the wadi from the rear. Four hours before the battle began, two battalions of the 4th Indian Division set out to infiltrate the Italian positions high on the hill.

In the lead were Gurkhas, doughty warriors from Nepal. Their principal weapon was the kukri, a long, curved knife with a blade sharpened on the inner edge. Shortly after midnight, on April 6, two sections of Gurkhas began scaling Fatnassa to secure the pathway leading along its ridgeline high above the wadi. One officer, waiting at the foot of the hill, recalled only silence until the Gurkhas reached the first Italian post. "Then," he remembered, "there came an eerie sound, an excited whimper not unlike hounds finding the scent." The Gurkhas charged grimly along the ridge through a sheet of machine-gun fire, leaping from rock to rock, hacking with their kukris. They secured the high ground, eliminating a key position of the Axis defense.

A few hours later, the British opened up with an artillery barrage described by the Italian commander, General Giovanni Messe, as an "apocalyptic hurricane of steel and fire." The 50th Division and the 51st Highland Division then struck at the center of the Axis line. Despite the forewarning of artillery, the Italians were surprised by the assault. They had expected their enemy to wait for a moonlit night to launch an attack. Instead it came in inky darkness, and the Italian defenders, thrown off guard, were quickly overrun. By 9:30 a.m. they were surrendering in huge numbers.

But the battle was far from over. The German 90th Light Division refused to yield its sector of the line. And that afternoon, as the British 8th Armored Brigade crawled cautiously around the base of a hill behind the captured Italian positions, its lead tanks were met head on and stopped by the guns of the 15th Panzer Division. All that afternoon, the 15th Panzer blocked a British breakthrough. Montgomery decided to wait until the next morning before trying to force the advance.

But that afternoon, the German divisional commanders brought discouraging reports to Messe: although they had blocked the British advance so far, they would not be able to hold out much longer. Messe agreed, and passed the word to Arnim. The Axis commanders then made a fateful decision: if the Italian forces were to be saved, they must pull back at once. The remaining Axis troops in the coastal region, at El Hamma and El Guettar, must also withdraw in mutual support to the north.

On April 7, the Eighth Army and the American II Corps discovered that the enemy had disappeared. Patton lashed his forces eastward to the coast for either "a fight or a bath." And that afternoon a symbolic encounter took place in the coastal plain southwest of the port of Sfax: a reconnaissance patrol of the British 12th Lancers, probing north, met up with an advance patrol from the American II Corps. On behalf of the Eighth Army, Sergeant William Brown, from Devon, said, "This is certainly a pleasant surprise." Replied Private Perry Searcy from Kentucky: "Well, it's good to see somebody besides a Nazi."

The Axis forces were now in full retreat up the coastal plain; no terrain would lend itself to a defense until they reached the high mountains ringing Tunis and Bizerte. And the two Allied armies, one hardened by desert warfare, the other learning quickly, would join in the pursuit and in the last, climactic battles that spelled the end of Axis domination in North Africa.

ONE MAN'S FOCUS ON THE WAR

Lieut. General George S. Patton watches American tanks advance at El Guettar in this picture taken by LIFE's Eliot Elisofon, whom Patton called "Hellzapoppin

STARING DANGER IN THE FACE

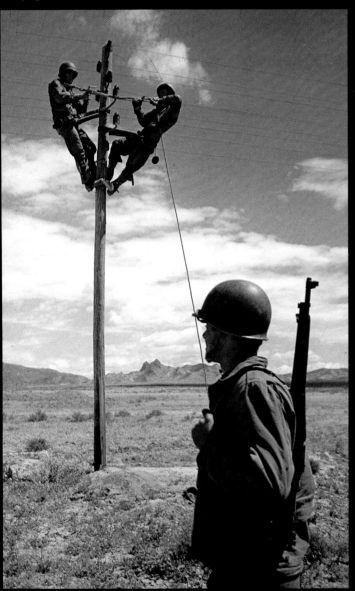

Elisofon turns a basically mundane scene—two U.S. Signal Corps soldiers stringing telephone lines along a Tunisian road—into a dramatic picture.

In North Africa as elsewhere, the War was thoroughly reported in words and pictures, and the people who covered it often faced the same dangers as the soldiers whose deeds they depicted. The job of combat photographers was especially risky, since a camera had to be where the action was to record it. One who braved those dangers in Tunisia was Eliot Elisofon of LIFE. During seven months in Tunisia he shot thousands of pictures, many in color—rare for that day. Some of the most striking appear on these pages. Along with excerpts from his reports to the magazine, they offer a remarkable, personal record of part of the hard-fought campaign that finally brought the desert war to an end.

At the front, Elisofon worked like an Old West gunslinger. "You shoot first and think afterwards," he said. "To delay is to lose the picture here." The two 35mm cameras he carried were always at the ready; if he didn't have time to focus, at least he could press the shutter release and hope. He aimed his lenses at all aspects of the war: at generals and GIs, at scenes of violence and the quiet moments in between.

Elisofon was enormously competitive and would do almost anything to get better pictures than his rivals. "Elisofon was afraid like the rest of us," said Ernie Pyle, America's best-loved war correspondent. "Yet he made himself go right into the teeth of danger." He shot photos from the bubble nose of a plane flying at 50 feet on a low-level bombing run and infiltrated German lines with infantrymen. Pinned in a slit trench for two hours by shellfire, he fumed because the barrage was so heavy he could not get up to take pictures of it. When a plane he was in crashed upon takeoff, Elisofon escaped just before it burst into flames, immediately began photographing the blazing wreck, and then fainted.

To Elisofon, who died in 1973, the picture was the crucial thing. "The great challenge," he said, "is to help the world to see."

TWO-FISTED ASSAULT ON AN ENTRENCHED ENEMY

"Nothing was lacking," said Elisofon, reporting back to his editors on an American attack on Axis positions near El Guettar in central Tunisia on March 30, 1943. "A tremendous amount of artillery of every type was brought into play. While all this artillery was working on the ridges, light tanks and half-tracks went in to feel out the enemy. After them came more than 100 medium tanks. The 155mm guns were firing away from a point so far back many soldiers attached to rear echelons wondered what they were firing at."

U.S. artillerymen hold their ears against the blast of their camouflaged 155mm gun, which, Elisofon said, could fire "20 rounds in less time than it took to shoot a dozen pictures."

American tanks grinding across El Guettar's sun-baked valley stir up clouds of dust. The murky conditions plagued Elisofon. "It is impossible to make pictures *without sand and dirt blowing into every part of your camera," he said. "I carry a shaving brush to clean the body of the camera and a small fine one for the lens."*

U.S. Signal Corpsmen try to track down a break in field-telephone wire caused by German fire.

IN PRAISE
OF UNSUNG HEROES

"I feel that war should be shown in relation to people and I try to cover as many aspects as possible," Elisofon said. He particularly liked to turn his lens toward "people who were not usually photographed in battle." Among these unsung heroes were "the poor guys" who carried ammunition to the front. "They would drive a 2½-ton truck to within three miles of the shooting, cover it with a net and at night sneak it up to the guns."

Elisofon also greatly admired the courage of engineers who searched for and disarmed the thousands of mines sowed by the Germans "They did this often under fire," he noted, "and a man wearing a headset to detect mines doesn't hear a shell coming."

He had no less admiration for the men of the Signal Corps, who had to work in dangerously exposed positions, and often alone, in order to keep vital communications open. "I remember," the photographer wrote, "one man walking along with a wire running through his hands looking for a break. One guy, pretty small in a very big landscape."

A group of American soldiers takes time out to watch the flaming remnant of an overturned armored vehicle still burning hours after the battle. It had been

A VALLEY LITTERED WITH THE WRECKAGE OF WAR

After a futile German counterattack at El Guettar, the floor of the valley resembled a graveyard for tanks, guns and half-tracks. Elisofon roamed the battlefield, taking pictures of the destroyed and captured equipment that littered the landscape.

He also indulged his insatiable curiosity, trying to discern something of the enemy's life and character from the debris of battle. A gourmet and avid cook, the photographer was fascinated to find in one German tank an unburned food box, and meticulously noted the contents: "It had three cans of sardines, two Portuguese and one Norwegian (from Stavanger), a can of German Limburger cheese, pressed meat, butter, black bread, fresh eggs (from the Arabs, no doubt), a can of British tea, sugar and dried milk."

destroyed either by a mine or by artillery fire.   *An American soldier inspects a German 150mm gun in a vast array of captured enemy weapons.*

Under the watchful eyes of a U.S. military policeman and several of their kibitzing comrades, newly captured Italians play cards in a POW compound. "They

Near a grainfield, wooden crosses mark a common grave for German dead.

COVERING THE AFTERMATH OF A LOST CAUSE

As the fighting at El Guettar progressed, scores of both German and Italian soldiers found their way into American prisoner-of-war compounds. "There were 897 prisoners taken the day I made my pictures," Elisofon recalled. "The Germans tried to hide from the camera and the Italians were strictly lens lice"—his way of saying that they competed to get into his shots.

Other Axis soldiers were less fortunate. Killed in action, they lay buried all over the valley *(above)*. Once Elisofon found "a magnificent German cemetery" containing 120 neat, stone-bordered graves. Some of the graves were decorated with helmets or marked with imposing replicas of the Iron Cross. A sign in the cemetery read: "These dead gave their spirits for the glory of Greater Germany." Elisofon was touched when he discovered an Italian grave, its headstone bearing a plastic-covered oval photograph of the dead soldier.

just ordered being photographed," Elisofon wrote after making the picture

7

On March 30, 1943, when General Siegfried Westphal, Kesselring's chief of staff, visited General von Arnim's headquarters in Tunis, he complained that Arnim's Army Group Africa, instead of concentrating on its job of fighting the Allies, was always looking over its shoulder. Yes, Arnim replied bitterly—looking for supply ships. "We are without bread and ammunition, as was Rommel's army before," he said. "The consequences are inevitable."

While Arnim's gloomy assessment would win him no good will from the German High Command or Hitler, who still maintained a façade of optimism about the outcome in North Africa, it was a true one. As the Allies drove Arnim's troops back into the northeast corner of Tunisia, their air and naval forces were devastating his lines of supply. Hitler himself had acknowledged that for the Axis forces to hold their Tunisian bridgehead they needed at least 150,000 tons of supplies a month. But since December, shipments had never averaged more than 75,000 tons a month, and in March they dropped to 51,000 tons. Besides suffering shortages of food and ammunition, Army Group Africa was running so dangerously low on fuel that soon it would have to save its gasoline for localized tactical operations and would be unable to make any major shifts in position.

Yet Hitler stubbornly insisted that the Axis presence in North Africa could and must be maintained. He had reasons for being so adamant. He deduced that the Allies would strike next at southern Europe (in fact, Allied planning for an invasion of Sicily was already under way). He recognized that such a move would be extremely difficult as long as Germans and Italians kept the Allies occupied in Tunisia and denied them the use of the valuable ports of Tunis and Bizerte. He also knew that the hold his ally Mussolini had on the Italian people was eroding. Workers demanding an end to the War and freedom from Fascism had already staged mass strikes in Turin and Milan. If Tunisia fell and the thousands of Italian soldiers there ended up in Allied prisoner-of-war camps, public reaction in Italy might lead to Mussolini's overthrow by anti-Fascists, dangerously exposing the southern flank of Hitler's Fortress Europe to an Allied onslaught.

The Führer's determination to hold the Tunisian bridgehead was faithfully translated into action on the ground by Arnim, who, despite his own doubts, was an obedient sol-

THE KNOCKOUT PUNCH

dier. While he privately conveyed his pessimism to the High Command, he addressed his officers and men in a spirit of optimism and admonished them to avoid defeatist attitudes. They had been pushed back from the Mareth Line and Wadi Akarit. But Arnim ordered that there be no retreat from the line held by Army Group Africa in mid-April, a ragged arc stretching from a point 25 miles west of Bizerte on the north coast to Enfidaville, below the Cape Bon peninsula on the east coast (map, page 166).

Along this 130-mile perimeter, the Axis dug in. While fending off sporadic attacks, Germans and Italians managed to mine passes and valley floors, fortify ridges and hillsides (sometimes using pneumatic drills to carve dugouts from solid rock), and place their artillery to command routes along which the Allies were most likely to make their major thrusts. The Axis troops worked with haste, knowing that those thrusts were sure to come soon.

Just which Allied forces would attack where had been a point of sometimes angry contention among the Allies since they had begun planning their big push. General Alexander, commander of Allied ground forces, had little confidence in the American troops (he had described them as "ignorant, ill-trained" and "mentally and physically soft") and had devised a plan that excluded most of them from the final action. The plan called for the major drives to be made by the British Eighth Army from the south and the British First Army—which had arrived in North Africa with the *Torch* invasion—from the west. One American division was to be detached from the U.S. II Corps and moved to the north of the First Army, under whose commander, Lieut. General Kenneth Anderson, it would serve. The main body of the II Corps, positioned between the two British armies, would take part in the initial attack but would be gradually pinched out of the offensive by the Eighth and First armies converging from the south and west.

On learning of Alexander's plan in mid-March, II Corps Commander George Patton and his deputy, Major General Omar Bradley, were enraged. Bradley flew to Algiers to protest to General Eisenhower, who as overall Allied commander in chief in North Africa could overrule Alexander. "I think we're entitled to function under our own command without being farmed out forever from ally to ally," Bradley

told Eisenhower. "Until you give us the chance to show what we can do in a sector of our own, with an objective of our own, you'll never know how good or bad we really are. And neither will the American people." He suggested that Eisenhower move the entire II Corps to the north of the First Army, and let the Americans go after Bizerte by themselves.

After considering the problems of shifting the whole of the II Corps across the busy supply lines of the First Army, Eisenhower agreed and quietly commanded Alexander to revise his plan. The shift was masterfully coordinated—particularly considering that on April 15, just about the time it got under way, the II Corps had a change of command (Patton, detached to work on the plans for invading Sicily, was replaced by Bradley). Almost 10,000 vehicles carried 100,000 men and their equipment from the Tebessa area to the vicinity of Tabarka, a distance of more than 150 miles across the British rear, without significantly interfering with the First Army's supply operation.

Meanwhile, the British were undergoing some reorganization of their own. On April 11, Montgomery tried to get an armored division transferred from the First Army to his Eighth Army. Alexander replied that, instead, Montgomery would have to yield an armored division and an armored car regiment of his own to the First Army. Because the mountainous terrain made Axis defenses strongest in the south, Alexander explained, Montgomery's attack was to be secondary, a diversion to draw opposition away from the main drive to Tunis by General Anderson's First Army. Montgomery understandably regretted that the Eighth Army, which had struggled so long in the desert, should have any less than the leading role now. On April 16 he wired Alexander almost plaintively: "All my troops are in first class form and want to be in the final Dunkirk."

At least Montgomery's Eighth Army had the privilege of striking the first blow in the offensive, code-named *Vulcan*, on the night of April 19. Two strongly defended prominences close to the village of Enfidaville—Djebel Garci, 1,000 feet high, and a 500-foot hill named Takrouna—were among the Eighth Army's initial objectives.

The 4th Indian Division struggled up the slopes and gullies of Djebel Garci for two days, repeatedly repulsing brutal counterattacks and suffering heavy losses. The division had secured only the southern portion of the hill before being ordered by Montgomery to halt the attack.

The New Zealand Division tackled Takrouna and met similarly fierce opposition. Takrouna's slopes were riddled with small caves in which German soldiers and Italians of the Folgore Parachute Division were holed up. The battle was waged with bayonets, grenades, knives—even rocks, hurled down from above. The first New Zealanders to reach Takrouna's summit were fewer than a dozen Maori soldiers led by Sergeant J. Rogers and Lance Sergeant H. Manahi. Roped together like mountaineers with scraps of telephone cable that they had found along the way, they managed to scale 20 feet of sheer rock face while under fire to reach the final pinnacle. The New Zealanders suffered 536 casualties taking Takrouna. Lieut. General Brian Horrocks, who was commander of the Eighth Army's X Corps, commented later that the capture of Takrouna was the most gallant feat of arms he witnessed during the entire war. He said he was "bitterly disappointed" when Manahi was awarded only a Distinguished Conduct Medal instead of the Victoria Cross for his deeds.

As costly as the hills were to assault, neither Djebel Garci nor Takrouna were of major significance. Behind them stretched more than 20 miles of similar mountainous country, and the Eighth Army could expect every peak to be strongly contested by the Axis. Two days after beginning the attack, a discouraged Montgomery paused; he spent the next four days regrouping his forces.

Unfortunately, the Eighth Army's attack had ceased before accomplishing its primary goal—drawing Axis forces away from the First Army, which had not yet started its drive toward Tunis. Arnim was convinced that the major effort would come from the west and had kept his strongest forces there. (On April 20, he had even dared to launch a spoiling attack against the British near Medjez el Bab, a key town along the main road to Tunis from the west, causing some damage, but not enough to forestall the Allied offensive.) Now, with pressure easing in the south, he could bring yet more troops to this part of the front.

On April 22 the First Army began its slow and arduous advance, characterized by tough slugging matches between British armor and panzers for little patches of level ground and costly infantry struggles for the hills. One dramatic conquest was that of Longstop Hill—the notorious peak

that had claimed 500 British and American casualties when the Allies tried without success to take it in late December, 1942. Longstop, which controlled two roads to Tunis, could not be bypassed.

The British began pounding Longstop with artillery on April 22, but the defenders bided their time in the relative safety of well-stocked dugouts that ran deep into the hillside. That night, when two battalions of the 36th Infantry Brigade moved up the western slopes of the hill, the Germans emerged from their burrows just far enough to slow the attack with heavy fire. By dawn the British had secured

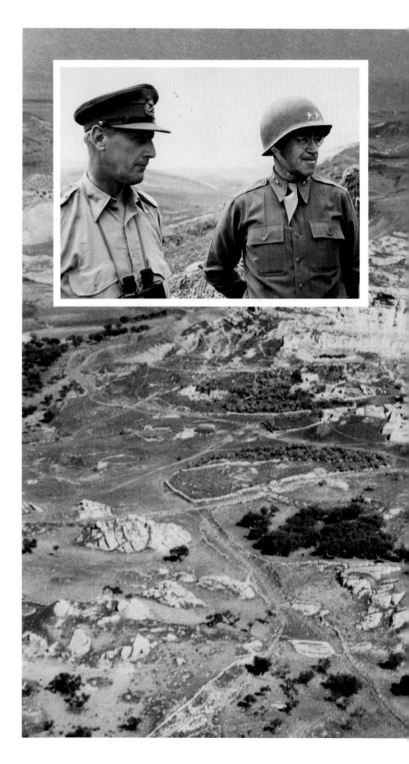

Hill 609, an Axis stronghold, dominates Tunisian terrain far different from the desert setting of earlier campaigns. Concerned that the Americans who were to take the hill would suffer high casualties, British Lieut. General Kenneth Anderson (inset, on left) suggested going around it. U.S. Major General Omar Bradley (inset, on right), believing it would be impossible to move troops past the hilltop guns, insisted on capturing it. When Hill 609 was finally taken, the British Eighth Army was being pinned down by other Axis positions on hills to the south. "Let's radio Monty," said Bradley, full of pride, "and ask if he wants a few American advisers."

only the lower slopes. On April 23 the 8th Battalion of the Argyll and Sutherland Highlanders took up the advance in broad daylight and were met by a sustained fusillade that exacted a stiff toll. After his commander was killed, a major named John Anderson stood up in the face of German fire and shouted "Come on!" Yelling, shooting, bayoneting and struggling through barbed wire, the Highlanders followed him up. When the battalion reached Longstop's western summit—ensuring the capture of the entire hill by the next day—it had been reduced to 30 men. Despite such courageous efforts, the First Army was able to advance its front little more than 10 miles in eight days of bitter fighting.

To the north the U.S. II Corps, which began its own advance on April 23, was soon engaged in a contest for another key hill. The battle for Hill 609—so called because French maps designated it by its elevation of 609 meters (about 2,000 feet)—dispelled doubt about the effectiveness of the GIs in North Africa. Known to Tunisians as Djebel Tahent, Hill 609 dominated not only lower surrounding hills but also the Tine River valley about five miles to the south. The valley—which soldiers called The Mousetrap because any force crossing it was easy prey for Axis artillery on the heights—was a natural route to Mateur, a gateway to the Tunisian coastal plain. General Bradley wanted to move the 1st Armored Division through The Mousetrap but could not do so until the 1st Infantry Division, under Major General Terry Allen, had cleared the enemy from the hills along the valley's northern rim. And Allen's advance was being stymied by savage artillery fire from Hill 609, which was reducing many of his companies to the strength of platoons.

Bradley sent for Major General Charles W. Ryder, whose 34th Infantry Division had done especially poorly in an operation with the British in the south. "Get me that hill," Bradley told Ryder on April 26, "and you'll break up the enemy's defenses clear across our front. Take it and no one will ever again doubt the toughness of your division." For four days the Americans repeatedly tried to dislodge the Germans from Hill 609 and the nearby lower hills, suffering heavy casualties each time. The tenacious defenders threw bundles of grenades known as "potato mashers" at the GIs and answered almost every gain by the 34th Division with a determined counterattack, often before the Americans could dig in. Then Bradley had an inspiration. For an attack early on April 30, he offered Ryder the use of Sherman tanks as mobile artillery support. Bradley later recalled that Ryder looked at him with "mild surprise"—tanks were not usually employed against hill positions—but accepted.

With infantry following in their wake, 17 Sherman tanks groaned up the slopes of 609 and began blasting the German strong points with their 75mm guns. Simultaneous attacks were launched against two crucial nearby hills. By the end of the day, the Americans had gained the summits and a reputation for toughness that soon spread throughout the Allied forces—a reputation they reinforced by fighting off ferocious German attempts to retake the hills.

The Americans paid dearly for the victory: 200 dead, 1,600 wounded, and 700 captured or missing. But the tactical rewards were substantial. Axis forces to the north, foreseeing that the American armored penetration made possible by the capture of 609 could imperil their rear, quickly fell back some 25 miles to the east. On May 3 the 1st Armored Division rolled through The Mousetrap and into the undefended town of Mateur.

While Axis soldiers attempted to defend their perimeter against a well-equipped and well-fed adversary, their sup-

ply problems assumed ominous proportions. During April, Allied warplanes pounced repeatedly on the lumbering Junkers-52 and Messerschmitt-323 cargo aircraft ferrying Axis supplies across the Mediterranean, and destroyed more than 200 enemy planes. On April 18, over the Gulf of Tunis, British fighters downed 38 of the German aircraft in a single encounter. By the end of April, desperately needed munitions had such high priority on the few Axis ships and planes reaching Tunisia that almost no food at all was arriving. Many of Arnim's troops were obliged to subsist on two slices of bread a day each.

The Allies, however, had no intention of laying siege to the northeast corner of Tunisia and starving the enemy into submission. On the same day that Hill 609 was taken, April 30, Alexander set in motion a scheme to renew the offensive, which seemed to have ground to a halt in all but the American sector. The plan, code-named *Strike*, called for a sudden, massive push by the First Army straight across the Axis bridgehead to Tunis in an effort to split the enemy's forces and seize the city before the defenders could damage its port facilities. Haste was necessary also to prevent the Axis from withdrawing behind the hills stretching across the base of the Cape Bon peninsula, a good natural defense line. While the First Army raced for Tunis, the U.S. II Corps was to press with similar speed toward Bizerte and the coast between the two cities.

To build up the muscle of the First Army, which was to deliver its big armored punch on May 6, Alexander ordered Montgomery to yield three of his crack units to Anderson: the 7th Armored Division, the 4th Indian Division and the 201st Guards Brigade. Some 3,000 aircraft were to support the attack.

Arnim knew by the Allied build-up where the heaviest thrust would come—the Medjez el Bab sector—but his shortage of fuel prevented him from shifting sufficient reinforcements to the area. For a week before the main effort, Allied aircraft, including American B-25s, softened up enemy positions with bombing raids. On May 4 the French XIX Corps, to the south of the First Army, advanced to secure the right flank of the corridor through which the British tanks would charge, and the First Army's own V Corps moved out to secure the left flank. In between them, the

A victorious Montgomery—tilting back in his camp chair for an aside with an aide—consults with his captives, Italian Marshal Giovanni Messe (seated at left) and German Major General Frecken von Liebenstein (seated at right), on assembly points for Axis prisoners. As they talked on May 13, 1943, thousands of Axis troops had already thrown down their arms and were streaming along the Cape Bon roads toward the British line at Tunis, in a procession that was spontaneous, leaderless and 80 miles long.

IX Corps of the First Army was poised, ready to spring.

At dusk on May 5, Allied planes began the heaviest air attack of the North African war. In the following 24 hours they flew 1,958 bombing and support sorties. (General Henry H. "Hap" Arnold, Commanding General of the U.S. Army Air Forces, who followed the action from his headquarters in America, later boasted, "We blasted a channel from Medjez el Bab to Tunis.") That same night the fire of 600 guns exploded across a 3,000-yard front astride the road from Medjez el Bab to Tunis. The weight of fire was enormous: 16,632 shells in two hours on the sector facing the British 4th Division alone. The projectiles crashing down on Axis positions, Lieutenant Nigel Nicolson later recalled, "burst like the flowering of a field of ruby tulips."

At 3:30 a.m. on May 6, the IX Corps moved out. First, carving a path for the armor, came the infantry: the 4th Indian Division on the left and the 4th British Division on the right. Behind them roared tanks of the 6th and 7th armored divisions. By 11 a.m. the enemy's frontline defenses had been cleared, and the tanks rolled on through the infantry to begin their dash for Tunis—juggernauts hastening to the kill, grinding cactus hedges to pulp and scattering goats that wandered across their route.

In the American sector, the II Corps' 9th Infantry Division, which had begun its advance on May 4, overcame the last Axis stronghold between it and Bizerte on May 6. The remainder of the II Corps launched its attack—aimed at the Bizerte-Tunis road—on May 6 and made steady progress in spite of tough opposition. Major General Ernest Harmon, commander of the U.S. 1st Armored Division, advised Bradley that he would have to sacrifice 50 tanks in order to break through the entrenched enemy to the coast. Bradley told him to go ahead. The final tally: 47 tanks lost. From the north, Major General Manton Eddy, commanding the 9th Infantry Division, complained that the road to Bizerte was "lousy with mines." Over his field phone Bradley was adamant. "Well then, get off your trucks and begin walking, but get the hell into Bizerte."

The urgency in the British sector was just as great. Alexander impatiently rebuffed Anderson's suggestion that, once the breakthrough was achieved, the First Army's armor should turn aside to mop up the battlefield. Both the 6th and 7th armored divisions, Alexander ruled, were to ignore any skirmishing on the flanks and drive for Tunis. "The rapier was to be thrust into the heart," he said later.

It was less a rapier than an inundation. The dam had collapsed and the Allied forces flooded toward Bizerte and Tunis. Hundreds of tanks sped for the two ports and the road between them—artillery and antitank guns, fuel and munitions trucks, and armored reconnaissance cars flowing with them. Down the Tunis road, swerving among the First Army vehicles, came Alexander driving his own jeep, his hands tight on the wheel, his face white with dust.

The Allied advance was so rapid that both sides were startled. As he hit Bizerte at 3:20 p.m. on May 7, American Lieutenant Gene Boutwell, in a jeep with two noncoms, discovered to his dismay that he had arrived 40 minutes ahead of the first Shermans. Two German submachine gunners he passed on the road were so taken aback that neither thought to open fire until the jeep was well past. "They must have been as scared as we were," Boutwell said.

In Tunis, which the British reached at 4 p.m., the confusion was great. Although it was raining, hundreds of Germans were moving about the streets or sipping drinks with their girl friends under the awnings of sidewalk cafés. In one barbershop some German soldiers jumped from their chairs, white cloths around their necks, chins lathered, to gape in awe at British armored cars rolling down the street.

There was scattered resistance in the Tunisian capital. British Colonel Freddie Stephens found himself besieged by French citizens pressing flowers, fruit and kisses on him— while the random stutter of machine-gun fire echoed across the city and rifle shots from snipers holed up in high buildings struck the pavement near his jeep. Some Germans were uncertain how to react: a major of the Hermann Göring Division, surprised just outside of Tunis, refused to believe the city had been taken until he was led to a radio set and heard the messages coming from the center of town.

Bizarre requests were made of the liberators. One officer was hailed by a Frenchman who asked him for chewing gum. "My wife is pregnant, and she has a craving for chewing gum," he explained. A beaming youngster told correspondent John MacVane: "We now can again see American films—Robert Taylor and Greta Garbo."

Inevitably, some citizens saw a way to turn a fast profit. Twenty-five troopers of the 15th Panzer Division, cut off by the River Medjerda from the 11th Hussars to whom they agreed to surrender, found the river too deep to wade. An Arab appeared with farm horses and offered to ferry the Germans across to their captors at 50 francs a head. The Germans reluctantly dug into their pockets and paid for their transport into captivity.

But the bulk of Arnim's forces, although disorganized and short of transport, fled toward the Cape Bon peninsula and the double line of defensible hills that ran across its base. If what was left of the Axis forces could get behind those hills and hold the two coastal passes that gave access to the peninsula—at Hammam Lif near Tunis on the north side and Hammamet on the coast to the south—Arnim might be able to delay the final Allied victory for months.

But Alexander struck swiftly to forestall this move. The 6th Armored Division rolled out of Tunis to Hammam Lif and with other British units spent two days forcing the pass there. On May 9 the division sped on toward Hammamet. This advance from Hammam Lif to Hammamet, which was reached on May 11, has been called one of the strangest and most impressive feats of arms in the entire war. Although the Axis had great numerical superiority in this area, they were stunned by the swiftness of the British armor. With no stops for taking prisoners, the 6th Armored's forces thrust through the surprised enemy, creating confusion among all who saw them. With the 6th Armored now holding the Hammam Lif-Hammamet line, the Axis forces were split, some bottled up on the Cape Bon side of the line while others were being surrounded to the west of it. With division cut off from division, regiment from regiment, the

Axis command structure broke down. Although dedicated German officers created ad hoc organizations to continue fighting, some men headed for the Cape Bon beaches seeking boats that might carry them to Italy.

In the bitter 11th hour, a stark order for Arnim arrived from Hitler: "The German people expect you to fight to the last bullet." Arnim conceived his own interpretation of "the last bullet." It would be the last shell fired by the last tank. Then the weapons would be destroyed and Army Group Africa would give up.

On May 11 the last seven tanks of the 10th Panzer Division, their desert-yellow paint peeling, ran out of fuel and fired a final defiant salvo toward the Hammam Lif-Hammamet line. The next day Arnim capitulated. Before surrendering he personally set fire to the big command vehicle Rommel had bequeathed him, captured from the British in the Western Desert two years before. To the German High Command, General Hans Cramer, the last commander of the Afrika Korps, dispatched a proud farewell message: "Munitions expended, weapons and war equipment destroyed. The Afrika Korps has fought to a standstill as ordered. The German Afrika Korps must ride again."

Surrender was a complex process, involving emotions as well as formalities. General Graf von Sponeck's 90th Light Division insisted on giving up to the New Zealanders, their doughty adversaries of two years' standing. To boost Italian morale, Mussolini promoted General Giovanni Messe, commander of the First Italian Army, to field marshal on the day he became a prisoner. Messe would surrender only to the veteran Eighth Army, not the fledgling First, and he was the last leading Axis commander to capitulate, on May 13.

To some fighting men this professional emphasis on protocol, following the slaughter of two and a half years, struck a jarring note. When the staff of Major General Fritz Krause, Afrika Korps artillery commander, arrived at General Harmon's headquarters wearing crisp dress uniforms and riding in Mercedes-Benz staff cars, Harmon commented, "You would have thought the bastards were going to a wedding." The men of the Hermann Göring Division, entrenched on a hillside, demanded a certificate saying that they were the last Germans to lay down arms on that front (it was not just pride; without communications, they were afraid they were being tricked into giving up while the fight continued elsewhere). Retorted an American battalion commander: "Brother, either you'll come down right now and cut out this monkey business or we'll carve that certificate on your headstone." The Germans came down.

In great sand-colored Wehrmacht trucks with the palm-leaf markings of the Afrika Korps, on bicycles and on burros, in horse-drawn gigs, some 275,000 Axis soldiers moved to areas designated by the victors as prisoner-of-war assembly points. Their feelings about surrendering varied widely. Major General Willibald Borowiecz, commander of the 15th Panzer Division, broke down and wept in General Harmon's headquarters. "I am a general without a command," he said. "My Panzers have been wiped out."

Some continued to display stubborn defiance. Private Tony Wittkop, a Philadelphia-educated Afrika Korps veteran, warned his captors: "Just wait until you try to land in Europe. We are not beaten yet, not by a long shot!" But many felt that the German High Command had let them down. On a Tunis street, one captured private took a portrait of Hitler from his pocket. "That's my Führer," he said as he tore the picture into pieces, "my Führer."

Troops on both sides were exhausted. After entering Tunis, some Allied soldiers simply lay down on the sidewalks and slept, despite the victory and liberation celebrations around them. They had only listless curiosity about the Axis troops streaming toward the prisoner-of-war camps.

No accurate calculation of Axis casualties in Tunisia has ever been made, but they probably totaled some 315,000—275,000 captured and 40,000 killed, wounded or missing in action. British losses, by contrast, numbered 35,940 dead, wounded or missing in action; American losses totaled 13,984; French, 16,180.

At 2:15 p.m. on the 13th of May, Alexander sent a message from Tunis to Churchill in London that the Prime Minister had waited almost three years to receive: "Sir, it is my duty to report that the Tunisian campaign is over. All enemy resistance has ceased. We are masters of the North African shores."

Masters—and more. The Allies had become a strong and confident team. This strength and unity was already being counted as an asset by planners who looked across the Mediterranean to Europe where yet another kind of war was soon to begin.

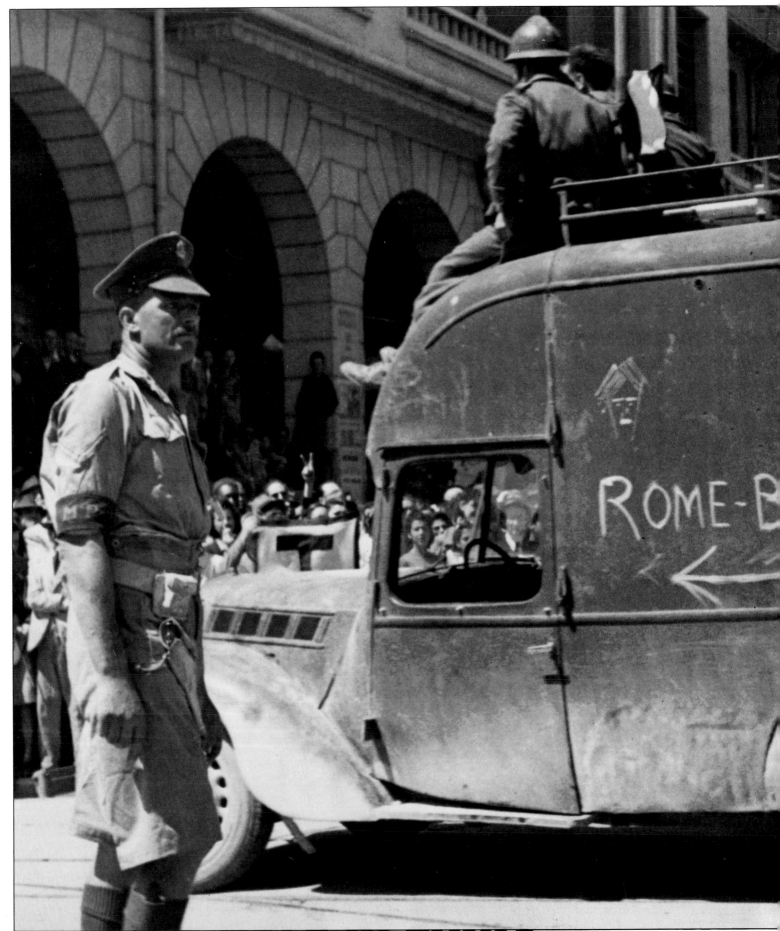

GRAND FINALE IN TUNIS

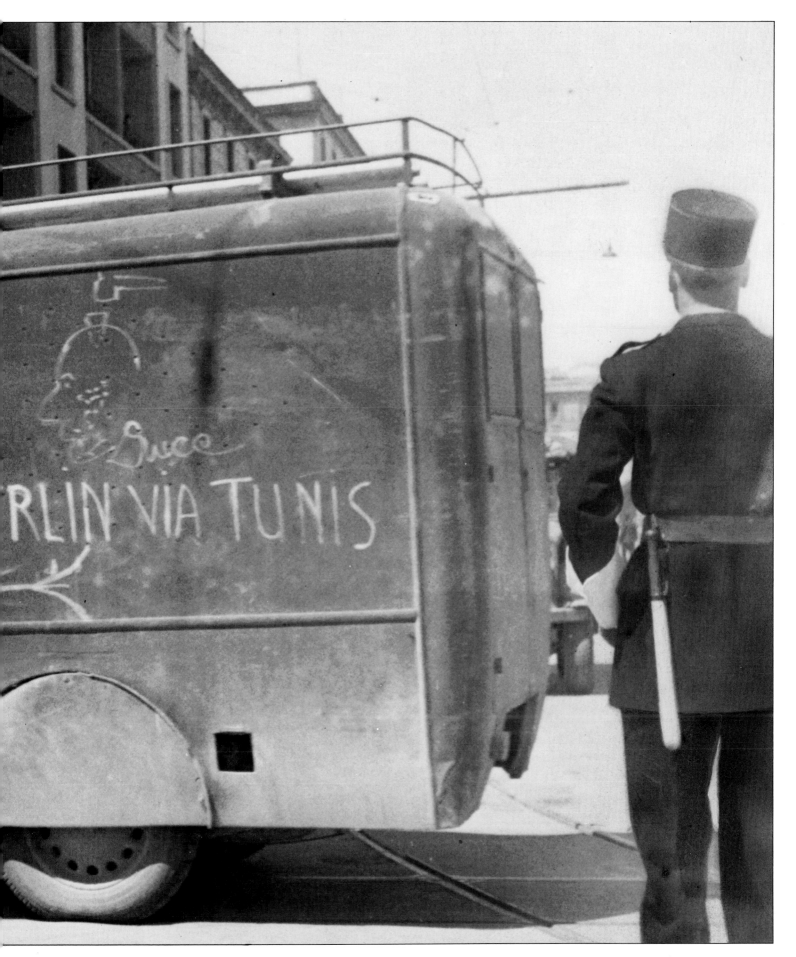

A sign on a van proclaiming the Allies' next destinations to be the Axis capitals in Europe elicits cheers from the liberated populace as the victors enter Tunis.

JUBILANT WEEKS OF VICTORY AND LIBERATION

The struggle in North Africa was virtually over. By late afternoon Wednesday, May 7, 1943, the Allies' first major victory celebration of World War II was building to a grand revel on the sun-washed boulevards of Tunis. Without waiting for the last German or Italian to surrender—that happened six days later—the old French colonial city unfurled the tricolors and plunged into festivity.

Tunis' jubilant population, doubled by refugees from the fighting and the horde of exultant, victorious soldiers who at last were out of the harsh North African deserts and mountains, gave itself over to wine, song and dance. Dowagers on balconies screamed "Vive!" while younger women smothered marching British and Free French troops with kisses, and showered the victors' tanks and trucks with flowers of the season—roses, lilacs and poppies. The Hotel Majestic, where Axis officers had resided two days before, now accommodated Allied officers—with the staff's apologies for the lack of hot water and electricity, and, since the restaurant cupboards were bare, with offers to warm C rations in the hotel kitchen.

While Tunis celebrated, there were reports of riots in Berlin. A Swedish newspaper said the families of Panzer Army Africa soldiers took to the streets of the German capital when they were refused news of the fate of their men in Tunisia, and troops had to be called out to put down their protest. In fact, most of the Germans in Tunisia were willingly crowding into prison compounds: at the gates of one barbed-wire enclosure in a Tunis suburb, a German infantry band serenaded the arriving captives with strains of Viennese *Lieder*.

The revelry continued for two weeks until May 20, when the Allies staged an official victory parade. The Americans, who had taken Bizerte on the same day that the British and French entered Tunis, came to town to join the review. For two hours, American, French and British troops, including veterans of Tobruk, El Alamein and Hill 609, marched through the crowded streets in a grand finale to the North African campaign.

Accepting hands eager to shake his, a smiling soldier marches proudly down a Tunis boulevard as victorious columns pour into the liberated city.

Allied riflemen, part of the official victory review, parade past British, French and American commanders in Tunis at the end of the North African campaign.

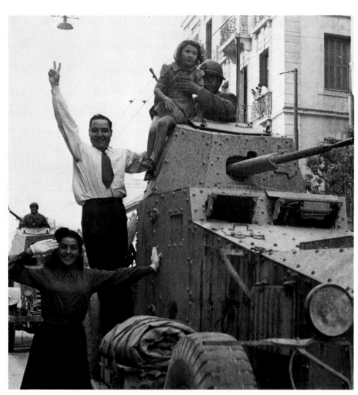

Jubilant French civilians accompany a British armored car as it enters Tunis. A small girl rides with the Tommy in the turret while her father, on the running board, flashes the "V" for victory sign, and a saluting woman runs alongside.

Dressed up in spring hats and suits to welcome liberation, Tunisian women wave to passing Free French soldiers who cling to their trucktops in order to get a better view of the crowds that turned out to greet them in the capital.

A group of smiling French Tunisians gather around a truck carrying impassive Gurkha soldiers—celebrated knife-fighters from the 4th Indian Division.

A wildly gesticulating throng—French and native Tunisians cheering the end of Axis occupation—jams an intersection during the boisterous Allied welcome.

In this aerial view, some of the 275,000 German and Italian soldiers who surrendered at the end of the North African campaign pour into a prisoner-of-war compound west of Tunis, near Mateur. Many of them arrived driving their own trucks, with white flags in clear view. Eventually, they were interned in POW camps in Canada, Great Britain and the U.S.

BIBLIOGRAPHY

Agar-Hamilton, John A. I., and Leonard C. F. Turner, eds., *The Sidi Rezeg Battles*. Oxford University Press, 1957.

Aglion, Raoul, *War in the Desert*. Holt, 1941.

Altieri, James, *The Spearheaders*. The Bobbs-Merrill Co., 1960.

Austin, A. B., *Birth of an Army*. Victor Gollancz, Ltd., 1943.

Badoglio, Pietro, *Italy in the Second World War,* translated from the Italian by Muriel Currey. Greenwood Press, 1976.

Barclay, C. N., *Against Great Odds*. Sifton, Praed, 1955.

Barnett, Correlli, *The Desert Generals*. The Viking Press, Inc., 1961.

Bartimeus:
East of Malta, West of Suez. Little, Brown and Co., 1944.
The Turn of the Road. Chatto and Windus, 1946.

Beddington, William Richard, *A History of the Queen's Bays, 1929-1945*. Warren & Son Ltd., 1954.

Bekker, Cajus, *The Luftwaffe War Diaries,* edited and translated from the German by Frank Ziegler. Macdonald & Co., 1967.

Bergot, Erwan, *The Afrika Korps,* translated from the French by Richard Barry. Allan Wingate Ltd., 1972.

Blumenson, Martin:
Kasserine Pass. Houghton Mifflin Co., 1967.
The Patton Papers, 1940-1945. Houghton Mifflin Co., 1974.

Borghese, J. Valerio, *Sea Devils,* translated from the Italian by James Cleugh. Henry Regnery Company, 1954.

Bradley, Omar N., *A Soldier's Story*. Henry Holt & Co., 1951.

Bragadin, M., *The Italian Navy in World War II,* translated from the Italian by Gale Hoffman. U.S. Naval Institute, 1957.

Brownlie, W. Steel, *The Proud Trooper: Story of a Regiment*. Wm. Collins, Sons & Co., Ltd., 1964.

Bryant, Arthur, *The Turn of the Tide, 1939-1943*. Doubleday & Co., Inc., 1957.

Butcher, Harry C., *My Three Years with Eisenhower*. Simon and Schuster, Inc., 1946.

Bykofsky, Joseph, and Harold Larson, *The Transportation Corps: Operations Overseas*. Office of the Chief of Military History, 1957.

Cameron, Ian, *Red Duster, White Ensign*. Doubleday, 1960.

Canevari, Emilio, *Graziani mi ha detto*. Magi-Spinetti, 1947.

Carell, Paul, *The Foxes of the Desert,* translated from the German by Mervyn Savill. E. P. Dutton & Co., Inc., 1961.

Carver, Michael, *El Alamein*. B. T. Batsford Ltd., 1962.

Cary, James, *Tanks and Armor in Modern Warfare*. F. Watts, 1966.

Chamberlain, Peter, *Afrika Korps*. Almark Publishing Co., 1970.

Churchill, Winston S.:
The Second World War, Bantam Books.
Volume III, *The Grand Alliance,* 1962.
Volume IV, *The Hinge of Fate,* 1962.

Clarke, Dudley, *The Eleventh at War*. Michael Joseph Ltd., 1952.

Clifford, Alexander, *Three Against Rommel*. George G. Harrap & Co., Ltd., 1943.

Cocchia, Aldo, *The Hunter and the Hunted,* translated from the Italian by M. Gwyer. U.S. Naval Institute, 1958.

Collier, Richard, *Duce!* Collins, 1971.

Connell, John:
Auchinleck. Cassell & Company Ltd., 1959.
Wavell. Collins, 1964.

Cowie, Donald, *The Campaigns of Wavell*. Chapman & Hall Ltd., 1942.

Crisp, Robert, *Brazen Chariots*. Muller, 1959.

Cunningham, Andrew, *A Sailor's Odyssey*. Hutchinson, 1951.

Davy, G. M., *The Seventh and Three Enemies*. Published for the regiment by W. Heffer, 1953.

D'Arcy-Dawson, John, *Tunisian Battles*. Macdonald & Co., 1943.

De Guingand, Francis:
Generals at War. Hodder and Stoughton, 1964.
Operation Victory. Hodder and Stoughton, 1947.

Destruction of an Army. Her Majesty's Stationery Office, 1941.

Eden, Sir Anthony, The Earl of Avon, *The Reckoning: The Eden Memoirs*. Cassell, 1965.

The Eighth Army: September 1941 to January 1943. Her Majesty's Stationery Office, 1944.

Eisenhower, Dwight D., *Crusade in Europe*. Doubleday & Co., Inc., 1948.

The Encyclopedia of Sea Warfare. Thomas Y. Crowell Co., 1975.

Esebeck, Hanns Gert von, *Afrikanische Schicksalsjahre*. Limes Verlag, 1950.

Esposito, Vincent J., ed., *The West Point Atlas of American Wars,* Vol. 2: *1900-1953*. Frederick A. Praeger, 1959.

Evans, Trefor E., ed., *The Killearn Diaries, 1934-1946*. Sedgwick and Jackson Ltd., 1972.

Farago, Ladislas, *Patton: Ordeal and Triumph*. Ivan Obolensky, Inc., 1964.

Farran, Roy, *Winged Dagger*. Collins, 1948.

Fearnside, G. H., *Sojourn in Tobruk*. Ure Smith Pty Ltd., 1944.

Felletti, Leonida, *Soldati senz'armi, le gravi responsabilità degli alti commandi*. D. de Luigi, 1944.

Fergusson, Bernard, *The Black Watch and the King's Enemies*. Collins, 1950.

Forty, George, *The Desert Rats at War*. I. Allan, 1975.

Freidin, Seymour, and William Richardson, eds., *The Fatal Decisions*. William Sloane Associates, Inc., 1956.

Gallagher, Wes, *Back Door to Berlin*. Doubleday, Doran & Co., 1943.

Gibson, Hugh, ed., *The Ciano Diaries, 1939-1943*. Garden City Publishing Co., Inc., 1947.

Graham, F. C. C., *History of Argyll & Sutherland Highlanders 1st Battalion, 1939-1945*. T. Nelson, 1948.

Halder, Franz, *Kriegstagebuch,* Vol. 5. W. Kohlhammer, 1962-1964.

Hastings, R. H. W. S., *The Rifle Brigade in the Second World War, 1939-1945*. Gale & Polden Ltd., 1950.

Heckstall-Smith, Anthony, *Tobruk*. Anthony Blond, 1959.

Hill, Russell, *Desert Conquest*. Jarrolds, 1944.

Holmes, Richard, *Bir Hacheim: Desert Citadel*. Ballantine Books, 1971.

Horrocks, Brian, *A Full Life*. William Collins Sons & Co., Inc., 1960.

Howe, George F., *Northwest Africa: Seizing the Initiative in the West*. Office of the Chief of Military History, 1957.

Howard, Michael, and John Sparrow, *The Coldstream Guards, 1920-1946*. Oxford University Press, 1951.

Icks, Robert J., *Tanks and Armored Vehicles, 1940-1945*. WE, Inc., 1970.

Ingersoll, Ralph McAllister, *Battle is the Pay-off*. Harcourt, Brace & Co., Inc., 1943.

Ismay, Hastings Lionel, *Memoirs*. Heinemann, 1960.

Jackson, W. G. F., *The Battle for North Africa, 1940-1943*. Mason/Charter Publishers, Inc., 1975.

Jacob, Alaric, *A Traveller's War*. Dodd, Mead & Co., 1944.

Jewell, Derek, ed., *Alamein and the Desert War*. Ballantine Books, Inc., 1967.

Jones, Vincent, *Operation Torch*. Ballantine Books, Inc., 1972.

Jordan, Philip, *Jordan's Tunis Diary*. Collins, 1943.

Kennedy, John, *The Business of War*. Hutchinson, 1957.

Keyes, Elizabeth, *Geoffrey Keyes*. G. Newnes, 1956.

Kippenberger, Howard, *Infantry Brigadier*. Oxford University Press, 1949.

Kirk, John, and Robert Young Jr., *Great Weapons of World War II*. Walker, 1961.

Lewin, Ronald:
Montgomery as Military Commander. B. T. Batsford Ltd., 1971.
Rommel as Military Commander. B. T. Batsford Ltd., 1968.

Lewis, P. J., and I. R. English, *The 8th Battalion, The Durham Light Infantry, 1939-1945*. J. & P. Bealls, Ltd., 1950.

Liddell Hart, B. H.:
ed., *The Rommel Papers,* translated from the German by Paul Findlay. Harcourt, Brace & Co., 1953.
The Tanks, Vol. 2: *1939-1945*. Frederick A. Praeger, 1959.

Lochner, Louis P., ed., *The Goebbels Diaries, 1942-1943*. Doubleday & Co., Inc., 1948.

Long, Gavin, *To Benghazi*. Australian War Memorial, 1952.

Macksey, Kenneth, *Beda Fomm*. Ballantine Books, Inc., 1971.

MacVane, John, *Journey Into War*. D. Appleton-Century Co., Inc., 1943.

Majdalany, Fred, *The Battle of El Alamein*. J. B. Lippincott Co., 1965.

Martineau, G. D., *A History of the Royal Sussex Regiment*. Moore & Tillyer, 1953.

Maughan, Barton, *Tobruk and El Alamein*. Australian War Memorial, 1966.

Maule, Henry:
Out of the Sand. Odhams Press, Ltd., 1966.
Spearhead General. Odhams Press, Ltd., 1961.

Mellenthin, Friedrich von, *Panzer Battles,* translated from the German by H. Betzler. University of Oklahoma Press, 1956.

The Memoirs of Field-Marshal the Viscount Montgomery of Alamein. The World Publishing Co., 1958.

Michie, Allan:
Honour for All. G. Allen & Unwin, Ltd., 1946.
Retreat to Victory. G. Allen & Unwin, Ltd., 1942.

Montgomery, Brian, *A Field-Marshal in the Family*. Taplinger Publishing Co., 1973.

Moorehead, Alan:
The March to Tunis. Harper & Row, Inc., 1943.
Montgomery. Hamish Hamilton, Ltd., 1967.

Morison, Samuel Eliot, *Operations in North African Waters*. Little, Brown and Co., 1975.

Murphy, Robert, *Diplomat Among Warriors*. Greenwood Press, 1964.

Mussolini, Benito, *Memoirs, 1942-1943,* edited by Raymond Klibansky and translated from the Italian by Frances Lobb. Weidenfeld & Nicolson, Ltd., 1949.

Neame, Philip, *Playing with Strife*. George G. Harrap & Co., Ltd., 1947.

Newton, Don, and A. C. Hampshire, *Taranto*. W. Kimber, 1959.

Nicolson, Nigel, *Alex: The Life of Field Marshal Earl Alexander of Tunis*. Weidenfeld and Nicolson, 1973.

North, John, ed., *The Alexander Memoirs, 1940-1945*. Cassell & Co. Ltd., 1961.

Onslow, William Arthur Bampfylde, Earl of Onslow, *Men and Sand*. Saint Catherine Press, 1961.

Parkinson, C. Northcote, *Always a Fusilier*. Low, 1949.

Phillips, C. E. Lucas, *Alamein*. William Heinemann Ltd., 1962.

Playfair, I. S. O., *The Mediterranean and Middle East,* Vols. 1-4. Her Majesty's Stationery Press, 1954-1966.

Poolman, Kenneth, *Illustrious*. W. Kimber, 1955.

Pyle, Ernie, *Here is Your War*. Henry Holt & Co., Inc., 1943.

Quilter, D. C., *No Dishonorable Name*. W. Clowes, 1947.

Rainier, Peter W., *Pipeline to Battle*. William Heinemann Ltd., 1944.

Rame, David, *Road to Tunis*. The Macmillan Co., 1944.

Ramsay, Guy, *One Continent Redeemed*. George G. Harrap & Co., Ltd., 1943.

Rissik, David, *The D. L. I. At War*. D. L. I. Dept., 1953.
Robinett, Paul McDonald, *Armor Command*. No publishers' information, 1958.
Rosenthal, Eric, *Fortress on Sand*. Hutchinson, 1943.
Roskill, S. W., *The War at Sea*, Vol. 2. Her Majesty's Stationery Office, 1956.
Schmidt, Heinz-Werner, *With Rommel in the Desert*. George G. Harrap & Co., Ltd., 1951.
Shirer, William L., *The Rise and Fall of the Third Reich*. Simon and Schuster, Inc., 1960.
Stamps, T. Dodson, and Vincent J. Esposito, eds., *A Military History of World War II*. United States Military Academy, 1956.
Stevens, W. G., *Bardia to Enfidaville*. New Zealand Department of Internal Affairs, 1962.
Strawson, John, *The Battle for North Africa*. Batsford, 1969.
Taggart, Donald G., ed., *History of the Third Infantry Division in World War II*. Infantry Journal Press, 1947.

Talbot, Godfrey, *Speaking from the Desert*. Hutchinson & Co., Ltd., **1944.**
Taylor, Henry J., *Men in Motion*. Doubleday, Doran & Co., Inc., 1943.
Tedder, Arthur, *With Prejudice*. Cassell & Co. Ltd., 1966.
The Tiger Kills. His Majesty's Stationery Office, 1944.
Tompkins, Peter, *The Murder of Admiral Darlan*. Simon and Schuster, 1965.
Truscott, Lucian K., *Command Missions*. E. P. Dutton & Co., Inc., 1954.
Verney, G. L., *The Desert Rats*. Hutchinson, 1954.
Walker, Allan S., *Middle East and Far East Australian Medical Services*. Australian War Memorial, 1953.
Walker, Ronald, *Alam Halfa and Alamein*. Historical Publications Branch, New Zealand Department of Internal Affairs, 1967.
Wellard, James Howard, *Man in a Helmet*. Eyre & Spottiswoode Ltd., 1947.
Wilmot, Chester, *Tobruk*. Angus & Robertson, 1944.
Yindrich, Jan, *Fortress Tobruk*. Ernest Benn Ltd., 1951.
Young, Desmond, *Rommel, the Desert Fox*. Harper & Brothers, 1950.

PICTURE CREDITS

Credits from left to right are separated by semicolons, from top to bottom by dashes.

COVER and page 1: Imperial War Museum, London.

ITALY'S REACH FOR GLORY: 6, 7—Istituto Luce, Rome. 8—Publifoto Notizie, Milan. 9—Bibliothek für Zeitgeschichte, Stuttgart. 10, 11—Istituto Luce, Rome. 12, 13—Istituto Italo-Africano, Rome, except inset, top left, Istituto Luce, Rome. 14, 15—Pietro Caporilli, Rome. 16, 17—Imperial War Museum, London.

A GAMBLE FOR HIGH STAKES: 20—Unedi, Rome. 22, 23—Map by Elie Sabban. 24—Roma's Press, Rome; Unedi, Rome—Stato Maggiore Aeronautica, Rome. 25—Roma's Press, Rome. 27—Map by Elie Sabban. 28, 29—Photo Trends. 30—Imperial War Museum, London.

THE DESERT FOX: 34, 35—Ullstein Bilderdienst, Berlin. 36—Courtesy Manfred Rommel. 37—Bundesarchiv, Koblenz. 38, 39—All courtesy Manfred Rommel. 40, 41—Courtesy Manfred Rommel; Bundesarchiv, Koblenz. 42, 43—Süddeutscher Verlag, Bilderdienst, Munich; Bundesarchiv, Koblenz. 44—Bundesarchiv, Koblenz. 45, 46, 47—Ullstein Bilderdienst, Berlin.

HELL'S OWN BATTLEGROUND: 48, 49—Istituto Italo-Africano/Luce, Rome. 50—PhotoWorld. 51—H. Roger-Viollet. 52, 53—Camera Press, courtesy Imperial War Museum, London, except inset, top left, H. Roger-Viollet. 54, 55—Süddeutscher Verlag, Bilderdienst, Munich—Robert Hunt Library, London. 56, 57—Keystone. 58, 59—Camera Press, courtesy Imperial War Museum, London; Transit Film, Munich, courtesy Bundesarchiv, Koblenz.

ROMMEL'S STUNNING BLOW: 62—PhotoWorld—National Archives, Rommel Collection (2). 64—National Archives, Rommel Collection. 66—National Archives, Rommel Collection. 67—Map by Elie Sabban. 68—Australian War Memorial. 69—P. I. from Black Star.

EMBATTLED MALTA: 72, 73—From *Message from Malta*, Office of War Information, courtesy National Archives, Motion Picture and Sound Record Branch. 74 through 77—Imperial War Museum, London. 78, 79—Courtesy Associated News (Malta) LTD.; Imperial War Museum, London. 80, 81—Camera Press, courtesy Imperial War Museum, London, except inset, top left, Photo Trends.

TRIUMPH ELUDES THE BRITISH: 84—Map by Elie Sabban. 85—Imperial War Museum, London. 86—Lega Navale. 88—H. Roger-Viollet. 91—Photoreporters.

LIGHT RELIEF IN CAIRO: 94, 95—Bob Landry for LIFE. 96 through 100—George Rodger for LIFE. 101—E. Chamma for LIFE. 102, 103—Bob Landry for LIFE.

THE CRUCIBLE OF VICTORY: 106—Photo Trends. 108—Imperial War Museum, London. 111—Map by Elie Sabban. 113—George R. Bradford, courtesy Arms and Armour Press, London, and Squadron/Signal Publications, Michigan (6).

THE BRUTAL POUNDING OF THE AXIS: 116, 117—Camera Press, courtesy Imperial War Museum, London. 118—Imperial War Museum, London. 119—Wide World. 120 through 123—Camera Press, courtesy Imperial War Museum, London. 124, 125—British Official except inset, bottom left, Wide World. 126, 127—Dever from Black Star; George Rodger for LIFE.

MONTY AT THE HELM: 128, 129—Imperial War Museum, London. 130—Courtesy Colonel Brian Montgomery. 131—Imperial War Museum, London. 132, 133—Courtesy Colonel Brian Montgomery (5). 134 through 137—Imperial War Museum, London. 138, 139—Wide World

AN ALLY JOINS THE WAR: 142, 143, 144—Navy Department, courtesy National Archives. 147, 148—U.S. Army.

TIPPING THE BALANCE: 152, 153—Imperial War Museum, London. 154—Navy Department, courtesy National Archives. 155, 156—U.S. Army. 157—Camera Press, courtesy Imperial War Museum, London. 158 through 161—U.S. Army.

AMERICANS TASTE THE FIRE: 165—United Press International. 166—Map by Elie Sabban; Imperial War Museum, London. 170—Eliot Elisofon for LIFE (3).

ONE MAN'S FOCUS ON THE WAR: 174 through 187—Eliot Elisofon for LIFE.

THE KNOCKOUT PUNCH: 190, 191—U.S. Army except inset, top left, Imperial War Museum, London. 193—Photo Trends.

GRAND FINALE IN TUNIS: 196, 197—Library of Congress. 198—Camera Press, courtesy Imperial War Museum, London. 199—Library of Congress. 200—U.S. Army (3). 201—Bob Landry for LIFE. 202, 203—U.S. Army.

ACKNOWLEDGMENTS

The index for this book was prepared by Mel Ingber. The editors of this book also wish to express their gratitude to Lieselotte Bandelow, Ullstein, Berlin; Bernard Bäter, Düsseldorf, Germany; Lieut. Colonel Oreste Bovio and General Rinaldo Cruccu, Stato Maggiore dell'Esercito, Rome; Commander Marc' Antonio Bragadin (Ret.), Rome; Rosario Casella, Rome; Commander Andrea Corsini, Rear Admiral Renato Fadda and Commander Leonardo Sansonetti, Stato Maggiore della Marina, Rome; Cecile Coutin, Curator, Musée des Deux Guerres Mondiales, Paris; Colonel Henri de Buttet, Saint Julien de Royaucourt, France; Admiral Luigi Durand de la Penne, Genoa, Italy; V. M. Destefano, Chief of Reference Library, U.S. Army Audio-Visual, Washington, D.C.; Edward Elisofon, New York, New York; Ulrich Frodien, Süddeutscher Verlag, Bilderdienst, Munich; General Adolf Galland (Ret.), Bonn-Bad Godesberg, Germany; Kyrill von Gersdorff, Deutsches Museum, Munich; Dr. Matthias Haupt, Bundesarchiv, Koblenz, Germany; Werner Haupt, Bibliothek für Zeitgeschichte, Stuttgart; First Lieutenant Heinz Hiltmann (Ret.), Koblenz, Germany; E. Hine, Department of Photographs, The Imperial War Museum, London; Julius C. Jefferson, Motion Picture Sound Recording Branch, National Archives, Washington, D.C.; Hans Klein, Bad Honnef, Germany; Dr. Roland Klemig, Director, Bildarchiv Preussischer Kulturbesitz, West Berlin; Franz Kurowski, Dortmund, Germany; Gustav Lamprecht, Clear, Alaska; Lieut. Colonel Brian F. Montgomery, London; Benedetto Pafi, Rome; Harry Postol, New York, New York; Helmut Regel, Bundesarchiv, Koblenz, Germany; Colonel Enrico Ripamonti, Captain Massimo Staccioli, Stato Maggiore dell'Aeronautica, Rome; Professor Dr. Jurgen Rohwer, Director, Bibliothek für Zeitgeschichte, Stuttgart; Manfred Erwin Rommel, Lord Mayor of Stuttgart; Joseph Schembri, Consul General and Carmel Sammut, First Secretary, Embassy of Malta, Rome; Jim Trimble, National Archives, Washington, D.C.; George Wagner, Archives Specialist, Modern Military Branch, National Archives, Washington, D.C.; General Siegfried Westphal (Ret.), Celle, Germany; Robert Wolfe, Chief, Modern Military Branch, National Archives, Washington, D.C.

INDEX

to invade Egypt, 18-19; declares war on Allies, 8; envies Hitler, 18; erosion of hold on Italians, 188; and German assistance, 33; and Graziani, 29; and invasion of Greece, 21; on losses in Egypt, 29; orders invasion of British East Africa, 20; orders invasion of Egypt, 8, 19

N

Neame, Philip: attempts to restore order during general retreat, 65; captured, 66; commands troops in Cyrenaica, 63
Nehring, Walther, 150
Nepal, Gurkha troops in Tunisia, 173
New Zealand: Germans surrender to, 195; losses at Takrouna, 190; troops in North Africa, 29-30, 68, 96, 114, *134-135*, 171, 172, 190
Nicolson, Nigel, 193
Norrie, C. W. M., 83, 90

O

O'Carroll, Walter, at Halfaya, 70
O'Connor, Richard Nugent, *30;* acts as adviser during general retreat, 65; advance into Libya, 30, 31, 32-33; captured, 66; commander in Egypt, 61; and defense of Egypt, 20, 23, 26, 29; on victory in Libya, 33
Olbrich, Herbert, 66, 68

P

Panzer Army Africa: advance to El Alamein, 93; assault on Bir Hacheim, 90-91; attack on El Alamein, 105; defense of Mareth Line, 163, 166, 168; defense of Rahman Track, 114-115; destroys Gazala line, 90-91; forces British back to Gazala line, 88-89; forces at El Alamein, 107; formed, 88; halts offensive in Tunisia, 167; losses at El Alamein, 105, 112, 115, 118, 122; matériel gained at Tobruk, 92; retreat from El Alamein, 115, *122, 124-127;* retreat to Tunisia, 118, 162; shortages at El Alamein, 112; supply routes to Egypt, 107; takes Tobruk, 91-92; unprepared for assault on El Alamein line, 109, 118; use of 88mm antiaircraft guns against tanks, 90, *91. See also* Army Group Africa
Panzer Group Africa: becomes Panzer Army Africa, 89; counters Operation *Crusader,* 84-87; forces, 83; Italian forces, 83; losses during *Crusader,* 88-89; retreats during *Crusader,* 88-89
Pardo, Leopoldo, at Halfaya, 70
Patton, George S., 168; accepts surrender of Morocco, 149; address to II Corps staff, 169; and dress code, 168; at El Guettar, *174;* headquarters in Casablanca, *144;* at invasion of Morocco, 146-147, 149; orders and stops bombardment of Casablanca, 147, 149; transferred to work on Sicily invasion, 189
Paulus, Friedrich, 69
Ponath, Gustav, 67
Primauguet, at Casablanca, 146
Pyle, Ernie, 146, 176

Q

Queen Elizabeth, 86

R

Raeder, Erich, 31
Ranger, in Operation *Torch,* 154
Rangers, U.S., 169
Revetra, Vittorio, 26
Richardson, Charles, 106
Ringler, Ralph, at El Alamein, 115, 118
Rintelen, Enno von, 33
Ritchie, Neil M., 87-88; commands Eighth Army, 87; loses respect of subordinates, 89;

ordered to destroy Rommel's forces near Knightsbridge Box, 90; orders retreat from Bir Hacheim, 90; plan for Tobruk, 91, 92; relieved of command, 93
Rogers, J., 190
Rommel, Erwin, *34-47,* 61, *66, 67;* advance on El Alamein, 92-93; on armor, 86, 113; and Arnim, 164-165; and attack on Gazala line, 90; and attack at Kasserine Pass, 164-167; and attack on Tobruk in 1942, 91-92; and Battle of El Alamein, 105, 111, 118; before Operation *Crusader,* 83; on British commando raids, 108; on British defense of Tobruk, 92; commands successful retreat during *Crusader,* 88-89; deceptions by, 60, 61, 64, 65; decides to attack Tobruk, 67; on early success, 65; ends first offensive, 69; family, *38, 39,* 61; forces British back to Gazala, 89; goggles, *34-35,* 66; halts offensive in Tunisia, 167; and Hitler, 37, 38, 112, 168; illness, 107; initial tactics against British, 61; intent of attack on Allied armies in Tunisia, 162; and invasion of France, *40-41;* made field marshal, 92; misjudges Auchinleck, 87; on nature of African war, 112; and Nazis, 38; nearly captured, 66; and Operation *Battleaxe,* 71; opinion of top officers, 61; ordered to delay early offensive, 63; ordered to hold El Alamein, 115; orders early offensive, 63, 64, 65; orders retreat from El Alamein, 115, 118; as photographer, 62; as pilot, *45;* plan for November attack on Tobruk, 84; protects northern sector at El Alamein, 114; reaction to Operation *Crusader,* 84, 85, 86; reaction to rebuff at Tobruk, 68; reaction to reinforcements sent to Tunisia, 149; relieved of command by Hitler, 168; returns to El Alamein line, 111; risk taking, 65; sent to Africa, 33; and siege of Tobruk, *46-47*
Roosevelt, Franklin D.: on alliance with French collaborators, 149; meets Churchill in Casablanca, *148;* and Sherman tanks sent to British, 104
Ryder, Charles W., 141, 192

S

Schmidt, Heinz-Werner, 60, 171
Shipping: Axis, attacked from Malta, 74; British, attacked from southern Italy, 31
Sidi Barrani: British attack on, 14-15, 23, 26-27; captured by Italy, 19, 20, 26, 27
Smith, Arthur, on Cunningham, 87
Somaliland, British, 8, 20
Somaliland, Italian, 8, 19
South Africa, troops in North Africa, 91, 98-99
Sponeck, Graf von, 195
Stark, Alexander, at Kasserine Pass, 165
Stephens, Freddie, in Tunis, 194
Streich, Johannes, at Tobruk, 68
Stumme, Georg, 107, 109
Sudan, 8, 20

T

Tanks: German mock, 61, *64,* 65; Grant (M3), 90, *113,* 150; Italian, 12, 21, *113,* 115; Lee, 151, *160-161;* Matilda, 20-21, *113;* Panzer III, 61, *113;* Panzer IV, 61, 104, *113,* 150-151; Sherman, 104, *113;* Valentine, 172
Terror, 30
Thoma, Ritter von: at El Alamein, 112, 115; and Montgomery, *136-137*
Tobruk, 28-29; Allied capture of, 31; Allied forces in, in June 1942, 91; battle for, in June 1942, 91; British defense, 66-68; British surrender, 92; defenses, 67; early German

attacks on, 67-68; German siege of, *46-47, 68-69,* 84; and Operation *Crusader,* 83, 87; supply route, 67; value of, 67
Torch, Operation, *152-161;* Allied forces, 140, 154; amphibious landings, 146-147, 152; assembly of fleet, 140-141; and desert offensive, 105; invasion of Algiers, 144-145; invasion of Casablanca, 146-149; invasion of Oran, 145, *152-153;* invasion of Tunisia in winter, 149-151; name, 141. *See also* Tunisia
Tunisia, map 166; advance by Allies, 150-151, 162-169, 171-173, *174-187,* 188-195; Allied forces invading, 149; Allied losses, 195; Allies enter Tunis, 194, *196-197,* 198; American vs. German armor, 150; Axis build-up in, 149; Axis prisoners in, 195, *202-203;* Axis surrender and losses, 195; battle of El Guettar, *174-175, 177-183;* battle at Kasserine Pass, 164-167; battles for Longstop Hill, 151, 190-191; British attack Mareth Line, 166, 171-172; British drive on Tunis, 192-193, 194; difficulties of invasion, 150; German defense of Mareth Line, 163, 168-169, 171-172; German final defense positions, 189; German offensive, 162-167; importance as base, 149, 188; importance of Kasserine Pass, 164; Tunis welcomes Allies, *198-201;* U.S. drive on Bizerte, 192, 193-194

U

United States, maintains relations with Vichy France, 141
United States, Air Force of: attacks on supply shipments to Tunisia, 192; attacks in Tunisia, 192, 193
United States, Army of: armor in invasion of Tunisia, 149, 150-151; and attack on Bizerte, 189, 193-194; at attack on Mareth Line, 169, 171; badly disposed in Tunisia, 163; confusion during Operation *Torch,* 146-147; defense of Kasserine Pass, 164-167; defense of Thala, 167; forces in Operation *Torch,* 140; and Hill 609, 190-191, 192; ill thought of, 189; inexperience of forces in Tunisia, 162, 165; invasion of French North Africa, 140-147, 149-151, *152-161;* losses at Hill 609, 192; losses in Tunisia, 164, 195; relations with French in North Africa, 159; in Tunisia, *174-183,* 186; at victory parade in Tunis, 198; withdrawal to Tunisia's Western Dorsal, 164

V

Valiant, attacked from midget submarine, 86
Victor Emmanuel III (King of Italy), *25*

W

Walney, and invasion of Oran, 145
Ward, Orlando, at invasion of Tunisia, 162
Warspite, 30
Waters, John K., 150
Wavell, Archibald, *30;* and aid to Greece, 22, 31; assigned to India, 71; and *Battleaxe* counteroffensive, 67, 70, 71; campaigns in Crete, Syria and Iraq, 70; conflicts with Churchill, 22-23, 31; on defense of Cyrenaica, 63; orders defense of Tobruk, 66; orders O'Connor to command during general retreat, 65; orders Operation *Brevity,* 70; and plan for counteroffensive in Egypt, 23, 26, 28-29; on timing of German offensive in Libya, 63, 64
Wechmar, Irmfried von, at El Agheila, 63-64
Western Desert, 50
Westphal, Siegfried, 188
Wimberly, Douglas, on cost of El Alamein, 115